Land, Conflict, and Justice

Territorial disputes have defined modern politics, but political theorists and philosophers have said little about how to resolve such disputes fairly. Is it even possible to do so? If historical attachments or divine promises are decisive, it may not be. More significant than these largely subjective claims are the ways in which people interact with land over time. Building from this insight, Avery Kolers re-evaluates existing political theories and develops an attractive alternative. He presents a novel link between political legitimacy and environmental stewardship, and applies these new ideas in an extended and balanced discussion of the Israeli–Palestinian dispute. The result is the first systematic normative theory of territory, and an impressive example of applied philosophy. In addition to political theorists and philosophers, scholars and students of sociology, international relations, and human geography will find this book rewarding, as will anyone with wider interests in territory and justice.

AVERY KOLERS is Associate Professor in the Department of Philosophy at the University of Louisville.

T0370821

Land, Conflict, and Justice

A Political Theory of Territory

AVERY KOLERS
University of Louisville

CAMBRIDGE
UNIVERSITY PRESS

CAMBRIDGE UNIVERSITY PRESS
Cambridge, New York, Melbourne, Madrid, Cape Town, Singapore,
São Paulo, Delhi, Dubai, Tokyo, Mexico City

Cambridge University Press
The Edinburgh Building, Cambridge CB2 8RU, UK

Published in the United States of America by Cambridge University Press, New York

www.cambridge.org
Information on this title: www.cambridge.org/9780521184120

First published 2009
First paperback edition 2010

A catalogue record for this publication is available from the British Library

ISBN 978-0-521-51677-8 Hardback
ISBN 978-0-521-18412-0 Paperback

For Nira, Karen, Adam, and Stella, with love.

Contents

List of tables

List of figures

Foreword and acknowledgments

Nearly everyone's back story is a saga of attachment to and alienation from land. The extent to which we are aware of this is usually the extent to which our back story is also a saga of near misses and lucky escapes. My paternal grandparents emigrated from Belarus, which has been controlled by at least four different states since they left. They were lucky to get out before the Golden Door closed, landing (like everyone else) at Ellis Island in 1918. My mother's family traces its roots in Jerusalem back to the expulsion from Spain in 1492. My mother remembers walking the long route to school to avoid tempting the Jordanian snipers atop the Old City walls. She arrived in North America in 1966. As for me, I grew up using Indian names for the city and country in which I was born and the lake on which the city sat, but learning next to nothing (or anyway, next to nothing that was true) about the prior inhabitants of the land on which I lived, or the circumstances under which it ceased to be their land.

At the same time, I have had the extreme good fortune to come out of that saga all but unscathed. Indeed, some might say that I have been too lucky: my parents are not Holocaust survivors; I have never had SCUDs or Qassams fall on my head; Canada was not, after all, torn in half by Québécois secessionism, and in fact seems to be in reasonable shape. Obviously, I prefer not to think of myself as too lucky. Rather, I hope that the emotional and biographical links to all these people and places have enabled me to bring to the question of territorial disputes in general a visceral appreciation for their life-and-death importance, and to treat each case with the kind of critical engagement (or wrestling) that one only attempts with loved ones.

I commenced work on this book in earnest in 2002, when I began corresponding with David M. Smith of Queen Mary, University of London, and when the University of Louisville awarded me the Olorunsola award for junior scholars. I used the Olorunsola money to visit David at QMUL and present there a paper that contained the germ of the approach I've developed here. In addition to what I have learned from his writings (and those of other geographers to whom he has guided me), Smith's comments on previous drafts of several chapters, his encouragement, and our shared puzzlement about these issues, have been abiding sources of inspiration. Several others also read drafts of multiple parts of the work at various stages. They include Karen Christopher, Andrew J. Cohen, John Cumbler, Cindy Holder, David Imbroscio, Linette Lowe, and David Owen.

My philosophical work on this subject dates back to the beginning of my dissertation project at Arizona, over a decade ago. Almost nothing of the dissertation survives. Nonetheless, I have been profoundly influenced by the work and tutelage of Allen Buchanan, Tom Christiano, and David Schmidtz, and I can only hope that some of the virtues of their work rubbed off on me.

The University of Louisville and the city of Louisville in general constitute an exceptionally friendly and stimulating environment. I am fortunate to have colleagues in various disciplines whose interests dovetail with my own in a variety of ways, whose ideas and knowledge have stimulated my thinking, and who have served as valuable sounding boards and readers of drafts along the way. In addition to those already listed, I am especially grateful to Tom Byers, Matthieu Dalle, Aaron Jaffe, Eileen John, D. A. Masolo, Rodger Payne, and Leigh Viner. I am also grateful to Cheshire Calhoun, Nancy Theriot, Wayne Usui, and Jim Brennan for solving the two-body problem on my behalf.

Speaking of which, the ten years of work on this subject have also been my first ten years with Karen Christopher – the last three of which we have shared with our son Adam (and now our daughter Stella). They are the light of my life.

Earlier versions of individual chapters have been visible or audible on a number of occasions, and in each case, participants, referees, commentators, and/or editors have contributed to improving arguments and clarity. Chapters Two and Three preserve elements of "Valuing Land and Distributing Territory," the paper I delivered at QMUL and, in modified form, as "Territory as Deep Diversity in Global Justice," at the 2003 Pacific APA Mini-conference on Global Justice. I am grateful to my APA commentator, Jeremy Bendik-Keymer, as well as the audience members at each session, particularly Shlomo Hasson at QMUL and Kristen Hessler, James Bohman, and Steve Scalet at the APA. Another part of Chapter Two is descended from my comments on Gillian Brock's

2004 APA paper, "Global Equality of Opportunity: Can We Formulate a Compelling Positive Version of the Ideal?" I am grateful to Brock for the paper that spurred the comments, as well as discussion afterwards, and to all the people who came down from the boycotted conference hotel to hear my comments and include me in the discussion of the paper.

I read part of an earlier version of Chapter Four at a Commonwealth Center for the Humanities and Society Faculty Research Forum at the University of Louisville in February 2005. The audience there raised a number of valuable comments. I presented a later version of Chapter Four as part of a symposium on "Geography and Justice" at the 2007 Canadian Philosophical Association, organized by Loren King, who also read a stimulating paper of his own. The audience members, who were kind enough to come to the session on the last afternoon of the last day, despite the beautiful Saskatoon spring weather – especially Jocelyne Couture, Jim Molos, and Kai Nielsen – were extremely generous with their ideas and comments.

Chapter Six is the most personal chapter, and section 6.3 in particular represents the culmination of a long and emotionally arduous journey. I am grateful to Karen Christopher, John and Judith Cumbler, Merle Bachman, Ira Grupper, Ibrahim Imam, David Imbroscio, Aaron Jaffe, Eran Kaplan, Lisa Markowitz, Julie Peteet, and Hank Savitch for discussion of some of the ideas there. Research and writing on the Israeli–Palestinian dispute have had a profound effect on my understanding of myself and my community. Innumerable friends and family members have helped shape my thinking on this issue over as many years as I have been conscious – Nira Kolers most profoundly of all (though that is the least of my debts to her). Inevitably, the process of research and writing has put me at odds with many of them, and with myself, and I have ended up very far from where I started. I hope the arguments here constitute adequate explanation of why I have reached the conclusions I have, and that these arguments and conclusions might spur others to undertake such a journey for themselves, even if they don't end up where I have.

Some material in Chapter Three previously appeared as "Valuing Land and Distributing Territory," in *Geographies and Moralities*, ed. Roger Lee and David M. Smith (Oxford: Blackwell RGS/IBG book series), 2004, 135–48.

Finally, I am grateful to John Haslam and Carrie Cheek, my editors at Cambridge, for supporting this project over a period of years and then bringing it to fruition; to the anonymous referees whose criticisms and suggestions spurred significant improvements to the arguments; to Jo Bottrill for his apparently boundless tolerance while turning the manuscript into a book; to Marjory Bisset, whose copy-editing enhanced clarity and whose queries got me thinking about language more deeply than I had in a while; to Natalie Weis, for providing a fresh pair of eyes on the proofs and saving me from numerous errors; and to what seems like a small army of people whose names I do not know, who interceded at one stage or another to move this project from proposal to manuscript to book.

Figures 6.4 and 6.7 are in the public domain. Figure 6.7 is taken from the Central Intelligence Agency *Atlas of the Middle East*, January 1993. Both figures are courtesy of the University of Texas Libraries, The University of Texas at Austin.

Figures 4.1, 6.3, 6.8, and 6.9 were drawn by D. J. Biddle of the University of Louisville Center for Geographic Information Systems. I am grateful to D. J. for taking on this project out of the blue and doing such an amazing job.

Introduction

Of elephants and living rooms

For at least half a century, since the major early works of Rawls, Feinberg, and others, political philosophy has been an absolutely vital intellectual enterprise. It has incomparably deepened our thinking on the meaning and value of democracy, equality, justice, and freedom. It has taught us to see the nature and importance of social institutions. It has forced us to confront and assess the morality of war and other forms of violence. More recently, it has thrown into question our assumptions about the boundaries of our moral communities and the quality of relationships both within and across them. But for all this, the enterprise of political philosophy has also nursed a number of shocking blind spots. Of those blind spots two are perhaps most dangerous.

The first is territory. The international relations theorist John Vasquez argues that territorial disputes are the most common cause of war, and that this explains "why neighbors fight" (Vasquez 1995). Just war theory has blossomed – or perhaps exploded is the better word – in the decades since Walzer's *Just and Unjust Wars*. But the territoriality of states and of the disputes that arise between them has been virtually absent from the work of political philosophers. Everyone knows that states are territorial, and most people agree that they are inevitably so. Yet theories of the state, of justice, and even of secession have traditionally had little or nothing to say about the relationship between states and territories, or the just resolution of the territorial disputes that arise between states, their neighbors, and their members.

Recent years have brought four classes of exceptions to this generalization. An *attachment* approach to territory, evinced by liberal nationalists such as David Miller (2000) and Tamar Meisels (2005), as well as proponents of indigenous peoples' rights (e.g. Tully 1994;

1

Ivison et al. 2000; Thompson 2002) holds that special linkages between groups and places can carry moral weight. A *conflict-resolution* approach (Levy 2000; Bose 2007) starts from the elements of territorial conflict and attempts to build a theory that can satisfy each claimant's most important demands. An *individualistic* approach treats territorial rights as more or less directly reducible to the interests and rights of individuals. Such accounts may foreground the territorial right in practice, but the justification itself nonetheless relies on individual interests that are themselves normatively individualistic, such as human rights or moral targets (e.g. Buchanan 2004), pre-political property rights (Simmons 2001), individual rights to resources (Steiner 1999), political association rights (Wellman 2005), or whatever. Finally, a *dissolution* approach (Pogge 2002) denies that territory poses any new problems, raising the issue only long enough to justify returning to domestic or global justice questions as before.

There is enough work now that it is no longer correct to say that territory is ignored; but what exists is, by and large, perfunctory and unsystematic insofar as it deals with territory and territorial rights as such. Indeed, the dominant approaches are dissolutionist or individualistic, and such approaches treat territory as generating no new ground-level problems for theories of global or domestic justice more generally. Thus, exceptions notwithstanding, territory remains a major blind spot of contemporary political philosophy, as marginalized now as ever.

The second major blind spot is the global climate emergency. There is perhaps no greater threat to the survival of human societies as we know them, other than the constant threat of nuclear annihilation. Yet – again with a few exceptions, such as Goodin (1992) and Dryzek (2000) – political philosophers have by and large proceeded as though climates did not exist. They have, at most, treated the climate emergency as a further issue to be dealt with after the core stuff was addressed. But in a real sense the core stuff doesn't matter as much as the climate emergency. As of the time of writing, the years since the original Rio Summit have been all but a total loss (Gardiner 2004). Already, some 150,000 deaths annually are attributable to climate change (Patz et al. 2005). Reports of melting permafrost, massive methane release, and a slowing Gulf Stream are the stuff of nightmare. Even if the Earth were to return to some climatic equilibrium, it would do so at a massive cost to human life and civilization. And we have no way of knowing how close we are to a tipping point that will take us into a new equilibrium that is much less favorable to human life.

It is not just that political philosophers ought to deal with territory and the environment, but that dealing with these things is crucial to getting good answers to the core questions on which political philosophers tend to focus. That is what makes these phenomena elephants in the living room, rather than, say, elephants in the zoo. The problem with having an elephant in the living room is that, if you don't take proactive steps to get it out while it's calm, it will eventually knock your house down. This book is an attempt to get the elephant out while it's calm. The book offers a theory of territorial rights that puts environmental sustainability – particularly stewardship of the climate and of ecosystem services that sustain civilization as we know it – at the core of legitimate state territorial claims.

Core ideas

This book develops what I earlier called an attachment approach to territory. In this respect it is cognate with certain liberal–nationalist and indigenous-rights views. But the ideas here are mostly unfamiliar to writers in both camps, as well as other philosophers and social scientists. This is, in other words, a bit of a strange book. I want briefly to lay out the main ideas, focusing particularly on the unfamiliar ones.

The first idea is that of an *ethnogeography*. This term is appropriated from a subdiscipline of geography that deals with describing the geographical beliefs of various cultures (Blaut 1979). I use the term to name, not the field of study, but its subject-matter – culturally specific conceptions of land. By conceptions of land I mean ontologies of land and our relationship to it; what land is, what about it is valuable, how humans interact with it. One particular point worth foreshadowing is that liberal writers such as Locke, Dworkin, and virtually everyone in between presuppose one particular ethnogeography, which I call the Anglo-American ethnogeography. Territorial egalitarianism, which is defended in various forms by Charles Beitz (1999) and Hillel Steiner (1999), as well as in Dworkin's (2000) broader egalitarianism about land, seeks to impose the Anglo-American ethnogeography on others who may not share it.

A related notion is that of the *ethnogeographic community*: a group of people who share an ethnogeography and whose land-use practices densely and pervasively interact. Territorial rights accrue, as I shall argue in Chapter Three, to ethnogeographic communities rather than to other sorts of groups such as nations or cultures.

A third core idea is that of *territory* itself, and of state territory or the idea of a *country*. As far as I can tell not a single other work in political philosophy pauses at any length to consider what territory is. Territoriality is in the first instance a strategy of bounding and controlling, and thereby making, geographic places. A territory is a geographic place that is bounded and controlled in part through geographical means such as the establishment of physical boundaries or other means of demarcation. To control a territory is to be able to make and enforce what the geographer Robert Sack calls the in/out of place rules, and the flows of people across the border and within the place itself. But not every territory is of concern here. The theory covers only *juridical* territories – territories that are bounded and controlled through rules of law. Roughly, a territorial right is a right to make viable one's ethnogeography by controlling a juridical territory, particularly through legal, political, and economic institutions.

Among juridical territories, only countries are appropriate candidates for statehood. A country is a juridical territory that has achieved a certain level of *resilience*. Resilience is an ecological concept denoting the capacity of a system to bounce back to an equilibrium. That is, a system is resilient insofar as it can absorb shocks and continue (or return to) doing the same thing as before (Walker and Salt 2006). The resilience of a territory is at a second level – it is achieved when a territory includes enough, or resilient-enough, systems that the human society in the territory can bounce back from the loss of a given system within that territory. For instance, the social-ecological system of the Goulburn-Broken Catchment in Australia is not resilient because, even as it suffers an epochal drought, it is also at risk of becoming waterlogged and hence infertile if even two consecutive wet years ensue, due to the rise of water tables and the salination of fields (Walker and Salt 2006). But Australia as a whole may nonetheless be resilient, provided it has a wide-enough array of systems to absorb the loss of any one. A territorial claim may be valid, but if the territory thereby claimed is not resilient then it is not a country; and if the territory is not a country, then the validity of the territorial claim cannot ground independent statehood. While any ethnogeographic community may be eligible for territorial rights, then, only valid claims to countries support claims to statehood or sovereignty.

Any attachment approach to territory reduces fundamentally to the criterion of attachment. The criterion derived here is *plenitude*, or fullness. Plenitude is in some respects cognate with other, better-known, attachment criteria such as *settlement* and *use*, but plenitude has the virtue of not presupposing any particular ethnogeography. The central challenge of Chapters Four and Five is to first specify the meaning of plenitude in the abstract, and then apply it meaningfully to territorial dispute-types. Plenitude has two aspects: empirical and intentional. A place is *empirically* full when it is internally diverse and distinct from other places. Think of the difference between a city and the rubble it may become in wartime. A place reduced to rubble is *empty*, rather than full, because, although there is no dearth of medium-sized physical objects, it is not internally diverse. The pre-war city, in contrast, is full insofar as it has distinct streets and buildings, economic and cultural activity, and so on. *Intentional* plenitude is a forward-looking notion, involving plans to achieve, maintain, or enhance empirical plenitude in perpetuity. Again, crucially, this need not require filling the place with people; it may rather involve preventing or limiting human encroachment to ensure that fisheries, forests, or wildlife habitats remain intact. Together with resilience, intentional plenitude puts the environment, and particularly long-term climate-related variables, at the center of the theory.

Plenitude is always from a perspective. As I drive through rural Kentucky, or walk through the City of the Dead in Cairo, I do not see much internal diversity. But others do. The place is full relative to their ethnogeography, but not relative to mine. This explains why they could, but I cannot, plausibly lay a territorial claim to it. All the same, the plenitude remains empirical because they would be able to use their knowledge of it in ways that could be third-party verified. They would, for instance, be able to mix their labor with the land in a way that would yield certain sorts of crops; they would be able to draw maps and solve drainage problems. We could begin to resolve territorial disputes not by asking who believes the place to be sacred, but by asking what is there, and seeing who knows.

It is now possible to state the core thesis of the book:

A territorial right exists if and only if an ethnogeographic community demonstrably achieves plenitude in a juridical territory; this right grounds independent statehood only if there is no competing right and the territory is a country.

The thesis is really quite simple; the complexity comes from explicating the core concepts and applying them to a variety of contexts. I
believe this book is significant not only because it is the first work of
political philosophy to offer a general and systematic theory of territorial rights, but because it goes far beyond most philosophical works
in the extent to which it applies the theory. A rigorous focus on territory generates some novel ideas about world order. Moreover, the
detailed and empirically informed application to the Israeli–Palestinian
dispute (Chapter Six) includes powerful critiques of the standard
solutions and offers two new proposals for the just resolution of the
territorial conflict.

A note on terminology

As should be clear from the conceptual neologisms laid out above, the
current theory departs in important ways from the main schools of
liberal political thought. These schools, then, come in for what I take
to be compelling critiques. Nonetheless, I have no stake in insisting
that this theory is not itself on some level a version of liberalism,
cosmopolitanism, nationalism, neo-Lockeanism, or whatever. The
theory here may be read as a corrective rather than an alternative to
any of these orientations. I do not purport to have discovered fatal
flaws with the very idea of cosmopolitanism or liberal nationalism.
Nationalists, for instance, may regard an ethnogeographic community
as a particular sort of nation; provided that other aspects of nationalism are modified as required by the theory, I need not protest.
Similarly, the attention to global problems and the attempt to discover a language for territorial claims that is universally applicable
without requiring imposition on unwilling others, may be taken for
hallmarks of cosmopolitanism. Again, I would take incorporation as
a compliment.

There are doubtless errors of argumentation and articulation in the
book. But, although the theory is an integral whole, I believe that it is
also severable: if one part is rejected, the rest of the theory may still
survive. For instance, if there is really no such thing as an ethnogeographic community – and this is a testable question of empirical
theory, as is, for instance, the (now quite dubious) existence of cultures (Kuper 1999) – the remainder of the theory may still provide a
useful basis for resolving territorial disputes between nations, states,

peoples, or whatever type of collective (or even individual) is shown to be eligible to assert territorial claims instead. Similarly, if plenitude is rejected, the theoretic structure and the strategy for resolving disputes may still be helpful to those who posit settlement, efficiency, sacredness, or other criteria. The theory is, then, ambitious; but in the likely event that it proves importantly flawed, it may provide a service by advancing the theory of territorial rights and providing some of the elements of an eventual solution to the problem. In doing so it may also help coax some dangerous elephants out of our collective living room.

1 | *Everything you always wanted to know about taking other people's land (but were afraid to ask)*

1.1 Territorial goods

Land is valuable in three basic ways. When stated, they are obvious, but they are so rarely stated in political theory as to require reaffirmation. First, we live on land – we, our homes, our belongings, and things we build individually and collectively, take up space. Hence the physical extension of *terra firma* is a good whose distribution matters to everyone. Second, land is composed of resources that we need in order to survive, prosper, and express ourselves; literally, the land constitutes both our physical bodies and virtually every material good we can find or fashion. Hence secure access to good land, land we can use to do the things we care about, is essential to our capacity to make our way in the world. Third, land and its properties – its location, its material composition, who or what lives on it – are essential to a vast array of world systems, such as nitrogen and carbon cycles, water purification and storage, ecosystems, and the production of oxygen, without which we would not exist. All the value of territory is built on these three foundations.

These three foundations have implications both for why anyone has a special interest in a particular place, and for how the world's land ought to be distributed among all potential claimants. Everyone has an interest in the sorts of places to which they have access. The universality of this interest is obvious in cases where everyone shares an interest in a single thing – access to freshwater, for instance. But even highly particular interests may be instances of the universal interest in place. People have an interest in access to land that supports the sort of life that they lead, whether that be a life of desert nomadism, of sedentary farming, or of suburban homesteading. These lives are integrated with their geographic and ecological underpinnings to a far greater degree than political theorists typically recognize. Territory both allows individuals and polities to foster the things they value and helps to shape what it is that they value.

Access to, and intelligent management of, territory is also valuable, not least for the capacity to absorb ecosystem shocks such as storms and droughts, as well as for attaining economic and other instrumental goods. For all the constitutive elements of territory, it remains the case that land contains natural resources that people need in order to survive, and the distribution of which may be assessed from the standpoint of justice. While a theory of territorial rights must give due respect to the constitutive goods and their local expressions, it must also recognize that stomachs must be filled. That stomachs are filled, bones grown, muscles manufactured, with highly particular forms of cuisine, speaks to the ways we make ourselves by making places. But everyone's stomach must be filled somehow, and a theory of territory that ignored this fact would be perverse. A theory of territory therefore must accommodate both the universal and the particular.

Extant discussions of state territoriality typically have little to say about most of the ways in which territory is a good. Contemporary liberal theories of the state focus on particular justifying functions, typically the procurement of public goods such as domestic tranquility and national defense. These theories have inherited a worldview in which people can be imagined to spring forth fully formed, like mushrooms (Hobbes 1998: 102), to set up their political institutions according to rational principles. In the most prominent recent case, that of John Rawls (Rawls 1999a), the character of the land on which the parties to the "original position" are to make their lives plays no role at all in the development of the theory. Indeed, it cannot do so, since the society is assumed to be closed, the boundaries fixed, and the relationship to land not in question beyond the matter of public versus private ownership of the means of production, which anyway is not decided in the original position. Those who purport to apply Rawls's theory to the globe as a whole have gone one further, treating territory as a good only because of the valuable natural resources that constitute it (Barry 1973; Beitz 1999; Pogge 1994). Rawls himself demurs, emphasizing that he takes his theory to be applicable only, or primarily, to modern constitutional democracies (Rawls 1999a: xi). That limitation may explain why the residents of Kazanistan (Rawls 1999b: 75–8), his imaginary Islamic hierarchical society, do not reach agreement on the comprehensive liberalism of *A Theory of Justice*, but it fails to explain why it is difficult to imagine nomadic, tribal, or even agrarian societies emerging from the original position with anything like Rawlsian social democracy.

Recently, some political theorists have begun to address the question of what kind of good territory is. Some of these have been liberal nationalists, who regard the national territory as a canvas on which the nation paints a picture of itself, or better, a lump of clay that it molds in its image (Miller 2000: 116; Moore 2001: 191; Meisels 2005: 86–90). This is indeed a relevant territorial good, at least if nations exist, but it seems to me to misplace the primary emphasis. The three fundamental ways in which territory is a good include this element of using territory for self-expression, but we must avoid focusing on this one to the exclusion, or even to the detriment, of the others. Other political theorists have focused on the role of territoriality in providing some of the state's essential public goods, such as security (Nozick 1974: 113–14; Simmons 2001; Wellman 2005, chap. 1), democratic deliberation (Kymlicka 2001), and efficiency (Kofman 2000). Here, territory is mere delimited physical extension. States so conceived are indeed, as Wellman puts it, inevitably territorial. But even more so than the nationalist view, this public-goods approach to territory ignores the fundamental ways that territory is a good.

Territory is both a highly particular good and a universal good. A theory of territorial rights must, therefore, look in two directions. It must be sensitive to the role of particular lands and territories in constituting identities, but it must also limit territorial claims, in both spatial extension and in the types of behavior they permit, in light of the ways that territory is a universal good.

1.2 The problem

A *territorial right* is a right of a group to control, or possibly to share with other groups in controlling, the legal system of a territory.[1] Not every territorial right is a right to an independent state. This is crucial, because not all valid assertions of territorial rights are valid assertions

---

[1] Obviously, not every territory is the territory of a state. I shall define territory in Chapter Three below; for now, I shall just stipulate that we are discussing juridical or political territory – the kind of relationship to land that states have.

of a right to sovereign statehood. In Chapter Three below I shall offer an account of how to tell the difference between these two types of rights. In the meantime we shall be discussing only the right to territory itself. Territorial rights may, of course, be legally recognized or not. Whether a given group's lacking recognized territorial rights grounds a legitimate grievance, however, depends on other considerations that we shall discuss below, including whether that group is the right sort of group to have territorial rights in the first place.

Territorial rights must in the first instance be group rights, and more particularly, rights of incorporated groups (Jones 1999; see also Meisels 2005, chap. 2). For we would normally expect the territory to be subject to the legal system of a particular polity, which polity was the bearer of the right to territory. The question would then seem to be which polities have such rights. But this imports further problems, because in many cases – such as those of Kurdistan and Palestine (at least prior to Oslo) – the putative right to a territory is the right to be constituted as a territorial polity. Thus to lay too much weight on incorporation as though that had to precede territoriality would be a mistake. We often speak of a mere (unincorporated) collective's having or lacking territorial rights, even if we do not know what sort of incorporated group it might form, if given the chance, or whether that sort of group is the right sort to have territorial rights. It is important to recognize that even nationalists, liberal or otherwise, speak this way; nations are typically not incorporated unless and until (sometime after) they have states bearing their names, but nationalists do not refrain from imputing territorial rights to those nations. Sometimes this sort of imputation is mistaken or wrongheaded, whether because the group in question is of the wrong sort, or because it lacks the right that we impute to it. Nonetheless, with appropriate caveats about the evidentiary value of our commonsense morality, a theory of territorial rights will have to either ground or explain away the most commonly asserted claims – those of Jews and Palestinians, Europeans and native peoples, Kurds, Québécois, Basques, and others. Such a theory will have to do so in part by explaining what sorts of groups these are – or more precisely, what sorts of groups they need to be in order to hold territorial rights.

But why do we need a theory at all? Why can we not just work to bring enemies to the table and find compromises that allow everyone to walk away with their dignity, bodies, and institutions intact? Why insist that they be groups of a certain sort and have claims of a certain sort? Or alternatively, why are principles of territorial justice not derivable from antecedent theories of justice already familiar to political philosophers? This chapter and the next take up these questions. The current chapter considers whether we are not best off dealing with territorial disputes as the need arises. To do this it engages principally with the work of Jacob Levy (2000). The next chapter considers available theories, primarily liberal cosmopolitan ones, that purport to derive implications for territory from theories already to hand.

1.2.1 Levy on territorial disputes

Jacob Levy (2000) broaches territory in the context of political conflict, his discussion driven by the aim of achieving tolerable resolutions rather than theoretic purity. More deeply than most others, however, Levy appreciates a crucial twist in territorial conflicts that political and economic conflicts do not typically raise: two groups may have not only distinct political aspirations and cultures, but incompatible conceptions of land. He contrasts what he calls the "nationalist and indigenous conception of land" with that of civic republicans and liberals (204–10). According to Levy, the former "elides the distinction between sovereignty and ownership," and "conceptualizes land as place, not property" (204). The liberal conception contrasts on both counts. This incompatibility in the two conceptions of land means that liberal polities may neither insist that indigenous peoples join the market like everyone else, nor simply accept the creation of large separate homelands. From a liberal perspective, Levy articulates the problem in terms of values such as social and geographic mobility, two of liberalism's sacrosanct "four mobilities" (208).[2] These two mobilities are vital both to individual interests as conceived by liberals, and to the social structure of a liberal society. Levy presses the question thus: "What does it do to a liberal and mobile society if an ever-growing portion of its land is held under a kind of indigenous entail?" (212).

---

[2] See Walzer (1990: 11–12). The other two mobilities are marital and political mobility.

Levy's concern is what to do when the two conceptions of land conflict in practice – that is, when liberals and nationalists (or indigenous peoples) have interests in the same land and are sharing the same larger society. He has in mind mainly liberal settler states such as the US, Canada, and Australia. He captures the problem through an analogy with freedom of religion. Just as a state can respect all religions only if it reflects none, so it can respect competing conceptions of land only by reflecting none: "At most [public] institutions could reflect or establish one such set of beliefs, but at the cost of not even respecting the others" (213). His solution is to "create those institutions which will allow each their own self-understanding while keeping their aspirations compatible with those of others."

Levy adopts Rawls's language of "overlapping consensus" to articulate his solution. The idea of an overlapping consensus is that, across deep pluralisms of religious and moral doctrines, everyone can maintain a commitment to the two principles of liberal justice. Each group may have distinct grounds for accepting these principles, but what's important are the conclusions, not the premises. Any group that, for whatever reasons, is able to maintain its commitment to liberal justice counts as reasonable and therefore tolerable to the liberal state (Rawls 1993). Levy applies this strategy to land rights. Liberals must give up their opposition to collective ownership and their commitment to an untrammeled market in land rights; but indigenous peoples must give up their absolute opposition to market alienability of land. For Levy, a market mechanism can serve to balance the extent of indigenous communities' attachment to land with the extent of liberals' interest in alternative uses:

It is not the case that every acre of traditional land is as sacred as every other acre; and while for some land possibly nothing could induce traditional owners to part with it, for other land the intensity of the preferences of others – as reflected, for example, in the price a mining company is willing to pay for a subdivision of the land – could result in a sale . . . A requirement that land be individually owned cannot be justified in terms acceptable to those who hold divergent views on the nature and uses of land, though alienability can be so justified as the measure that allows for the mutual adjustment of projects and uses (214).

Levy's solution, while potentially promising in some land disputes, is beset by several crucial difficulties. In the remainder of this section

I shall detail these difficulties by dividing them into two categories – *claims* and *claimants*. This division yields a six-category framework by which to assess theories of territorial rights.

Territorial disputes are distinctive because they involve parties that are not working from a shared conception of land. It may be helpful to distinguish between territorial disputes proper and what we might call mere boundary disputes, such as that between Britain and the United States regarding the upper boundary of the Oregon Territory (source of the famous and bizarre battle cry, "Fifty-four-forty or fight"). Mere boundary disputes occur because two conflicting parties want a piece of land for the same reason – a tax base, national security, a source of natural resources, or even a shared conception of sacredness. Territorial disputes proper are at their core disputes between conflicting ontologies of land, or as I call them, ethnogeographies.[3] One great virtue of Levy's discussion is his recognition that the liberal conception – no less than the nationalist or indigenous conception – is itself a particular ethnogeography. Unfortunately, Levy's political liberalism of land ultimately fails to do justice to this insight. For the distinct ontologies are not fully analogous to differences of religion in Rawls's political liberalism; and the disanalogies are fatal.

1.2.2 Claims

Levy grants an initial disanalogy: whereas in Rawls's account, each reasonable party accepts the two principles of justice as a fully justified and fully integrated part of a larger comprehensive doctrine, in Levy's account the two sides accept the collective-ownership-with-alienability overlap simply for political reasons. That is, they accept this constraint on their conception of land (and of the good society) simply because they would rather not fight about it. Levy denies that this difference turns his account into a mere "*modus vivendi*, changed whenever the balance of power changes" (215). He instead stakes out a middle ground: it is possible to accept the overlapping consensus neither for one's own internal moral reasons, nor for mere balance-of-power reasons, but "for the reasons offered by the stand-alone political justifications." That is, it is possible to balance the arguments

[3] Briefly, an ethnogeography is an ontology of land and of our relationship to it. I elaborate on this notion in Chapters Two and Three below.

Levy gives for alienability – the four mobilities, the dynamic society, the appropriate measure of relative interests – with the arguments he offers for collective ownership and relaxed evidentiary rules in indigenous-title cases. Levy then concludes that "[t]he relationship of Lockeans and indigenous persons to the 'political liberalism' of land may well be like the relationship of 'neither-reasonable-nor-unreasonable' to political liberal toleration."

But the difficulty goes deeper than that. In Rawls, the basic ground rules are set by a shared commitment to an identical set of principles. No one is asked to give up any of their core commitments, and the state is not taken to have basic interests beyond the promotion of justice as articulated in the (universally shared) two principles. In Levy, the liberal state has a clear agenda – maintaining the four mobilities underlying liberal dynamism – and uses the market to set ground rules. The state is thus based on unshared values – values that indigenous groups cannot be expected to endorse. Granted, in Rawls, the principles of justice are liberal, so Rawls initially seems to have the same problem. But the adjective "liberal" is ambiguous. Rawls's principles are liberal as opposed to illiberal, but not liberal in the sense that they are the exclusive property of liberals. Precisely their ecumenism is what (allegedly) makes it possible for all reasonable groups to live by them. But the four mobilities and market alienability of land are not ecumenical in the same way. Rather, these values are the exclusive property of the liberal conception of land that Levy's gloss on political liberalism aims to transcend.

To be sure, Levy gives reasons for his liberal ground rules, but these reasons cannot be expected to compel indigenous peoples the way they compel liberals. For instance, the four mobilities argument – at least as Walzer articulates it – is an argument about a specific political culture with a specific set of values: "Liberalism is, most simply, the theoretical endorsement and justification of [these mobilities]" (Walzer 1990: 12). And the dynamic society that the four mobilities underwrite is even more clearly a specifically liberal value – as Levy recognizes, citing Gandhi as an opponent (209). (It may be right, but that is beside the point; the point is that it is unshared.) Levy's solution can work consensually only in cases where the value and interpretation of dynamism are both shared – that is, for mere boundary disputes. But for fully fledged territorial disputes, it can work only by imposition.

We can grant that some indigenous and nationalist groups will indeed share the commitment to dynamism and hence be "neither-reasonable–nor-unreasonable" in the requisite way. Still, what do we do about those groups that are wholly "unreasonable" – those indigenous groups, say, who refuse to alienate any of their land, or who claim a right of return to most of the land from which they were expelled, or those comprehensive liberals who cry "individual market alienability or bust"? In the context of religious pluralism, the political liberal simply denies unreasonable groups a place at the table, and hopes or expects that such groups will constitute a small minority of the citizenry.[4] Such a solution might work for Rawls's limited purposes, which imagine religious pluralism against a shared, but now rejected, history of religious conflict with no decisive winner. Indeed the lack of a decisive winner is precisely the impetus for the moral-psychological evolution that Rawls describes.[5] But the struggle for land that pits liberal settler states against indigenous peoples lacks any such historical balance. The history of conflict has not resulted in a "hurting stalemate," nor have liberal attitudes evolved to the point that settlers "are willing to have their advantages only under a scheme in which this works out for the benefit of" indigenous peoples (Rawls 1999a: 90). To the contrary, attitudes may have evolved in a way that runs decisively contrary to indigenous peoples' benefit – or at least to appropriate territorial settlements. Recent polls of non-indigenous Canadians, for instance, found widespread "support for doing 'away with Aboriginal Treaty rights and treat[ing] Aboriginal people the same as other Canadians'" (Cairns 2005: 57). That is: individual market alienability or bust.

Thus we cannot expect that the wholly "unreasonable" – comprehensive liberals who insist that all land ought to be alienable, or indigenous peoples who want all their land back, or who think none should be alienable – will constitute a tiny minority. And while not-unreasonable liberals may be willing to brush aside wholly unreasonable liberals, it is hard to see the justification for expecting that

---

[4] This issue has been a source of much debate among proponents and critics of political liberalism, not least because it downplays the resort to coercion and takes for granted that the unreasonable will be a small minority. See Scalet (2000).

[5] See Rawls (1993, esp. pp. xxii–xxv).

unreasonable indigenous peoples, after half a millennium of genocide, white rule, ethnic and ethnobiological cleansing, will calm down and see it the liberals' way – especially when that involves the liberal state's setting the ground rules and pursuing its parochial agenda. To the contrary, it is fully understandable why those indigenous leaders who are willing to be not-unreasonable are widely regarded as having been co-opted (Alfred 1999: 73–9).

Levy's analogy with Rawls's overlapping consensus is, then, severely strained, because the Rawlsian framework cannot do justice to the unshared worldviews or conceptions of land that characterize the sorts of territorial disputes Levy wants to address. But there is a further difficulty having to do with the role of history and the status quo. As Levy notes, because sacredness may come in degrees, indigenous peoples might be enticed to trade off some amount of sacredness for some amount of access to capital through land alienation. Any such agreement would inherit the baggage of 500 years of colonialism, hence reflecting the unjustly worsened bargaining position of indigenous peoples. One obvious site where such baggage has consequences is in the question of which land is to be sold. A significant portion of the territory of contemporary settler states was never ceded by treaty or sale – let alone by fair treaty or fully voluntary sale – from the prior inhabitants. One plausible response to Levy's proposal, then, is to treat that land, the stolen land – places like Nashville and Seattle – as less sacred, and charge the current settlers for it now in a sort of collective title repair.

Lest this proposal be taken as a joke, recall that Levy's concern is to avoid "a form of indigenous entail," with ever-larger sections of territory being taken off the market. But under current conditions, this worry risks coming across as more than a little farcical. Indian reservations constitute a tiny percentage of US land territory. They represent a significant portion of only a handful of American states, mostly west of the Mississippi. And even in these states, the significant percentage raises no risk of overwhelming the sacrosanct liberal mobilities. The only way to work up any genuine worry about indigenous entail is to envision the return of stolen land. While this does indeed change the terms of the equation, it also undermines Levy's proposal to mediate indigenous land claims by putting the land on the market. If our fear is about stolen lands, but Levy's solution is about as-yet unstolen lands, then the solution is irrelevant to the problem.

To summarize the critique of Levy on claims: his "political liberalism of land" misses a crucial disanalogy with Rawls, namely that the
Rawlsian overlapping consensus is built around shared principles and
a neutral state, while Levy's is built around exclusively liberal principles and a partial state. So the solution gets hung up on the problem
of translating between ethnogeographies, opting to impose the Anglo-
American ethnogeography endorsed by the liberal state. A deeper
implication of this is that Levy fails to take seriously the possibility
that certain claims may be fully convincing to one side but seem
absurd to the other. (One thinks here of Manifest Destiny, the doctrine of *terra nullius*, and the hypothesis that indigenous peoples did
not improve the land.) I have further argued that Levy's proposal
misses its mark because it fails to take the status quo seriously as a
problem in its own right, with, in the case of indigenous rights, 500
years of historical baggage. Levy assumes that each interested party is
currently where it wants (or has any right) to be, and remaining disputes are over control, not settlement or placement. Thus he might
have a reasonable response if, say, the Cherokee insisted on slightly
expanding their holdings in Oklahoma, or attaining greater autonomy
there; but not if they asserted a territorial right to Atlanta.[6]

The two key arguments – about ethnogeography and status quo –
overlap on the problem of degrees of sacredness. Levy assumes that
the most sacred regions of two or more groups will conveniently be
found in different places, and so territorial disputes can be settled by
accommodation at the margins. Cases such as those of Jerusalem and
Kosovo, where both sides regard the disputed territory as central to
their destiny, suggest that Levy's political liberalism of land can at best
be a partial solution. On the flip side of this coin, Levy's political
liberalism of land ignores any possibility that claims might be assessable for comparative validity. Three vices result: the view marginalizes
some claimants whom Levy must regard as unreasonable but who are
clearly not, such as indigenous people who demand that all treaties be
respected; it mainstreams some unreasonable claimants, such as the

---

[6] It might be replied that he has a perfectly reasonable answer to a Cherokee claim
to Atlanta: "No." Or perhaps, "How much is it worth to you?" But these
answers presuppose an account of how to deal with claims to *unheld* or *formerly*
held lands, and this is precisely what I have argued that Levy lacks. (More on
this in 1.2.4 below.)

Québécois who assert that Quebec's borders, including Cree territory, are sacrosanct; and perhaps worst of all, it has no basis for distinguishing the two: a Palestinian claim to Jaffa will be neither more nor less plausible than a Mexican claim to Baltimore – or, for that matter, a Mexican claim to Mexico City.

1.2.3 Claimants

For Levy the basic reason to accommodate indigenous and nationalist claims has to do with a particular fact about those who make the claims. The problem is that the particular fact has only to do with the political or persuasive power that these groups can muster, and the effectiveness of territorial compromise as a means of taming that power. It has nothing to do with the sorts of groups these are. That is a basic element of Levy's methodology. But in this instance it is inadequate. As John Bern and Susan Dodds (2000) argue, how we understand the nature of the group that makes a claim – for instance, as indigenous, as a nation, or as something else, and within these categories, what exactly it means to be indigenous or a nation – contributes to determining how that group's interests can be represented. Moreover, part of the project of respecting claimant-groups, and particularly indigenous groups, rests precisely in affirming the kind of group that it is – for instance, affirming its indigeneity, or nationhood – and the special status of such groups in the history of a country.[7] The risk of postponing all the work of representing group interests until the competing claimants present themselves is then twofold. It cannot sort the wheat from the chaff; and it cannot affirm the goodness of even the best wheat. That is, Levy's account entails a criterion of eligibility to assert territorial claims – of which sorts of groups are the right sort to do so – but his criterion is both too restrictive (for barring groups that cannot make others feel their pain) and too permissive (for permitting any group that can do so). For this

---

[7] A number of authors assimilate indigeneity to nationhood – at least in the case of those groups, such as the Mohawk, the Cree, and the Navajo, which are large enough that political self-determination seems feasible. See Alfred (1999); Cairns (2005). Other authors reject the language of indigeneity. See most prominently Waldron (2003). Still others defend indigeneity as a discourse and an identity, hoping to get beyond the sorts of questions that Waldron raises. See Maaka and Fleras (2000).

reason I would argue that, from a theoretic perspective, Levy loses the focus on territory; from a practical perspective, this loss of focus risks exacerbating rather than limiting territorial disputes, particularly by giving small groups an incentive to turn fearsome.

A related point has to do with the nature of the attachment that any group might have to the land it claims. As a version of political liberalism, Levy's multiculturalism of fear does not subject competing claims to normative evaluation. To be sure, normative analysis plays a significant role in Levy's account, but that role is epistemological – to understand competing claimants' arguments in order better to mediate competing interests. The result is that Levy has no account of why anyone might have a specifically territorial grievance, or seem justified in claiming territory – let alone why they might claim a particular territory as a solution to a particular grievance. But if the nature of attachment to the claimed territory is not open to normative assessment, then just any link to land (or none at all) is as good as any other, provided the sorts of groups in question can accommodate one another through Levy's proposed political liberalism of land.

Levy's view is unsatisfying here because the only criteria by which claimants are assessed are their presence and their not-unreasonableness: that is, that the liberals both need to and can reach a peaceful accommodation with them. But the foregoing paragraphs suggest three lines of critique. First, as we noted, Levy's criterion of who is eligible to assert territorial claims is both too restrictive and too open. Nothing in Levy's view prevents his accommodating, say, suburbanites, the working class, or redheads through territorial compromise; nothing in his view requires paying any attention to, say, Cherokee demands to return eastward. Levy may of course endorse this result: say that there is nothing special about territory, and so nothing special about territorial compromise other than that it sometimes works where other sorts of compromise do not. But this response effectively endorses the liberal (proprietary) conception of land, as against the indigenous/ nationalist (place) conception. It therefore belies his distinction between "reflecting" and "respecting" the competing conceptions of land; it reflects the liberal conception and disrespects the indigenous one.[8]

---

[8] To put the point in James Tully's helpful terms, Levy attempts to replace "constitutional nationalism" with Esperanto constitutionalism, but ultimately falls back into the nationalist version. See Tully (1995: 7).

In addition to the demand that the state respect all ethnogeo-graphies by not reflecting any, an improved eligibility criterion would also serve as a principle of order for political conflict both within and across borders. Currently, in international law, the criteria for recognizing the legal standing of nonstate collective actors are arbi-trary or based on ill-founded concepts (Cassese 1986: 85–99; Ranjeva 1991: 101–2). Domestically – even with the recent flowering of indi-genous-rights law – whether the state recognizes the existence of indigenous peoples as distinct and distinctive societies within its borders is largely a matter of sheer luck or shifting political winds. A criterion of eligibility would provide a principled basis for singling out all and only those claimants whose assertions of territorial rights are worthy of respect. Eligibility, in other words, serves both to make good on the commitment to respect competing conceptions, and as a first filter on territorial claims.

Beyond eligibility we may wonder in what the claimant's attach-ment to the territory must consist if it is to generate territorial rights in a particular place (see also Simmons 2001: 308). Is it enough to appeal to the liberal mobilities, or to sacredness, to justify subjecting a certain tract of land to one community's jurisdiction rather than another's? These universal criteria might suffice, if territorial claims were solely about convenience and global equality. But if there is more to terri-torial claims, how is attachment to be relevantly demonstrated? Subsidiary to this is whether and how attachments are to be uniquely fixed. A given group might have links of various sorts to a variety of places. For instance, the Israeli Declaration of Independence claims that Eretz Yisrael was the place where "'the Jewish people came into being,' and it was there that 'the people's spiritual, religious, and political image was forged,' where 'it lived a life of sovereign inde-pendence . . .'"[9] This assertion of a territorial claim seems plausible enough on its face – albeit more accurate with respect to the West Bank than to the territory of Israel proper – but only the criterion of historical sovereign independence links the Jews solely to the biblical land of Israel, as opposed to Iraq (Mesopotamia, Babylonia) or the Sinai peninsula. It could be argued that by the other criteria, Iraq and the Sinai (or indeed, the condition of being diasporic: see Boyarin and

---

[9] Cited in Gans (2003: 100).

Boyarin 2002; Kaplan 2005: 34) are in fact more important. So a plausible attachment criterion must determine which sorts of links matter for territorial rights, and thereby link each claimant group to a single place rather than several places.

Finally, Levy's political liberalism prevents our asking what makes attachments to particular territories normatively significant. For political liberalism, once a claimant group's presence and not-unreasonableness are established, the normative basis of its claim is not open to evaluation. The not-unreasonableness of a group has to do with its willingness to accept the liberal state's basic interest in promoting the four mobilities; thereafter, the group's territorial claim is equally worthy of respect no matter what its foundation. There is a normative element to this, because the not-unreasonableness criterion serves as an eligibility screen. Once eligibility is established, any criterion whatsoever may ground a particular claim. By the same token, the reasonableness of a religious group, for Rawls, is a matter of its attitude toward the two principles, not to any other aspect of its comprehensive view. It may believe that God is a round square; Rawls does not care. But religions do not compete for access to each other's gods. In contrast, any number of groups, such as newfangled cults or putative Lost Tribes of Israel, might emerge from the woodwork and insist on territorial attachments of ancient or recent provenance, claiming to find some piece of ground sacred. It may be charitable to treat any claim seriously if its proponents are serious about it. But this charitable cast of mind risks producing more territorial conflicts among more competing claimants than it could possibly solve.

1.2.4 Framework

The critique of Levy brings out three demands to be laid upon any theory of territorial rights in respect of its treatment of territorial claimants. The eligibility problem demands an account of which sorts of entities can have territorial rights, and thus qualify to assert valid territorial claims. The attachment problem asks on what basis a claimant can support a putative link to the territory in question. A resolution of the attachment problem should also account for the individuation of attachments – the uniqueness of a group's attachment to this land and the geographic limits on such claims. And the normativity problem asks why each group's claim is a moral one rather than just a matter of ideology or convenience.

Political liberals might reject these criteria on the grounds that, since land is a scarce resource, it must first and foremost be subject to principles of distributive justice. From the standpoint of distributive justice, Levy's opposition to what he regards as excessive indigenous entail establishes a bare minimum; possession of large unused tracts, after all, may be regarded as an expensive taste not worthy of weighing on the scales of what each is owed (Dworkin 2000: chap. 1).

The problem with this reply is twofold. First, the three criteria are justice criteria, and their applicability is due precisely to the scarcity – inasmuch as there is competition for it – of land. We need to know how to evaluate claims, and in particular, in a non-arbitrary fashion. We must avoid endorsing the right of the stronger, and we must have a basis on which to rule out groundless claims that would risk people's access to what is one of the most basic goods that anyone can have – the land on which they live. Eligibility, attachment, and normativity are crucial here. Such criteria must determine who has standing to assert a claim to territory; on what they might base their claim to a particular territory; and why this claim should be treated as a claim in justice.

Second, political liberalism, surreptitiously or otherwise, is already committed to positions on these questions. As we saw above, Levy has an account of eligibility (presence), a "revealed preference" account of attachment (willingness to pay or to forgo offers of payment), and an account of normativity that validates just anything an eligible group asserts as a land claim and backs up with a willingness to pay (or to refuse rich reward). (By the same token, just any belief held as religious by a reasonable religious group counts as a religious belief to be respected by the liberal state.) So Levy's account has, or can be read as having, positions on these three criteria. Not only, then, can we give good reasons for imposing these criteria on liberal (and other) theories; we can also discern these criteria – albeit unremarked and underdeveloped – within those theories. Our criteria are not imposed or idiosyncratic, but derived as part of a rational reconstruction of the notion of territorial rights.

Let us return, then, to the issue of claims, discussed in 1.2.2 above, and systematize the bases of our concerns. Claims may fall anywhere along three axes that we may call the *status quo* axis, the *worldview* axis, and the *epistemological* axis. Their particular positions along these axes need not themselves make claims more or less valid. But our ability to locate claims along these axes may be essential to our ability to evaluate them, and hence one test of a theory of territorial rights is that it be able to respond to claims anywhere along all three axes. That is, the theory need not (should not) say the same thing no matter where on each axis a claim falls, but the theory's prescriptions should be equally plausible and well-grounded at any point on the axis. It is worth explicating the three axes at greater length and identifying some positions along them.

The status quo axis measures, with respect to two variables, how the world desired by the claimant compares to the world as it stands. The two variables are settlement and political control. A claim is *conservative* when lodged by a group that already both inhabits and controls the relevant territory. For instance, the English claim to England is conservative. A claim is *radical* if the claimant seeks a change in both variables. Diaspora nationalists and displaced peoples may make radical claims to be able to repopulate and control their putative homeland. Colonialists and expansionists also make radical claims, as would a group that wanted to abandon a territory. Finally, in *revisionist* claims, only one variable is at issue. Disenfranchised inhabitants seeking statehood – such as Palestinians claiming the West Bank – make a revisionist claim. Similarly, nonresident controllers of a territory make revisionist claims when they argue either for settling the territory themselves or for ceding the territory to another controller. So to continue with the West Bank example, in Israeli politics both the extreme right advocating the ethnic cleansing of the Territories, and proponents of a two-state solution are territorial revisionists they just seek opposite revisions.

We can now more clearly articulate one of the problems with Levy's view, insofar as it aspires to resolve territorial disputes in general. Even as the prospect of radical claims is what raises fears of indigenous entail, his view can ultimately speak only to conservative and revisionist claims. But a viable theory of territory cannot be silent on radical claims – whether or not those reflect efforts to rectify prior expulsions.

The worldview axis measures how important the place in question is to the claimants. A territory may be some group's putative heartland or hinterland. Competing claimants may each regard the same spot as their heartland (as, say, Jews and Muslims do Jerusalem), or they may have disputes in a place that is hinterland for one or both of them. Claims to putative heartlands are *central*, whereas claims to hinterlands are *marginal*. The degree of centrality may shift over time as populations shift and different aspects of a people's history become salient to its members. Centrality may also vary by sub-group or even individual member. The worldview axis directs us to assess competing claims on the grounds of how much a particular spot matters to the claimants. In the event that some spot is central to both or all claimants, the worldviews are *territorially incompatible*. For instance, the Muslim claim to *al-Aqsa* Mosque is incompatible with the claim of those Jews who seek to build the Third Temple on that spot. Though a matter of degree, full-blown territorial incompatibility is extremely rare, since territorial rights are distinct from full sovereignty as well as property rights; the group that has a territorial right to a place does not thereby have untrammeled ownership or destruction rights over particular buildings, or rights to the outright exclusion of the members of other groups. A territorial right is not a sufficient condition for such further rights to exist. Nonetheless, territorial incompatibility in a weaker sense – the larger cases of Jerusalem and Kosovo are examples, as are perhaps indigenous burial sites and old African–American cemeteries discovered in central cities or on building sites – do occur. A theory of territory therefore ought to be able to speak to territorial incompatibility, despite its rarity.

Like every other view of which I am aware, Levy's view presupposes – or just hopes – that territorial incompatibility does not occur. To get his proposal started, recall, Levy must emphasize that not every territory is equally sacred. More than that, he must assume that central regions of two or more groups will conveniently not overlap, and so territorial disputes can be settled by accommodation at the margins. He therefore has nothing to say about incompatible cases such as Jerusalem and Kosovo.[10] Plausible theories of territorial rights

---

[10] The prospect of competition over mutually central places suggests a further issue in Levy's approach – the group that is willing to sell the place might want to put restrictions on the uses to which its purchasers may put it. That not all places are equally sacred does not immediately imply that all less-sacred places are equally profane.

must non-arbitrarily weight claims having a variety of degrees of centrality. Such theories must also have strategies for rendering incompatible claims compatible, or else be able to justify the deployment of significant coercive power in defense of their decisions.

Understanding which places are central as opposed to marginal to a particular group requires either that we take the claims of groups at face value, or that we actually examine the competing ethnogeographies – the grounds on which the claimants justify their assertions, the character of the connection they feel to a particular land, how they determine the limits of the "most sacred" as opposed to the "less sacred" land, and why the limits are where they are. In other words, a theory of territorial rights must grapple with the epistemological axis, which measures how easy it is for nonmembers to understand and assess a given claim. A group's claim is *transparent* to the extent that nonmembers can assess it, *translucent* or *opaque* to the extent that the unshared moral language or assumptions of nonmembers render the claim impossible to assess. Transparency is a relative criterion, in two senses: being about how a claim is perceived by an audience, it is by definition a relation rather than an intrinsic property; and (more importantly) various parts of the audience may share more or less of the worldview that such claims manifest. For instance, sedentary populations may find a claim of longstanding occupancy perfectly transparent, while nomadic populations, failing to see any special value in permanent settlement, may find it at best translucent. Similarly, the promises of a divine messenger or text may be transparent to audiences who share the claimant's religious tradition, but translucent or opaque to others. Plausible theories of territorial rights must not assume that all claims are fully transparent, but must have non-arbitrary grounds for deciding even translucent and opaque claims.

We have articulated six criteria for assessing territorial-rights theories. Three of these apply to their assessments of territorial claims: such theories must have non-arbitrary grounds for deciding claims at various points on the epistemological, status quo, and worldview axes. The other three criteria apply to their accounts of territorial claimants: such theories must explain who is eligible to stake territorial claims, in what legitimate attachments consist, and precisely what is normatively significant about attachments of that type. To demand that a theory meet these criteria is, arguably, to depart altogether from political liberalism. For we now make more demands of putative claimants than merely their presence and their (not-un) reasonableness; and we make more demands of claims than that they can be reconciled with other not-unreasonable claims. This departure will seem, to many, to be a virtue of the framework.[11] It is not yet, however, to depart in any particular direction or to any other particular orientation. What I have said so far may be endorsed from a variety of perspectives, liberal and otherwise.

1.3 Territory, sovereignty, property

Throughout this chapter I have presupposed that territorial rights are distinct from both property rights and sovereignty – and hence, a theory of one will not constitute a theory of the others. Chapter Three below offers a full analysis of territory, but I want here briefly to support the presupposed distinction.

Historically, the most popular conceptions of territorial rights – in both political philosophy and international relations theory – have endorsed some version of the *domestic analogy*. This analogy treats the state either as analogous to a person (such that territory is the person's body), or as identical to the sovereign (such that territory is the sovereign's property).[12] Recent years have brought a number of powerful arguments against the domestic analogy, regarding both the empirical theory of the state and its moral standing (Beitz 1999: 154–61; Buchanan 2004: 31–7). Nonetheless, the analogy is a useful jumping-off point for clearly distinguishing these concepts.

Consider first the property-rights version of the domestic analogy. In recent years critics have cataloged the divergences between property rights and territorial rights. For instance, territory is held in trust for a population, including future generations and future immigrants; thus territorial rights have at their core a stewardship element that is typically absent from or peripheral to property rights. Further, territorial rights exclude certain activities, such as wholesale eviction of people who do not own their land, and the destruction, willy-nilly, of

---

[11] Political liberalism has come under sustained and powerful liberal critique from at least two sides. One valuable critique from the standpoint of comprehensive liberalism is Tan (2000). From the perspective of postcolonial liberalism, see Ivison (2002).

[12] On the bodily version of the analogy, see Walzer (1992: 58–63). On the property version, see Locke: (1988: II, sec. 45).

religious treasures or other objects of great significance to insiders or outsiders. Property rights permit these behaviors. On the other hand, territory may include airspace, waterways, and other non-land entities and processes that are not normally susceptible of ownership. Indeed, territorial rights include the power to determine whether something is to be the object of property rights, and hence a piece of land is no less the state's territory just because a private citizen or even a citizen of a foreign country owns it. To the contrary, its being owned is an affirmation of its being under a jurisdiction. The two relations, in short, confer different rights, obligations, and powers on their bearers.

A. J. Simmons (2001: 318) claims, however, that territorial rights may be understood "by subtraction" from prepolitical or natural rights, including but not limited to property rights. The idea is that Lockean contractors surrender to the state all and only those rights that are required for effective territorial sovereignty, including, for instance, the rights to make binding laws and to cross the land in order to defend against invasion and, notably, the right to remove one's property from the state after the contract has been signed. Then, assuming (i) the lack of internal dissenters, and (ii) an "international understanding" that internal unowned places (such as lakes or forests) are common only to the members of the state (314), it follows that territorial jurisdiction and sovereignty are derivable from individual natural rights.

Simmons assumes that the contractors surrender all and only those rights that they must in order to build "a peaceful, stable society" (2001: 313). This is meant to explain why they surrender all and only the particular prepolitical rights they do, including the controversial right to exit. But there is a prior step: they can hand over any right only if that right is in fact prepolitical. In some cases at least, the only reason to suppose that the relevant rights are indeed prepolitical is that they would have to be, if the contractors are to be able to create a polity by consent in the Lockean fashion. That is, even if we grant the face validity of the Lockean contract orientation, and thus grant that property rights in some fashion may be prepolitical, the derivation of territorial rights requires highly specific assumptions about the content of prepolitical property rights. For instance, if states have territorial rights in their airspace (whether or not this includes the geostationary orbit above them), then these must be included in someone's prepolitical property rights. But, at least above a certain very low altitude, it is impossible for individuals to mix their labor with air-space.[13] (They may have a strong interest in keeping enemy aircraft out of it, but the question is how this interest could ground a right, be it property or territory.) The same goes for underground natural resources as well as rivers and lakes that form interstate boundaries. It is possible to treat airspace as included in the property right to the land below, but – and this is the point – there is no good Lockean reason to do so other than the need to derive territory from it by contractual consent. Thus the Lockean contract is both *explanandum* and *explanans*.

Simmons could perhaps avoid this circularity by building in more assumptions about the international understanding that he admits is already dubious when applied to internal commons, or by denying that any state has the rights in question, for instance to airspace or underground resources. But either strategy puts more pressure on his view: the former because it reduces the explanatory power of the property theory, the latter because it further divides the Lockean theory from settled judgments about the legitimate claims of legitimate states.

Finally, Simmons denies that there are any enormous or mysterious differences between territory and property (2001: 318–19), but enormity and mystery are not the point; the point is rather that territory cannot be derived from property. His view cannot, except arbitrarily, resolve the aforementioned divergences between territory and property. The state may not evict tenants en masse; the state may not wantonly destroy objects of great worth; the state has positive obligations to outsiders and future generations that property owners lack. But these limitations on territorial rights are not due to subtraction from property rights, they are due to the addition of consideration of non-owners, including those who do not consent to the state and do not own land in it – in some cases, because they do not yet exist. In short, property and territory are distinct, and territory is not derivable from property, even in the broadest Lockean sense of the term.

---

[13] Or at least: if it is possible, then the identities of those who do so in a given place may diverge quite sharply from the identities of those who own the underlying ground. That one state has jurisdiction over the latter will then not preclude another state's having jurisdiction over the former.

The bodily-integrity version of the domestic analogy – in which the state's relation to its territory is analogous to a person's relationship to her body – has suffered much the same fate as the property version. Assuming the bodily analogy, the harm principle implies that it would be wrong to interfere, without consent, with any purely internal action that the state might take. Using the state's body for any purpose inconsistent with self-determination constitutes a kind of enslavement. It seems to follow that the state has an absolute exclusive right to control any and all events inside its territory.

Although there are some respects in which the analogy is apt, these respects do not ground the moral shift required to generate sovereignty. The obvious disanalogy is that, unlike human bodies, the state's body is inhabited by the bodies of other people and animals that are worthy of inherent moral consideration. Indeed, it is the moral worth of the inhabitants that justifies the moral worth of the state, not vice versa. So the bodily-integrity version of the analogy cannot support a move from territoriality to sovereignty.

To be sure, I have attacked only the most extreme version of the view, the view that state sovereignty permits the state to do absolutely anything it wants within its territory. But the invalidity of the inference does not do anything to the premise that the state has a right to its territory; it merely undermines the conclusion about sovereignty. Sovereignty, in other words, remains at issue even if we presuppose territorial rights; and that is all we need to see that the two are distinct. There are other ways to see the distinctness. Numerous claims to territorial rights, most importantly the claims of indigenous peoples, are typically severed from any aspiration to sovereign statehood. If territorial jurisdiction can be accorded without sovereign statehood, then the two are distinct.

It follows that territorial claimants may be satisfied even without attaining sovereignty. Thus in the first instance, territorial rights establish not sovereignty but *standing*. Standing denotes a status of commanding recognition – being competent to press one's own claims – in a legal institution. Christopher Stone defines standing in terms of four necessary and sufficient conditions. Some person or other entity S has standing if and only if: (i) *"some public authoritative body* is prepared to give *some amount of review* to" apparent violations of S's rights; (ii) S "can institute legal actions *at its behest*"; (iii) "in determining the granting of legal relief, the court must take *injury to* [S] into account"; and (iv) "relief must run to the *benefit of S.*"[14] In the first instance, this book is about how to determine who has standing based on territorial rights, and how to deal with it when they do. Independent statehood is one strategy, but it is not the only one or even, often, the best.

---

[14] Stone (1972: 459), emphases in original. Stone's conditions are stated in terms of a thing's being a holder of legal rights, but he uses this interchangeably with standing.

2 | *Land and territory in political theory*

If political theory has been mostly silent about territorial rights, this might be because territorial rights do not exist. Cosmopolitan political theorists treat borders as (at best) pragmatic markers for the division of moral or political labor; borders are morally secondary, and the territories they enclose are morally justifiable, if at all, only by appeal to the equal interests of all individuals everywhere (Goodin 1988; O'Neill 2000; Scheffler 2000; Pogge 2002). Post-modern political theories may reach a similar conclusion on different grounds. Post-modernists deny the existence of prepolitical identities or sharp differentiations of identity across borders (Bishai 2004). For this reason, the idea of territorial rights must be fundamentally confused, because rights can exist only where the right-holders can be identified independently of the rights. If either of these approaches to global politics is right, then we have good reason to abandon the search for some theory that will meet the six criteria laid out in Chapter One.

Such arguments come in stronger and weaker forms. The weaker rejections of territorial rights adopt an *individualistic* approach. Such views, which are the subject of sections 2.1 and 2.2, hold that territorial rights, including the sorts of claims raised by indigenous peoples and others involved in ethnic/territorial conflicts, should be understood as derivative (at one or more removes) upon important individual interests. In such approaches, territorial rights may indeed be important political resources, but do not demand any special theoretic apparatus. Individualists hold that their approach to territorial rights would accommodate the overall interests of territorial claimants better than a theory that posited the existence of territorial rights as such, because such a theory would have to sacrifice certain other morally important goods – such as freedom of movement or political association – simply in order to keep territories integrated.

Individualistic approaches include Lockean views such as that of Simmons, which we discussed in Chapter One above. Non-Lockean individualists have adopted two general strategies for deriving territorial rights; each strategy is the subject of a section of this chapter. Perhaps the most straightforward strategy involves what is often called the *public goods argument* for the state. This strategy appeals to the moral importance of certain functions for which states are putatively necessary. Daniel Kofman and others have argued, within this framework, that some public goods are essentially territorial. If this is right, then perhaps we can divide up the earth's surface simply by appeal to the effective pursuit of these public goods. This strategy would obviate the eligibility requirement by allowing anyone who can secure territorial public goods for a population to claim territory. Other theorists, such as John Rawls, posit another kind of entity, such as a People, and limit eligibility that way. Section 2.1 argues, however, that public goods theories of territorial rights, though able to account for important aspects of international organization, also leave important gaps in specifying the goods to be achieved through a regime of territorial entities. Further, such theories can provide no attachment criterion for territorial claims, and so cannot explain the special valence of claims to particular places.

Section 2.2 discusses what is perhaps the most prominent individualistic approach, that of Allen Buchanan. Buchanan argues that claims to territory are a crucial element of international institutions as we know them, and that individuals, states, and the system as a whole have a strong interest in territorial stability. Nonetheless, he argues – indeed, on these very grounds – that rights to territory are subject to an extraordinary status quo default, which can be overcome only as a remedy for ongoing, serious human rights violations (Buchanan 2004: 337). I shall argue, however, that Buchanan presupposes the very sorts of territorial rights that he denies are necessary. Moreover, the strong interest in territorial stability does not adequately account for the interest in territorial claims and, again, the link between people and particular places. Buchanan thus fails to explain (or explain away) both attachment and eligibility.

The stronger form of argument against the existence of territorial rights adopts a *dissolution* approach. Such arguments hold that territorial rights should be repudiated outright and replaced with some alternative, for instance, a global property-rights regime, a single (possibly federative) international system, a set of jurisdictional divisions organized purely on the basis of convenience, or a wide distribution of jurisdiction among a number of levels of government. The essence of dissolution arguments is that territorial rights are a fiction, and the world system would be morally preferable if it rejected them altogether. I shall address such arguments in section 2.3. Finally, in section 2.4 I shall develop the concept of an *ethnogeography*, which I mentioned in Chapter One. In particular, I shall explicate what I call the Anglo-American ethnogeography. Fundamentally, opponents of territorial rights, whether individualistic or dissolutionist, typically go astray because they presuppose this particular ethnogeography and treat it as universal – that is, they fail to recognize that their conception of land is *a* conception of land at all. Only by understanding ethnogeographies can we appreciate what a theory of territory is a theory of; only by appreciating the particularity of the Anglo-American ethnogeography, and fairly accommodating those who do not share it, can we get beyond the surreptitious imposition of this particular conception of land on all who do not share it.

2.1 Public goods arguments

Ever since Hobbes, the most prominent defense of the state in Anglo-American political theory has been the appeal to a particular set of essential functions for which the state is necessary. On this view, commonly known as the *public goods argument*, the state's main purpose is to resolve collective-action problems and provide public goods that markets or nonstate modes of coordination could not provide. Public goods are by definition those benefits that cannot be only partly provided and from which individuals cannot be selectively excluded; prominent examples include national defense, clean air, and domestic tranquility. Due to their non-excludable character, the creation of public goods engenders collective-action problems such as free-riding. According to public goods theorists of the state, the importance of such goods, combined with the impossibility of overcoming collective-action problems in an anarchic state of nature, provides the best justification of the state. On this view, the state is justified only if, and because, it efficiently or justly solves collective-action problems that would otherwise prevent persons from effectively pursuing their interests (Rawls 1999a, sec. 42; Morris 1996).

Some public goods are essentially territorial. By explicating the public goods that a particular regime of territorial rights generates, it may be possible to circumvent the eligibility and attachment problems, defending such rights without appeal to national identity or sacred lands.

Typically, public goods arguments pay little attention to location; in addition to national defense, the public goods enumerated have to do with public welfare systems, resolutions of coordination problems such as which side to drive on, and the prevention of free-rider problems such as tax cheating, insider trading, etc. But Kofman (2000: 217; see also Lomasky 2001: 65–6) claims that the emphasis on indivisibility "conceals another [feature], namely that [public goods] are inherently territorial." That is, indivisibility is indivisibility *in a territory*. It is possible to exclude Atlanta from the national defense of Jerusalem, but it is not possible to exclude only one house on Elm Street from the national defense of all the others. But the territoriality goes further: public goods must not only be produced, but be produced fairly, and this entails that the entire legal and political system – including all three branches of government – must have "identically bounded jurisdictions." Indeed, "the very clustering of functions [is] itself a public good" (Kofman 2000: 218).

The commitment to both justice and efficiency in public-goods provision entails the inherent territoriality of public goods, which territoriality in turn supports undivided state sovereignty. Granting that the state is justified by appeal to public goods, and extrapolating this justification to the system of states as a whole, we can extrapolate Kofman's argument to the question of territorial rights.

A public-goods orientation might permit an end-run around our framework, which requires accounts of eligibility, attachment, and normativity. The problem of eligibility can be avoided by respecting the claim of any "dominant protective agency" capable of providing specific public goods (Nozick 1974: 16; see also Hampton 1996: 97) in any given territory. And attachment and normativity can be replaced with the notion of internally provided and globally provided public goods, respectively. (A state's claim will be normative for others if that state or the system of states as a whole provides global public goods.) So the challenge confronting the public goods argument is this: does placing a particular group in a particular spot provide any public goods both (i) for its members (attachment), and (ii) for nonmembers (normativity)? Three main public goods seem most likely to fill the bill: political development, self-determination, and global efficiency. Take these in order.

2.1.1 Political development

In *The Law of Peoples*, Rawls defends the territorial sovereignty of "Peoples" with an argument from political development. Using an analogy between territory and property, Rawls argues that stable territorial boundaries provide a way to hold Peoples responsible for their environmental stewardship: "the point of the institution of property is that, unless a definite agent is given responsibility for maintaining an asset and bears the loss for not doing so, that asset tends to deteriorate" (Rawls 1999b: 39). In our context, the argument could run thus: when Peoples "take responsibility for their territory and its environmental integrity, as well as for the size of their population" (*Ibid.*), this responsibility can be expected to engender a kind of political maturation, with a focus on environmental sustainability – a public good for their members. And a world of mature polities, each of which takes responsibility for its environmental integrity, is a global public good. One virtue of this premise is its (in-principle) empirical testability: successful stewardship, not mythical identity, is the criterion of eligibility and attachment.

Testing the political development argument requires that we identify the mature polities and see whether their maturity is a result of their having taken responsibility for their bounded territories. But what is maturity? Perhaps it can be inferred from traits like democracy, durability, and stability. The longest-standing major democracies (under some definition) are those of Britain and the United States. These states have exercised stable jurisdiction over their bounded territories for a long time. But they have also exercised various forms of control, direct and indirect, over external territories, so their homelands have not been effectively bounded. Moreover, they have failed, to different degrees, to attain environmental sustainability. Each country is causally dependent on overseas environmental rapacity and, even so, each is itself under serious domestic ecological stress. Stewardship has failed.

Perhaps, though, maturity should not be identified with duration, because imperial expansion seems to cause a prolonged (and petulant) national adolescence. Instead, we should find some specific criterion of maturity and see whether this is necessary or sufficient for successful stewardship. But this turns political maturation into an evaluative concept and, moreover, one that is multiply realizable – some mature polities might be democratic, some nondemocratic; maturity may be compatible with violations of some human rights or the establishment of a religion; etc. Unless we simply define "mature" as "some political system that has successfully taken responsibility for its territory by exercising stewardship," we have no criterion for assessing the plausibility of the hypothesis.

The stewardship argument could be salvaged by treating territoriality as identifying a merely necessary condition of the public good of maturity, rather than a sufficient one, and chalking up the failure of longstanding stable democracies to practice effective stewardship to their failing to satisfy some additional necessary condition(s). Even so, we still need an account of the nature and possibility of the further, as-yet-unidentified, necessary condition(s) of political development.

2.1.2 Self-determination and democracy

Perhaps one of the other two public goods arguments could shoulder this burden. The self-determination argument hypothesizes that any polity's self-determination is a public good for its members that can be achieved only in its homeland, and peaceful implementation of the principle of self-determination is a global public good. The initial problem with this is its empirical first premise. Is it true that territorial self-determination can be effectively achieved only in homelands? To the contrary: as New-World settler states demonstrate, self-determination for the settlers was possible outside Europe; indeed, the settlers forged new national identities in these places, proving that the importance of a specific territory to a particular group is at least as often a result of its being sovereign there. The premise might be plausible if consideration were limited to extant identities, in which case the example of the settler states' ability to forge new national identities would actually prove the point, rather than undermine it: once removed from the mother country, all these people failed to maintain their prior national identities. But the truth of the empirical premise has then been purchased at the cost of the plausibility of the public goods claims. The ossification of national identities is not a public good for nations themselves or still less for the world as a whole. If self-determination is a public good, that is in part because it permits members collectively to shape their evolving identity.

But it may be argued that the crucial issue with self-determination is not national identity but democracy, and democracy requires territoriality. On this view, the subject matter of democratic decisions comprehends a particular class of public goods, which Thomas Christiano calls the "collective properties of society." Christiano offers a functional and counterfactual definition of collective properties: they are all and only those "propert[ies] of individuals' lives in a society" which are such that "in order to change one person's welfare with regard to this property one must change all or almost all of the other members' welfare with regard to it" (Christiano 1996: 60). Such properties are characterized by four features: non-exclusivity, publicity, inevitability, and alterability. Among the collective properties of any society are the distribution of wealth, the system of property rights, the degree of environmental protection, educational systems, etc. (Christiano 1996: 59–61).

It might be argued that not only are collective properties territorial as Kofman explains, but that they carry with them quasi-natural territorial limits. For instance, the topography of one region may mean that air pollution gets concentrated there, in which case that region is a quasi-natural territorial jurisdiction for regulating air pollution. But the topography of another region may mean that air pollution from there causes major problems downwind, and so people downwind ought to have a say in air-pollution legislation as well. In either case, if democracy requires that all and only those subject to the relevant collective property ought to have a say in it, then topography determines the stakeholders for decision making about air pollution.[1]

Such issues are important considerations in the political division of labor, but the problem for the public goods argument is that the conditions that make some area the quasi-natural jurisdiction for one collective property might be highly particular, and inapplicable to others. What holds for air pollution might not hold for water. Consider the situation of St. Louis, Missouri. Air pollution from St. Louis blows eastward to Illinois, Indiana, Kentucky, and beyond. Thus it would make sense for St. Louis's air-pollution regulations to be

---

[1] I made this argument in Kolers (2002: 35). I no longer accept it, for reasons discussed in the text.

subject to collective decision-making with the citizens of states to the east. But water pollution in St. Louis flows south to Tennessee, Arkansas, and eventually the Gulf of Mexico. It would make sense, then, for the citizens of those southern states to have a vote in St. Louis's water-pollution rules. (By the same token, residents of St. Louis ought to have some say over water pollution in Minnesota.) To divide quasi-natural jurisdictions based on each collective property would require indefinitely many criss-crossing, subject-specific jurisdictions, no one of which is the obvious candidate for other, entirely nonnatural collective properties such as the distribution of wealth. And most importantly for the public goods argument, such criss-crossing divisions would destroy the jurisdictional unification that Kofman thought necessary to provide public goods in a just and efficient way.

2.1.3 Global efficiency

Consider, then, the third public goods argument. The global efficiency argument holds that nations are able most efficiently to use those territories with which they are intimately familiar – such aspects as soil, growing seasons, underground resources, etc. Efficiency of use reduces marginal environmental impacts and permits a more successful geographic division of labor, bringing about greater global economic benefits. Furthermore, nations are likely to be intimately familiar with only one or a very few territories. Therefore national self-determination in territories with which nations are intimately familiar is a public good. Recall the gap left open by the political development argument: the need for one or more further necessary conditions of attaining the public good of maturity. The global efficiency argument could stand alone, but it might also fill this gap.[2]

---

[2] Note that the global efficiency argument is distinct from – indeed runs directly counter to – the "efficiency argument" deployed by Locke and many others in defense of European encroachment upon indigenous lands. See Tully (1994, chap. 5). For discussion see Kolers (2000) and Moore (2001, 181–84). For a limited defense see Meisels (2005, chap. 5). Another interesting element of the global efficiency argument is that it associates local self-determination with successful globalization, two theoretic strange bedfellows that have been linked by economic geographers and social theorists such as Saskia Sassen. See Lee and Wills (1997); Sassen (1998, chap. 10).

The problem with the global efficiency argument is that efficiency is always relative to some good. If the relevant parties do not agree on the nature or prerequisites of the good, efficiency arguments do not apply. So far from filling the gap in the political development argument, the global efficiency argument presupposes that the gap has already been filled. Only if we know which goods the territorial states system uniquely or most effectively produces can we appeal to the system's efficiency in producing that good.

We have considered three possible public-goods attempts to explain away territorial rights. Public-goods arguments are individualistic because they attempt to derive territorial rights from public goods, which are themselves goods because of their service to individuals. But this derivation does not succeed. We can accept Kofman's public-goods argument for the territorial state as such, with enforceable boundaries somewhere or other, and still have no account of who ought to be where, or why their claim to be there should be treated as normatively significant. On the other hand, we might even reject Kofman's public-goods argument, and still think that indigenous and national groups have territorial rights. That is, on one popular formulation, to have a right is to have a "trump" that forbids certain ways of promoting the common good (Dworkin 1977). Thus the public-goods account might fail for territorial rights whether or not it succeeds at justifying the territorial state as such.

2.2 The ethics of the international system

As part of his broader moral theory of international institutions, and particularly international law, Buchanan (2004) provides an alternative individualistic approach to territorial rights.[3] Buchanan accepts only conservative claims to territorial rights – claims made by extant states to territory they already hold – except when territorial rights are needed to remedy longstanding human-rights violations, and in a very few other contexts (351–2). Claims to territory based solely on the special link between people and land may (but may not) legitimate some form of special consideration within a state, but cannot themselves justify independent statehood. Rather, Buchanan argues that

---

[3] Unless otherwise noted, parenthetical page references in this section refer to Buchanan (2004).

the international system should permit nonconsensual territorial revisions only as remedial mechanisms. Remedial rights are by definition those rights that exist to remedy rights violations or morally intolerable circumstances.

What international law ought to recognize has not been part of our discussion thus far, but in order to get at Buchanan's underlying assumptions about territorial rights, we must briefly discuss institutional arrangements such as autonomy agreements, secession, and statehood. The question for us is whether a remedial-right-only theory of secession, of the sort that Buchanan defends, can proceed by assuming that rights to territory exist only a) as legal fictions designed to further certain compelling state interests such as territorial integrity, or b) as remedies for systematic assaults by the state on the human rights of its members. According to Buchanan, in the current world order, recognizing any nonremedial right to unilateral secession would generate perverse incentives, render the international system incoherent and anarchic, set unreachable and counterproductive moral targets, and treat states as though they were floating atoms rather than highly structured parts of an institutional framework (348–50). If Buchanan is right, then proponents of freestanding territorial rights should give them up, because the interests that such rights putatively protect are better protected without them. I want here to meet Buchanan's challenge by showing why his theory cannot replace and explain away territorial rights: he ultimately presupposes them.

Buchanan's primary analysis of attachment to territory occurs in his discussions of state legitimacy and the right of substate regions to secede. Buchanan understands internal political legitimacy in terms of a permission-right to attempt to rule, not as a claim-right to obedience. Internal legitimacy is therefore defined as being "morally justified in ... [making a] (credible) attempt to achieve supremacy in the making, application, and enforcement of laws within a jurisdiction" (233). But such legitimacy is distinct from recognitional legitimacy, which is "the judgment that a particular entity should ... be recognized as a member in good standing of the system of states, with all the rights, powers, liberties, and immunities that go with that status" (261). Because it purports to bind outsiders to respect the territorial claim of insiders, we can read the account of recognitional legitimacy as, most straightforwardly, an attempt to solve the normativity

problem – that is, to explain what about a particular group's territorial claims ought to compel other groups that have potentially
competing claims. In Buchanan's view, states are legitimate when they
wield political power "for the sake of protecting basic human rights
and in ways that do not violate those same rights" (248). They earn
recognitional legitimacy by being internally politically legitimate
and respecting human rights in their foreign policy, provided they do
not come into existence by usurping any other recognitionally legitimate entity.

So far, so good: recognitional legitimacy offers a solution to the
normativity problem – that is, shows how (territorial) claims can
be articulated and morally defended across borders and between
competing claimants. But does this account for, or explain away,
eligibility and attachment? How would Buchanan determine which
sorts of groups can claim territory, and in what their relevant connection to it consists? Buchanan purports to solve these problems in
his theory of unilateral secession. For Buchanan, a theory of secession
is fundamentally a theory about legitimate claims to territory, because
"secession is not merely the repudiation of the state's political
authority . . . it is the attempt to appropriate territory claimed by an
existing state, and to exercise the functions characteristic of states
within that territory, with the implication that the state's claim to this
territory is invalid" (348). He therefore proposes a territorial thesis
about secession: "Unless a theory can provide a plausible account of
the validity of the claim to territory by those to whom it ascribes the
right to secede, it fails" (337).

Recall that Buchanan defends a remedial-right-only theory of
secession, in which states may suffer unilateral secession only if they
are guilty of certain grievous crimes. Secession from a legitimate state
constitutes usurpation and hence precludes recognitional legitimacy.
But what kinds of crimes are sufficiently grievous to justify their
victims' secession? Buchanan enumerates three: (i) genocide or massive violations of the most basic individual human rights; (ii) unjust
military occupation or unjust annexation; and (iii) persistent violations of intra-state autonomy agreements (351–2).[4] We might add

---

[4] Based on his discussion, Buchanan seems to include under (iii) the state's
persistent failure to enter into autonomy agreements when they are called for.

that autonomy agreements could be either (a) territorial or (b) non-territorial.

Both (ii) and (iii)(a) are recursive. Regarding (ii), if the state has occupied or annexed some territory unjustly, this presupposes that some previous political entity in that territory was recognitionally legitimate, or that some other group, which for some reason has a right to try to be recognitionally legitimate in that territory, is being denied this opportunity. For instance, to say that the US and UK have unjustly stolen the island of Diego Garcia from its inhabitants – not merely occupying their island, but evicting them – is to presuppose that the islanders were the legitimate claimants when the US and UK arrived, or that they have the right to rule there now. So condition (ii) falls back upon the account of recognitional legitimacy. As for (iii)(a), a group's entitlement to substate territorial autonomy presupposes that the group has the right sort of claim to the substate territory in question – that is, has the right to be party to an autonomy agreement in that place. When justified by (iii)(a), the right to secede is an enforcement mechanism for a right to intra-state autonomy which may itself be remedial: the state had its chance to get off easily, but failed to hold up its end of the bargain (404; 415–21). So understood, a right to territorial autonomy must have two features. It must be an exclusive right, that is, it must be the case that this group, not some other, has the right to determine the political status of the place; and it must be a specific performance right, that is, this group must have a right *that there be* an autonomy agreement, rather than none. Absent these presuppositions, failing to make an autonomy agreement with some group would be like failing to incorporate a city, and failing to respect such an agreement would be like revoking a municipal charter. Unless the entity has the right to such territorial autonomy, abrogating or suspending such an agreement in itself raises no claim of injustice.[5]

One difficulty in this case is location. In the case of indigenous peoples, autonomy agreements might do any of three things. They might, first, just fortify an indigenous group's autonomy on the land it now has – for instance, by establishing remaining lands as an autonomous reservation, or by preventing further encroachment on an

---

[5] There might, of course, be *procedural* injustices in the way the agreement or charter is revoked. But in the absence of a right to such an agreement or charter, there would be no *substantive* injustice in its non-existence or repudiation.

extant reservation. Second, such agreements could restore to indigenous groups some or all of their prior holdings, for instance, rights delineated in treaties that the state has violated (419–20). Finally, such agreements could establish an indigenous group's control over land that it wanted, but had never occupied. How would Buchanan choose among these options? He offers no moral account of which choice is appropriate, and when, and no account of attachment that can distinguish claims of the third type (to land that the group never occupied, but wanted) from claims of the first type. And claims of the first two types presuppose that we can determine which lands the group previously held *by right*.

Buchanan could argue that there is no further fact here, no objectively preferable form for such agreements to take. But much of the moral force of indigenous claims, in particular, is precisely the appeal to the further fact that land was stolen.[6] To deny that there are further facts about which lands indigenous groups previously held by right; why they had a right to enter into the treaties they did; and why invading Europeans had obligations to negotiate, sign, and uphold those treaties, is to undermine the ground on which indigenous groups' claims are built in the first place.

In other words, the recursive conditions (ii), unjust occupation or annexation, and (iii)(a), abrogation of territorial autonomy agreements, presuppose a prior account of what we might call candidate legitimacy – the right to try to become recognitionally legitimate in a place. And that is a matter of eligibility and attachment to territory. Buchanan's conditions therefore cannot themselves ground the relevant attachment to territory.

It might be thought that the recursive conditions (ii) and (iii)(a) fall back on the non-recursive conditions (i) and (iii)(b). As we noted, the latter is no help because by definition it pertains only to nonterritorial self-determination. But (i) also makes no reference to territory or place in any sense, so it can provide no account of attachment, either.

Buchanan may reply that my criticism asks for something he explicitly rejects, namely some sort of primordial right to place. On

---

[6] Buchanan writes, "the argument could also apply to groups that are not classified as indigenous. It just so happens that the circumstances that make the arguments applicable probably most often obtain in the case of indigenous peoples" (416).

his view, he might argue, the right to place itself – like the right to intra-state autonomy in general – exists only as a remedial right. And thus, a status such as candidate legitimacy is at most a status conferred upon or recognized in certain groups on a purely pragmatic basis, much as the United Nations currently grants international subject status to national liberation movements and international organizations (Cassese 1986: 85–99). The recursive conditions (ii) and (iii)(a) could therefore fall back on a purely pragmatic account of recognition for national liberation movements.

This answer, however, repeats and even worsens the original problem. Buchanan's account of recognition is explicitly designed to make recognition, in both internal and external contexts, a reward for good behavior or a remedy for gross injustice. To retreat under pressure to a pragmatic account of candidate legitimacy is to lose much of the normative bite of the theory. Buchanan's explanation of why we need a moral theory of recognition in the first place is based on the moral implications of recognition – the fact that any position on recognition, including a purely pragmatic one, is a moral position susceptible of critique on moral grounds (266). To be sure, international organizations and national liberation movements do not in themselves have all the advantages and capacities that states do, but international subjecthood itself brings a number of advantages whose distribution is also a moral issue.

Buchanan might, however, offer the following example by way of a further reply. Recall the first putatively sufficient condition for a remedial right to secede – namely, massive human rights violations. Suppose a brutal dictator ruled a multinational state, but the dictator perpetrated gross oppression indiscriminately – systematically violating the rights of all his subjects, not merely those of an ethnic, religious, or territorially concentrated subgroup. It would, we may suppose, be impossible to distinguish the victims from the perpetrators on any basis except for the arbitrary fact of membership of the ruling party. Buchanan's condition (i) here would justify revolution, not secession, because the oppression does not take a discriminatory form. But now suppose that some ethnic group with a territorial base, citing its putative right to territory, decided to try to secede rather than join the general resistance. We might accuse the secessionists of a kind of injustice: the rest of the population has not oppressed this group, only the regime has, and the secessionists owe it to their fellow victims to join in the rebellion, rather than to pull out. Indeed we can give international-institutional reasons for this conclusion: if aggrieved parties can gain recognition on their own, despite leaving their fellow victims in the cold, they face a perverse incentive to divide broad-based resistance movements, and dictators could cut their losses by emancipating restive minorities. Buchanan could then conclude that territorial rights are uniquely remedial – and moreover, indicated only when the oppressive conditions are discriminatory.

But why do would-be secessionists have so strong an obligation not to abandon their fellow victims? I grant that it might be better if they did not. However this course of action may be supererogatory. The mere fact of shared citizenship is hardly morally significant given the nature of the regime. A natural duty of justice might ground such an obligation to remain, but if so, why don't people in other states have a parallel obligation to try to immigrate (or to merge their territories with that of the oppressive state), so as also to share the burden? If there is no such obligation for outsiders, it follows that the natural duty of justice can be adequately discharged from across international boundaries; and if so, the existence of such a duty is no argument against secession.

Buchanan attempts to capture all the moral force of territorial claims without the risk of chaos or morally intolerable outcomes that territorial rights seem to carry, and without having to appeal to religious worldviews or national myths. Unfortunately, he is unable to capture all this moral force. His account of recognitional legitimacy presupposes, but fails adequately to address, a deeper kind of legitimacy, analogous to standing in the law. Standing, in territorial rights contexts, can be explained only with an account of which sorts of entities are of the right sort to make valid territorial claims, and in what their attachment to territory consists. If the argument in this section is successful, then, it shows that Buchanan's individualistic approach fails because it presupposes the rights it purports to derive.

2.3 Dissolutions

Dissolutionists do not try to satisfy territorial interests at all, but instead try to banish them, on either of two grounds: that there are no prepolitical identities (or at least, none with territorial significance); or that territory is simply one mechanism for distributing rights over land

and its constituent resources, and such distributions are best handled within a cosmopolitan – that is, an individualistic and universalistic – theory of justice. I shall accommodate, rather than rebut, the first grounding in the chapters to follow; territorial rights do not require prepolitical identities. This section deals with the second ground, as represented by cosmopolitan egalitarians. In particular, I shall focus on cosmopolitan attitudes regarding land.

The core of the argument is that cosmopolitans endorse universal principles that embody a kind of egalitarianism, but in the process ignore the diversity of goods that follows upon geographic diversity, and diversity in the ways people interact with land. By failing to recognize the geographic constraints to global institutions, cosmopolitans end up treating global order on a world-state model even as they (almost unanimously) explicitly reject a world state. This failure is a symptom of a deeper problem: the tacit endorsement and universalization of what I have called the Anglo-American ethnogeography.[7] The result is actually anti-egalitarian; cosmopolitans fail by their own lights.

Cosmopolitanism is a family of theories characterized by opposition to various forms of what we may call *statism*.[8] *Moral* cosmopolitanism rejects statism about moral principles such as justice. *Institutional* cosmopolitanism is the stronger thesis that conjoins moral cosmopolitanism with the rejection of statism about political organization. My quarry is institutional cosmopolitanism, but since moral cosmopolitanism is a proper part of that, I must characterize both.[9] I shall do so by looking at the two forms of statism that they reject.

Each form of statism has both domestic and international versions. Consider first statism about political organization. The international version of this view endorses a billiard-ball conception of the international system, in which states are morally and empirically opaque units of the international system (see Barry 1982, Rawls 1999b, Walzer 1992). The domestic version assumes away domestic diversity, treating national solidarity as causally necessary for the success of

---

[7] See Chapter One.

[8] Moral cosmopolitans include Beitz (1999), O'Neill (2000), Nussbaum (2000), Tan (2000), and Buchanan (2004); institutional cosmopolitans include Moellendorf (2002), Caney (2001), and Pogge (2002).

[9] Hereinafter *cosmopolitanism* refers to institutional cosmopolitanism, unless otherwise noted.

state institutions, particularly those that require good faith, forbearance, or redistribution. This view is also known as the states-need-nations argument (Miller 1995: 90–4). Now turn to statism about justice. The international version denies that any robust principles of distributive justice could succeed across state boundaries (Christiano 2006). The domestic version regards national boundaries as significant moral boundaries and denies that claims of international justice affect the theory of domestic justice except at the margins (Rawls 1999b; Freeman 2006).

Institutional cosmopolitanism starts from the assumption that all individuals everywhere have an initially equal claim on our moral attention. This equal claim must be expressed in the basic principles of any global institutional framework – for instance, through a doctrine of universal human rights, capabilities, or distributive justice. And though states may be provisionally useful as sites of limited democracy and minimal social justice, globalization decreases their value even in these respects. Cosmopolitans tend to endorse a proliferation of levels and forms of government, though most are content to leave some power at the state level provided states earn their moral keep. So cosmopolitanism and statism diverge sharply on a number of important axes.

The problem of territory reveals that the two views have perhaps more in common than at first meets the eye. Specifically, territory brings out a level of diversity that cosmopolitans cannot accommodate. As a result, the rejection of statism appears to be less a departure from than a refinement of that view. In effect, as we shall see, institutional cosmopolitans assume away a particular kind of diversity. They regard global citizenship in some form as necessary for the success of global institutions, which makes the view into a version of statism about domestic organization, albeit with a larger state. Cosmopolitans regard traditional state boundaries as incompatible with justice, which is a version of statism about international justice – albeit, once again, with a world state. At least some cosmopolitans regard the boundaries of global institutions – the global basic structure – as significant limits on moral concerns, which is a form of statism about domestic justice (See Buchanan 1993). In other words, cosmopolitans typically endorse at least two versions of statism, but simply expand the scope of the domestic well beyond the boundaries of states as we know them (see Kolers 2006).

Not only do cosmopolitans then ignore distance, they assume that there is only one global politico-economic system – one global basic structure within which all currencies of distribution are commensurate. Ironically, that is, for all their attention to the global context, cosmopolitans succeed only insofar as they domesticate the international sphere. This is what makes cosmopolitanism in effect a refinement of statism, rather than a departure from it, or so I shall argue in the remainder of this section.

2.3.1 Global equal opportunity

Equal opportunity principles take the following general form:

EO: All [*scope*], regardless of [*circumstances*], should have the same chance of [*benefit*], given the same [*inherent condition*] and [*choice condition*].

That is, opportunity egalitarians reject inequalities of benefit, among some range of people, that are causally due to circumstances, but permit inequalities that are causally due to inherent or choice conditions. Each theory then fills in the blanks in slightly different ways. For cosmopolitans the scope reaches all persons everywhere; circumstances usually include unchosen "suspect classifications" such as race, sex, religion, and place of birth; the benefit may be cashed in terms of income, quality of life, standard of living, or some other metric; inherent conditions may include innate talents, ambitions, and job-specific physical features such as height; and choice conditions include what persons set their minds to, such as specific careers.

We have a reasonably clear idea of what fair equality of opportunity looks like within a society – that is, where the scope is limited to citizens or residents of a single society. But it is much less clear what equality of opportunity would look like on a global scale. Consider the version that Darrel Moellendorf defends. In his view, such equality requires that "a child growing up in rural Mozambique would be statistically as likely as the child of a senior executive at a Swiss bank to reach the position of the latter's parent" (Moellendorf 2002: 49). This formulation – which uses a counterfactual or statistical interpretation of equal opportunity – is intuitively very problematic. Assuming that the Swiss bank is not moving to Mozambique, why should Mozambicans have to move? Why insist that they be capitalists? What about Mozambique's 1.6 million Muslims, whose religion forbids the taking of interest (for instance, by Swiss bankers)?

I dwell on Moellendorf's example only because it perspicuously brings out cosmopolitans' key assumptions. The unwillingness, or failure, of the Mozambican to move to where the jobs are is counted as part of the choice condition and thus excuses inequality. But what is the alternative? Surely it is not to ensure that Maputo becomes as much a center of global finance as Zurich (or vice versa). Not only would it be impossible to ensure that each country has its own center of global finance (or of anything global), it would demand even more of the Mozambicans – not just individual mobility but fundamental social change – and hold failures to develop in precisely this way against them. Moellendorf could, instead, limit his point to earnings rather than to the particular job, although, this concession would effectively undermine fair equality of opportunity, which demands equal access to influential offices and positions, not just to money. Even limiting the point to earning power presupposes a single, all-encompassing economy, a single system of education and qualifications, and again holds the failure to attain this kind of education against the Mozambican who does not do so. In short, Moellendorf's proposal for global equality of opportunity is, surreptitiously, a version of domestic organization statism. It can understand equality only against the backdrop of a standardized form of development, education, and/or mobility that rejects global diversity.

Arguably, where Moellendorf goes awry (apart from any objections to opportunity egalitarianism in general) is in the attempt to universalize the scope criterion from the matrix above. Gillian Brock (2005) raises a forceful dilemma for all such attempts to universalize the scope of equal opportunity. Her dilemma allows us to generalize the critique of Moellendorf's view and show that global opportunity egalitarianism is inevitably committed to domestic organization statism.

Brock's dilemma: either benefit covaries with scope – that is, also becomes universal – or it does not. Suppose first, with Moellendorf, that it does not. This assumes that everyone would want the "western" good if given the chance. But not everyone's conception of the good includes moving to Zurich and becoming a banker, and so some people will not even try. But then inequalities that arise as a result are treated as choices rather than circumstances, and hence not unjust. People are in effect penalized because they do not want the putative benefit that has been made equally available to them. Instead of "free to be you and me," the cosmopolitan's motto becomes "free to be just like me."

Now suppose benefit and scope do covary. This requires positing a culturally neutral or sufficiently vague specification of the benefit condition – something that everyone does want. Simon Caney, for instance, posits standard of living, as understood using the capability approach, as the appropriate universal benefit (Caney 2001: 120; also cited in Brock 2005: 17). But Brock points out that in this case the benefit fails to protect against systemic differences of opportunity organized around, say, gender, caste, or race. Brock imagines a society where the options open to men include being "a witchdoctor, a storyteller, or a circus performer." whereas the options open to women include being "a witchdoctor's wife, a storyteller's wife, [or] a circus performer's wife" (2005: 18). She supposes that the two sets of roles would carry similar standards of living. But this, too, does not look like equality of opportunity. If scope and benefit covary, circumstance conditions like caste or gender become inherent conditions, and hence inequalities based on caste and gender are permitted.

Brock's dilemma turns on the fact that scope variations affect other variables: if benefit covaries with scope, then (as in Caney's case) circumstances are treated as inherent conditions. If benefit doesn't covary with scope, then (as in Moellendorf's case), circumstances are treated as choice conditions. Either way, the theory must permit inequalities that the theory itself rejects as unjust: inequalities based on differences of circumstances. The problem for opportunity egalitarians is that it doesn't seem possible to put nationality or citizenship in the circumstance box without moving something else into either the choice or the inherent box. That is, we cannot universalize the scope of equality without causing the circumstance box to dissolve, and hence holding people responsible for things that they ought not to be held responsible for.

2.3.2 Global equality of resources

Resource egalitarians differ from opportunity egalitarians in that the latter permit inequalities on the basis of choice or inherent conditions, whereas the former treat inherent conditions as part of a person's circumstances and hence impermissible bases of inequality. Resource egalitarianism revises EO thus:

ER: All [*scope*], regardless of [*circumstances*], should have the same chance of [*benefit*], given the same [*choice condition*].

Ronald Dworkin (2000: chap. 2) is the most prominent resource egalitarian.[10] Provided that all parties start out with equal resources, trade freely, and are duly compensated for unfortunate circumstances, Dworkin holds, market distributions embody equality. A resource is such because it can be used to buy any material object other than a person, and buyers themselves determine the identities of material objects – they can purchase any object or part thereof, except for persons. It is crucial that persons cannot be bought, for otherwise the market would generate the "slavery of the talented": highly talented persons would either be purchased by others, in which case they would be slaves, or be forced to pay a high price to purchase themselves, thereby using up much of their purchasing power before they owned anything else, thence becoming wage-slaves in order to buy what the less talented – those for whose talents there is less market demand – already own.

In terms of our schemata EO and ER, Dworkin differs from both Moellendorf and Caney because Dworkin allows no distinction between inherent conditions and circumstances. But Dworkin's specification of the benefit condition is also distinctive: by giving persons power to determine the nature of the benefits, Dworkin finds a middle position between Caney's vague, universal specification, and Moellendorf's specific, particular one. Dworkin is, in this sense, an individualist about benefit.

Dworkin imagines, as a heuristic device, a group of castaways bidding on shares of an uninhabited island upon which they have been shipwrecked. Will Kymlicka (1993: 186) has shown that Dworkin's auction story presupposes that the shipwrecked persons share a culture and expect to be undifferentiated citizens of a shared polity. Kymlicka therefore tweaks the auction story to accommodate the

---

[10] Dworkin is not a cosmopolitan; I focus on his account of resource egalitarianism because it is especially clear and highly developed, and, like Rawls's difference principle, is available to cosmopolitans even if the progenitor of the theory rejects cosmopolitan application.

existence of a minority culture. But I want to note a distinct problem, which persists even under Kymlicka's reformulation. By imagining an uninhabited island to which everyone is a newcomer, both Dworkin and Kymlicka put off-limits all the questions that arise when conceptions of the good co-evolve with land: jurisdiction, sacred landscapes, burial grounds, long-term occupancy, staple-crop cultivation, non-instrumental or collective attachments to land – indeed, any kind of attachment that develops over time. Dworkin would balk at such attachments, admitting that some people are luckier than others in the total stock of goods available (Dworkin 2000: 69). But to do this is, I shall argue, to make the same mistake as Moellendorf: to enshrine one conception of the good in the benefit condition, even though many people will not regard the benefit it specifies as choiceworthy, and thence allow inequalities on the basis of adherence to that particular conception of the good, thereby holding people responsible for something they should not (by the theory's own lights) be held responsible for.

Suppose we tweak the auction story further, in hopes of achieving territorial resource egalitarianism. In our case, such a strategy would require not only people of different cultures, but also the array of different places that they had arisen from – not only Bedouins, but the desert; not only Inuit, but the Arctic; not only sedentary farmers, but temperate plains. The most appropriate way to tweak the story is then to drop the whole idea of a shipwreck and pretend that, in a fit of conviviality, the people of the world got together to start afresh and divide the Earth equally.

Suppose, then, Bedouins (*badawiyyīn*, from-the-desert) bid on Arabia. To their chagrin, however, would-be oil barons bid up the price. The misfortune of wanting land for cultural reasons, when others want it for economic reasons (which the Bedouins do not, by hypothesis, share), would require the Bedouins to overspend just for a place to live that supports their livelihood. Having done so, the Bedouins would be required to change their lifestyle, drilling the oil in order to make up for necessities they could not afford because their habitat was extraordinarily expensive. But it was precisely to avoid changing their lifestyle that they bid on that land in the first place. Just as Dworkin put persons off-limits to avoid the slavery of the talented, this global auction must put land off-limits, to avoid what we might call the slavery of the resource-rich. But since all or most resources are contained in land, it is hard to see that there could be any global auction at all.

The slavery of the resource-rich underscores the instability of the distinction between choice and circumstance. On the one hand, if oil is valuable, then the Bedouins can change their way of life to take advantage of the good fortune of living on top of trillions of barrels of oil. It is hard to see this as a burden. But to portray the discovery of saleable underground oil as good fortune rather than nuisance, burden, or threat (which would be historically more accurate), undermines Dworkin's individualism about benefit. It turns out that resource egalitarianism presupposes a version of statism about domestic organization. For all parties are treated as having the same relationship to political and economic institutions. Furthermore, changing their way of life in order to take advantage of this "good fortune" is portrayed as, at worst, an incidental cost, even if it requires a fundamental change of livelihood: Bedouins as Beverly Hillbillies. Their traditional livelihood must be portrayed as up for sale to whoever offers enough money to finance their "modernization." Dworkin thus makes the same mistake that Levy made: to enforce a conception of land as a commodity, thereby imposing one ethnogeography on all. But Dworkin's mistake is more serious, since he cannot even carve out space for relatively more sacred places, in principle insulated from markets.

A Dworkinian solution to the slavery of the resource-rich would be to let parties insure against being too richly resourced for their own good. Insurance compensates the unlucky for their bad luck. But what exactly is the bad luck here? Dworkin must, it seems, treat attachment to a resource-rich place as an expensive taste, rightly expensive "because it has an alternative use which is highly valued by [world] society" (Roemer 1996: 132). The question is whether the taste is voluntary or involuntary. I submit that it cannot rightly be treated either way. It is surely possible for Bedouins to modernize and drill their oil, so it seems unfair to compensate them for voluntarily holding a resource that others want. On this view, they must, as Dworkin says, pay for the opportunity costs of their lifestyle for others.[11] But it seems equally unfair (and environmentally dubious) to demand that they drill, and charge them for not doing so.[12] Persons'

---

[11] Beitz (1999) and Steiner (1999) share this view.
[12] As Pogge (1994) and (2002) agrees.

interest in living in a certain way on land of a certain type can plausibly be treated only as a choice or ambition, something that must bend, in one direction or the other, to the dictates of the market. But it has the moral weight of a circumstance, for it is unfair to demand that people live wholly otherwise than they do. Under Dworkin's theory of equality it can become too expensive to live one's own life (as, say, a Bedouin), and when it does, resource egalitarians must recommend dropping that life for another.

Why is it wrong to do this to people? There are two fundamental reasons. One straightforward reason is that each lifestyle represents a more-or-less rational response to the array of conditions that people confront in different places over time. The pressures they face vary, and their responses vary along with them, and then feed back to alter the nature or severity of those pressures, meanwhile generating new pressures to which people must respond in turn. Among such pressures are internal and external population pressure; the quality and quantity of soil, sun, air, and water; flows of people, goods, and capital both within and across communities; and cultural matters such as the ideological or religious alignments of a given population and its neighbors. Over time, and even across generations, there is a certain amount of path-dependence, earlier decisions shaping and constraining later options. The institutions presupposed by liberal egalitarianism have their roots in the responses of Celts and Anglo-Saxons to the various pressures that they faced in northwest Europe in the medieval period (Hargrove 1980), as revised and reshaped by the rise of enclosure, the centralized state, the industrial revolution, imperialism, the liberal revolutions, etc. over the next millennium (Olwig 2002; Tully 1994). Thus the first problem with globalizing resource egalitarianism is that it takes one set of responses that made, or make, a certain amount of sense in a particular context (with a particular set of pressures and a particular history), and assumes that these responses will make the same sense when totally divorced from the context in which they arose. The view is therefore imperialist, if only in a thin sense of the term: it takes a set of social, political, and economic institutions from one place and drops them onto another place, ostensibly for the benefit of the recipients, but without due input from the putative beneficiaries.

The broader consequences of such an imposition might even be extremely positive in the short- or long-term, but that does not change the fact that it is an imposition and it is carried out with attention to (at best) only one type of consequence, namely, the existence of market-oriented egalitarianism. The global egalitarian defends a form of "semi-consequentialism" (Pogge 1989: 47). The view is deontological because it prioritizes a conception of equality over the maximization of global utility, thereby seemingly prioritizing the right to the good; but it is consequentialist because it is willing, paternalistically, to impose this conception of equality and to do so without due attention to other consequences for language, culture, or the environment. The second problem, then, is that the view devolves into a kind of equality-consequentialism, maximizing (one interpretation of) equality rather than ensuring that equality serves as an appropriate check on attempts to achieve other goals. Other aspects of people and other relationships among them must be sacrificed in order to ensure that they are equal according to the understanding of the theory.

The subjection of all persons and all ways of life to the same egalitarian order forces onto everyone a single relationship to every kind of thing, and a single sort of role in the political economy – namely, universal commodification and market consumption, respectively. In the case of resource egalitarianism, when we universalize the scope, conceptions of the good based on long-term attachments to particular lands must all count as mere choices.

Choice is a legitimate basis of inequalities only if the benefit is defined in such a way that everyone can be expected to regard it as choiceworthy. But there is no such thing, in the real world, as a universal benefit, or if there is, it doesn't help anyone: benefit always has to be specified with attainable outcomes that people value. So benefit conditions, and hence choice conditions, must vary from place to place. Further inherent conditions such as talent are relative to the nature of the benefit and the distribution of capacities across a population (Rawls 1999a: 89). From place to place, then – and across times – differently specified benefits cut across social categories in different ways, so that the inherent, choice, and circumstance conditions have to have different contours from one context to the next. The variables captured in the schemata of egalitarianism – benefit, choice, circumstances, inherent conditions, and scope – are highly unstable and highly interactive. Across times and places, then, the theory of equality, whether of opportunities or resources, may need to vary not just its conception of benefit but its metaphysics. Conceivably, one feature (say, nationality, ethnicity, religion, or gender) may come out as a circumstance for one scope at one time, and as an inherent or choice condition for another.

Perhaps, though, we are led astray by thinking of a broadening of scope from domestic to international. The language of scopes suggests differences of degree: domestic justice is like global justice, only smaller. But this may be as dubious as Socrates' assumption in *The Republic* that personal morality is like political morality, only smaller. The scopes may differ not primarily in size, but in nature. And if that's right, then there is no immediate reason to think that what seems just in one scope will seem just in the other. The global egalitarian owes an account of why the analogy should hold. Note that arguments such as those of Moellendorf, Beitz, and Pogge, to the effect that there is a global basic structure, do not make the case, but only restate it – domestic basic structures are like global ones, only smaller and typically more integrated – and in doing so, risk committing themselves to a form of domestic justice statism, albeit on a larger scale (see also Freeman 2006: 38–9).

2.3.3 Beyond domestic organization statism

Cosmopolitan egalitarianism is merely a refinement of, not a departure from, statism about political organization (because diversity must be assumed away in order to give concrete meaning to equality) and statism about justice (because the fundamental political and economic institutions must be assumed to be the same everywhere in order for justice to be achieved). Cosmopolitanism is thus committed to one or another interpretation of equality that is unattractive by the lights of cosmopolitanism itself, and worse, is arguably incoherent. Cosmopolitans owe an account of how to get beyond these forms of statism while remaining committed to their fundamental moral commitment: normatively individualistic moral universalism.

We might try to tweak Dworkin's theory again in order to achieve this. Suppose the auctioneer attempted initially to divide up the world into different homelands, and then allowed each society to carry out its own internal auction. This proposal presupposes a separate method of fairly dividing the Earth into homelands. How could this be done? The auctioneer might allocate the same amount of land, measured in hectares, to everyone, and then let them choose their homeland. But people who live in different ways need different kinds and amounts of land to live equally well. People convert space into well-being at different rates, depending on the kind of space and the kind of life they lead, and thus the nomadic Bedouin and the sedentary farmer would not be equally well served with equal-sized tracts of land. This point generalizes: there is no single variable equalization which embodies equality of territory. Ultimately, whether and to what degree any amount of land can be considered a benefit to anyone depends not on its intrinsic value, but on whether it allows people who live a certain way to live on it that way in relative security and prosperity.

It may be objected here that my argument is committed to a meta-ethical view called "deep distributive pluralism," which denies the possibility of international consensus on distributive justice principles and infers that such principles ought to be excluded from the theory of global justice (Buchanan 2004: 204–8). But my view is not committed to this version of meta-ethical relativism, whether conceived as limited to distributive questions or as covering all moral issues. I am committed to a normative ethical position that could also be called *distributive pluralism*, in which interpersonal distributive comparisons are difficult if not impossible when societies differ in their basic social and geographic organization. But this is not an especially strong claim. First, not all states differ in this way. Certainly the countries of the Organization for Economic Cooperation and Development are quite similar in the character of their basic structure, including the fact that most if not all of them are environmental "neo-Europes."[13] Valid interpersonal comparisons should therefore be possible among them. But taking a broader range of states, interstate distributive questions are indeed difficult at best, since income and wealth – even if measured in purchasing-power-parity dollars – open different doors in different ways in different places. Moreover, even purchasing-power parity does not reflect the effect of macroeconomic and transnational structures and events that may force people off their land and into cities, or in other ways make them less able to shape the places they live and the trajectories of their lives. My point is not that there is no global basic structure, or that principles of distributive justice cannot

---

[13] That is, they have relatively good soil and temperate climates, and their biome is largely European in origin (see Crosby 1993).

exist to apply to that basic structure. Rather, basic structures go deeper than cosmopolitans have seen, because the basic structure includes land, the patterns of its use, and our capacity to shape and reshape it over a lifetime. Cosmopolitans, however, have appealed primarily to the existence of shared economic and political structures to show that there is a global basic structure. As long as the basic structure ignores geographic differences and the ways land affects social organization and individual identity, the theory of global distributive justice will be shallow at best.

Consider Dworkin's desert-island auction. The auction ultimately works only because, and insofar as, all the castaways share or can be held responsible for failing to share a peculiar conception of land, which I've called the Anglo-American ethnogeography. The reason that cosmopolitanism ends up as a form of statism is that it is committed to the universal imposition of this ethnogeography.

2.4 The Anglo-American ethnogeography

An ethnogeography is a culturally specific ontology of land and our relationship to it.[14] The Anglo-American ethnogeography is that tradition of understanding land – epitomized by Locke, Dworkin, and the dominant strain of Anglophone political philosophy in between – according to which land is a passive instrument of the human will, essentially worthless until value is inserted into it by "mixing labor."[15] Because value is imbued in land solely through economic or instrumental activity, land is important only as a store of natural resources or economic potentialities:

> For 'tis *Labour* indeed that *puts the difference of value* on every thing . . . I think it will be but a very modest Computation to say, that of the *Products* of the Earth useful to the Life of Man 9|10 are the *effects of labour*: nay, if we will rightly estimate things as they come to our use, and cast up the several Expences about them, what in them is purely owing to *Nature*, and what to *labour*, we shall find, that in most of them 99|100 are wholly to be put on the account of *labour* (Locke 1988: II,V,40).

---

[14] Blaut (1979) uses the term to mean the study of various cultures' geographic beliefs, a kind of geographical ethnography.

[15] See Locke (1988: II. V, 40–43). See also Hargrove (1980). For a brilliant exposition of this ethnogeography see Russell (2004).

Critics have challenged Locke's calculations and his failure to see land and labor as having interactive rather than additive effects (Cohen 1996: 179; but see Russell 2004). But the view is not internally inconsistent; the problem lies not in the calculations but in the ethnogeography. Because value is imbued in land solely through economic or instrumental activity, land is taken to have importance only as a store of natural resources or economic potentialities.

Consider the use of market value. Market mechanisms purport to measure values, but they do so only after imposing some values and obscuring others. Anything that nature provides – such as the extra warmth enjoyed by northern Europe due to the Gulf Stream – is assumed to be free and inexhaustible (Brown 2000). Indeed, this is the kernel of truth in neoclassical attempts to treat discoveries as creations. Before anyone discovered a use for petroleum, rock oil was a smelly nuisance that reduced the resale value of land on which it was found. Thereafter, petroleum was gold. Soon after that, it was petroleum as we know it today (Simon 1998: 242). These fluctuations did not reveal anything about the real value of the land; they did not actualize some "natural, intrinsick Value" (Locke 1988: II,V,43) that was latent in the land. Rather, the market changed in some way, and that change imposed values on certain pieces of land. Any one piece of land has an infinite number of properties, and changes in social circumstances can cause the values of those properties to fluctuate.[16]

If, therefore, markets impose rather than measure value, then it is impossible to compare land holdings fairly in the absence of a single shared economy, or fixed conventions about land values. If land holdings are noncomparable across economies, though, then global egalitarianism, be it resource or opportunity egalitarianism, is guaranteed to slip back into domestic organization statism. For there is no way to convert land into dollars and distribute it equally, without shoehorning everyone into the same economy.

The plurality of ethnogeographies is, then, crucial for global justice. Arriving on the desert island, Dworkin's castaways have no antecedent relationships to any land. They all treat land as the inherently

---

[16] Why not say that the market *actualizes latent* values? The supposedly latent values would themselves be economic, so *explanandum* and *explanans* could not be kept separate. It is more accurate to say that the market imposes value.

worthless, passive object of human action. But people in real life face the exact opposite situation: we are all engaged in mutually formative relationships with the land on which we live. Land is as it is (partly) because we make it so, and we are as we are (partly) because land makes us so. Antagonists in territorial disputes are often fighting not just for a piece of land, but for their ability to be who they are and live as they "always" have. Territorial rights are important because they respect this fact; cosmopolitan egalitarianism founders on its failure to respect it.

In general, cosmopolitans do not recognize that they are assuming a culturally specific conception of land, or still less, that there are alternatives to it. Just as traditional statists assume the state or the nation, cosmopolitans assume the Anglo-American ethnogeography; that view thus appears natural. In the light of this conclusion, the problem of universalizing the Anglo-American ethnogeography can be restated more precisely as having two stages, each destructive. In the classical or Lockean stage, universalizers refuse to recognize the validity of other ethnogeographies, licensing the obliteration of peoples who affirm them (Bryan 2000; Pratt 2001). In the cosmopolitan stage, universalizers try to respect everyone by treating them as if they endorse the Anglo-American ethnogeography, and equalizing their holdings accordingly. The result is to obscure other ethnogeographies, mismeasure the values of distributive shares, force people off their lands under the guise of market choices, and ultimately commodify both land and people.[17]

2.5 Applying the framework

Theories of territorial rights may be assessed in terms of the three problems for claimants – eligibility, attachment, and normativity – and their implications for claims at various points along the epistemological, worldview, and status quo axes (see Chapter One above). These sets of criteria remain relevant even though cosmopolitans reject territorial rights altogether. The challenge then becomes whether cosmopolitans can explain them away.

---

[17] The two stages are analogous to Mills's (1997: 73) diagnosis of the two stages of Global White Supremacy: the (initial) *de jure* stage and the (ongoing) *de facto* stage.

Institutional cosmopolitans reject eligibility altogether as a criterion for territorial claimants. For cosmopolitans, eligibility is about legitimate authority and just distribution. There is no more question of eligibility to assert claims to places than there is a question of eligibility to assert a right to live under legitimate authority or get one's fair share of collective resources. For the same reason, for cosmopolitans there is no issue of attachment beyond property rights or, at most, legitimate expectations. These positions are justified in large part by the cosmopolitans' commitment to normative universalism – justice without borders. To deny attachment altogether is surely counterintuitive to anyone who discerns a difference between, say, a Cherokee claim to part of Georgia, and a Mexican claim to part of Maryland. To see this difference is not to defend or deny either putative rights claim, but just to recognize the intuitive pull of differential attachments. The same can be said for eligibility. We may be favorably disposed toward a territorial claim lodged by an indigenous group, a nation, or some other kind of group. And we may reject outright any territorial claim lodged by, say, a corporation such as the Pullman Company (Walzer 1983: 295–303). Again, to note these different dispositions is not to offer a theory justifying them. Cosmopolitans deny the intuitions underlying our nuanced attitudes about attachment and eligibility. This denial is rendered necessary by the cosmopolitan position on normativity. But normative universalism, at least as applied in cosmopolitanism, turns out not to be the strength that it at first seemed. On the contrary, the cosmopolitan interpretation of moral universality hides a universalization of the Anglo-American ethnogeography, one that universally imposes a particular conception of land.

But perhaps cosmopolitans could develop an account of eligibility and attachment that remained universalistic and individualistic. This strategy would require them to explain the eligibility of individuals – to cash out territorial rights as ultimately individual rights – and to solve the problem of attachment by determining what gives an individual a right to live and vote in a place. Steven Rieber treats the right to territory as the right to live and vote in a particular place – a right for which individuals are paradigmatically, if not uniquely, eligible. He then offers the following list of factors "that are generally thought to contribute to the normative right to live within a particular territory:" birth; past long-term residence; being the offspring of persons with either of these properties; likelihood of future long-term residence; or linkage via ancestry or other special ties (Rieber 2004: 540). Rieber eventually endorses most of these connections on grounds that people generally "have a strong interest in being able to live near those whom they care about," and that they "also develop ties to their place of work, ties that can last many years; therefore they have a strong interest in living in the territory where they work" (Rieber 2004: 541). Finally, he notes the sometimes excruciating difficulty of emigration, implying that, even though emigration is possible, it is too much to expect of people that they emigrate.

Stateless people, however, are living proof that the rights to territory and to vote are both conceptually and normatively distinct sorts of rights. Such people may be granted citizenship and voting rights in their adopted states, but their having accepted these rights neither adequately discharges nor undermines their claim to a homeland. Indeed the interest in a national homeland may be partly justified precisely by appeal to the assimilationist pressures of absorption into the majority society of another state. The interest in a self-determining homeland may persist even if the exile never exercises her "right of return," or even visits (Gans 2003: 52–8). Thus the individualistic strategy of translating territorial rights into a voting-rights issue cannot provide a satisfactory account of eligibility or attachment.

Cosmopolitans thus fail adequately to respond to the three claimant-related problems we set out in our theoretic framework: eligibility, attachment, and normativity. Consider, then, the cosmopolitan position on the status quo, worldview, and epistemological axes. In the first place, cosmopolitans cannot recognize the status quo axis at all, because it is simply a question of property rights or the theory of legitimate authority. A conservative claim (to territory that one currently both inhabits and controls) is simply a claim that the current order is politically legitimate and distributively just. A radical claim (to be able to inhabit and control territory that one currently neither inhabits nor controls) is simply a claim that the current regime is politically illegitimate, and that property has been stolen and its rightful owners displaced. And revisionist claims (to political or residential change, but not both) are either claims that an otherwise just order has suffered a large-scale theft of property, or that the current residents lack the right sort of say in their government. For cosmopolitans, diaspora nationalism is identical to colonialism.

The worldview axis – how central or marginal the territory is to the claimant – is unrecognizable to cosmopolitans, because the intensity or importance of someone's desire for some object has nothing to do with whether she has a right to it. But as we saw in the challenge to both Moellendorf and Dworkin, treating all such worldview questions as mere preferences is inadequate. Finally, for cosmopolitans, the epistemological axis – the putative strength of cosmopolitanism – turns out to be a weakness because cosmopolitans cannot recognize their own conception of land as a particular ethnogeography, and hence cannot recognize alternative ethnogeographies as having any significance at all. All claims must be fully transparent to Anglo-Americans, or else they cannot be recognized as moral claims in the first place. But this fact brings out the parochialism underlying cosmopolitan universality. Cosmopolitanism represents a significant simplification of the schema we developed in the first chapter. But this simplification requires cosmopolitans to deny the deep diversity in global justice.

To summarize, the Anglo-American ethnogeography, as embodied in Locke, Dworkin and nearly every mainstream Anglophone political theorist in between, treats land as the passive object of human activity and ignores all forms of value that are not easily priced on the market. These assumptions ignore the dynamic, bi-directional relationship between people and land – the mutually formative interactions between people and their habitat – and therefore hide the fact that it is impossible fairly to compare the holdings of persons across economies or ethnogeographies. Cosmopolitan political theory purports to depart from statism, because cosmopolitans apply the principle of moral equality universally instead of only domestically. On closer analysis, however, it becomes clear that cosmopolitans are merely rejecting one version of statism while pursuing a different version. For the method whereby cosmopolitans approach the global context simply universalizes certain culturally specific assumptions about the basic structure. This is particularly problematic for territorial justice, because land forces political theory to come to terms with deep diversity.

This chapter has argued that the individualistic approach, which seeks to derive territorial rights from more fundamental individual rights and interests, and the dissolutionist approach, which purports to undermine territorial rights altogether, fail. It may still be possible decisively to overthrow statism, as cosmopolitans desire. Ironically, however, doing so requires not simply treating the international as the domestic, but articulating the deep diversity that territory introduces into global justice. Because the Anglo-American ethnogeography is culturally particular, genuine universalism requires facing and accommodating, rather than simply globalizing it. The remainder of this book constitutes an effort to do that.

3 | *Groundwork*

A theory of territorial rights must in the first instance provide an account of the subject and the object of territorial rights. That is: who can have territorial rights, and precisely what does one have when one has them. In terms of the framework developed in Chapter One, the former question is a restatement of the eligibility problem. While there is a sense in which the who question is prior to the what question, knowing more about the nature of territory will help clarify eligibility.

We already know something about how to answer these two questions. From the two previous chapters we know that territory is neither identical to nor derivative upon property. The two clearly intersect, but neither concept exhausts the other, and neither provides a sufficient basis for causal or justificatory accounts of the other. Certain rights that property owners have, such as eviction of tenants or wanton destruction, go beyond the rights that territorial rights-holders have. But this does not support grounding territory in property, because territoriality involves structuring internal property relations and creating classes of things that can be owned. But fundamentally, to treat territory as identical to or constructed out of property is to take a side in favor of the Anglo-American ethnogeography (or in Levy's terms: to reflect the liberal conception of land), and to impose that on all.

But these claims are mostly negative; they tell us what territorial rights are not, but not what they are. Section 3.1 builds a recursive account of the concept of a country. The concept of a country has been more or less ignored in political philosophy, but I take a country to be paradigmatically the kind of territory about which one can make a plausible case that it should be a state. There is no requirement that all countries be states; there is, however, very good reason to insist that only countries should be states. A country is a kind of territory, and so the concept of a country is built out of the concept of a territory. But whereas the analysis of territory and territoriality is conceptual in a straightforward sense, the last step – from a particular

66

kind of territory to a country – involves a normative judgment requiring an independent argument. The notion of a country is therefore normative in a way that the notion of a mere territory is not. The normative content of the concept is inadequate to ensure that any state controlling a given country is a morally tolerable state; that goes beyond what we can plausibly insist on as part of the analysis of the concept of a country. That is, the notions of state, legitimate state, and just state go well beyond the concept of a country. I do not suppose that the theory here will exhaust the moral demands we may put on political entities. But I do insist that inattention to the normative element in the notion of a country, due to the previously noted fact that political theorists pay too little attention to territory, constitutes an important gap in the theory of the state. My argument is that the two complement each other, and that neither is sufficient on its own. Political theorists who ignore territory present an incomplete picture of the moral justification of political power – they understate the demands we may place on those who wield it.

In a nutshell, the thesis of this chapter is as follows. Recall the notion of an ethnogeography, or culturally specific conception of land. In effect, territory is a *manifest ethnogeography* – that is, a conception of land made concrete through acts of bounding, controlling, and shaping space, and being shaped by it in turn, over time. A *territorial right*, then, is a right to manifest one's ethnogeography – to have one's ethnogeography made viable through political, legal, economic, and other institutions. The entity that can have such a right is what I call an *ethnogeographic community*, which is a group of people marked out by their shared conception of land and their densely and pervasively interacting patterns of land use. So defined, a territorial right has no necessary link to sovereignty. Ethnogeographies can be made concrete in a variety of ways. Whether a territorial right should be realized through control of a state is a further normative question settled by consideration of competing claims as well as by whether the territory in question is a country. A necessary condition of a country is that it meets a standard of sustainability.

3.1 The concept of territory

The concept of state territory has received almost no sustained attention in its own right in political philosophy. One reason for this has to do with the institutional conception of the state that has been dominant in political philosophy perhaps since Aristotle. (Or perhaps it has just made a comeback in the modern era.) In this conception, the state is identified with the particular institutions or, in Aristotle's version, constitutional form, rather than with its land, people, or anything else (for recent examples, see Morris 1996; Copp 1999; Wellman 2005). A state is "an association of citizens in a constitution," and thus, "when the constitution undergoes a change in form, and becomes a different constitution, the city will likewise cease to be the same city" (*Politics*, III.3.1276b1–3). There is without doubt some truth to this; clearly, Iran became a new state when it reconstituted itself as the Islamic Republic of Iran in 1979. But equally clearly, there is more to the story; the Islamic Republic does not pop up out of nowhere and just happen to be located on the same spot as the previous kingdom. Both the kingdom and the Islamic Republic form temporal stages in the history of a place called Iran or Persia. If you purchased a book called *A History of Iran*, only to find that it either ended or began in 1979, you would be right to complain that you had been misled. The Aristotelian emphasis on the constitution and the modern emphasis on basic institutions miss all this.

Obviously, Aristotle is not solely to blame, and indeed, comes off better than most. Mainstream political theory since Locke has inherited the Anglo-American ethnogeography, according to which land is wholly passive, and worthless without human valuation. As we noted in Chapter Two, discussions of global distributive justice either explicitly (Beitz 1999; Pogge 1994; Steiner 1999) or implicitly (Moellendorf 2002) assume that land just is natural resources that may be of greater or lesser value, such that either before or after they are exploited, their value must be distributed fairly. The moral thesis about distribution may be true, but as we saw, the conceptual thesis is false. Uncovering the assumed ethnogeography explains how a claim that is, from one perspective, so obviously false, can gain such currency as to seem not even to need defense. Indeed, it is shocking, but after all not surprising, to note that Allen Buchanan found it necessary to remind his readers, in a major philosophical journal, that human beings "have bodies that occupy space, and the materials for living upon which they depend do so as well" (Buchanan 1997: 47).

There is little debate that states are inevitably territorial; as Christopher Wellman puts it, territoriality "is the only way for them to perform their functions" (Wellman 2005: 14). Such functions essentially include protecting people from the depredations of the state of nature by making and enforcing a coherent system of laws. But this notion of territoriality has to do solely with using territory as a means by which to act on people. By parity of reasoning, delivering pizza is inevitably territorial because the restaurant is at some geographic remove from the delivery site, and the driver must cross the intervening space in order to perform his or her legitimate function. This account of state territoriality is not inaccurate, so far as it goes – the state uses space to perform its functions – but it does not go very far. As I shall argue, it misses what is peculiar to the state in respect of territoriality: states are not just inevitably but inherently territorial.

Most fundamentally, state territory – a country – is a kind of place.[1] The territoriality of the state consists in the fact that the state serves as a placemaker. Of course, each of us is a placemaker. We make places by bounding and controlling space. We demarcate places by promulgating basic rules of who or what may be in the place and how it may be used (Sack 2003: chap. 2; Cresswell 2004). Arguably, our capacity to do this is bound up with our capacity for agency and experience altogether (Malpas 1999). As embodied, needy creatures, we are constituted by our interactions with places; we make ourselves by making places. In interacting with our environment we both shape it and are shaped by it. As each of us does this, the state functions as a higher-order placemaker, making places by harnessing or determining citizens' agency, shaping its citizens by setting ground rules for the kinds of places they can make, and creating a spatial background against which the citizens act. The state makes itself and its citizens by making its place.

To say that the state makes its citizens is to reaffirm Derek Parfit's "non-identity problem," according to which the policy decisions we make today determine who exists in the future (Parfit 1984: 352). The

---

[1] I shall use *state territory* and *country* interchangeably. For obvious reasons, the notion of *land* is often invoked in discussions of territory. But territories may include things that are not terra firma, such as territorial waters and airspace. I therefore use the more accurate notion of *geographical place*.

territorial aspect of public policy and individual identity adds another level of interest to this problem. Discussion of the non-identity problem typically takes the relevant criterion of identity to be the particular gametes that join to create particular organisms: state policies influence which people will reproduce with which other people, when. But when we treat the state and its citizens as constituted by their interactions with places, we engage with a thicker notion of identity. How the state and its citizens make places influences what sorts of people the citizens will be, what sorts of things they are likely to care about, to believe, to want, etc.[2] Thus the territoriality of the state is important because it is partly constitutive of the identity of the citizens of that state. In missing this element of territoriality, political theorists share Hobbes's assumption that individuals appear on the scene fully formed, like mushrooms (Hobbes 1998: VIII,1,102). In what follows I attempt to remedy that error by offering a recursive analysis of the idea of a country, and arguing that only countries ought to be able to have states.

3.1.1 *Juridical territoriality*

In the first instance, territoriality is a strategy whereby an agent makes and controls geographical places. Not all places are geographical. For instance, the internet is a place that is subject to various strategies of control, but it is not geographical and thus not a territory.[3] Places in social structures, too, such as one's position relative to ownership of the means of production, are nongeographical places. Geographical places are those that normally remain fixed relative to the Earth's surface. Such places include (among other things) rooms, buildings, parks, and cities, as well as countries. Like other places, geographic places need not be equally discernible to all; an unsuspecting boater might enter and exit the Bermuda Triangle without ever having had any idea that she was there. But the Bermuda Triangle is still a place, provided that it is *re-identifiable*.[4] Re-identifiability does not require

---

[2] For discussion in a specifically environmental context see Sagoff (1988: 63). See also McGirr (2001).

[3] One could perhaps regard the internet as a virtual geography, but a virtual x is a non-x.

[4] Anti-realists might be inclined to strengthen the epistemic point into an ontological one, saying that the placeness of the Bermuda Triangle is relative to the observer: it is a place only for those who can discern or respect its

that boundaries be rigid, but it puts a vague upper bound on their fluidity.

Territoriality, then, is a strategy regarding geographic places, understood as re-identifiable places that are normally fixed relative to the Earth's surface. But what sort of strategy is it? The geographer Robert Sack, in his classic work on the subject, defines human territoriality as "the attempt of an individual or group to affect, influence, or control people, phenomena, and relationships, by delimiting and asserting control over a geographic area" (Sack 1986: 19). Control over a place is partly a matter of establishing and enforcing what Sack calls the "in/out of place rules" – the means of regulating spatial flows within, into, and out of it (Sack 2003: 66). Sack uses the example of a parent who tells his children not to handle delicate plates in the kitchen (Sack 1986: 16). If the children are still able to enter the kitchen, and the only means of controlling access to the plates is the injunction regarding the plates themselves, then the parent is not using the place to control the people, and hence, is using a nonterritorial strategy. The strategy becomes territorial when the parent asks or commands the children not to enter the kitchen, thereby using the place itself – its walls, doorways, and distinctive flooring – to constrain the children and protect the plates.

The territoriality of control strategies is itself complex. Within strategies of control we may distinguish between strategies of *demarcation* and strategies of *enforcement*. When the parent tells the children not to enter the kitchen, he is using a territorial demarcation strategy, as described above, but a nonterritorial enforcement strategy (namely, relying on their obedience). If, instead, he locks the kitchen door, his enforcement strategy is also territorial, because the enforcement mechanism relies not on the children's deference to his authority but on his making a geographic place inaccessible to them. While states (and other agents) often resort to territorial enforcement strategies, such as guarded borders, they are not necessary; provided the demarcation strategy is territorial, the place may count as a territory.

The use of territoriality in a geographic place is insufficient on its own to create a territory. Several further necessary conditions must hold. First, the territorial strategy can establish only semi-permeable

boundaries. I speak in realist terms, but I can remain agnostic about this; those with anti-realist tendencies may read the translation into the text.

boundaries. The kitchen in the above example may be inaccessible to children but accessible to mice and parents. Boundaries that were fully impermeable would establish hermetic seals. Territorial boundaries are morally and politically significant precisely because they are differently permeable to different people and things. One aspect of political power is the power to determine who or what can cross under what conditions. Second, the territorial means in use must govern the flow of (among other things) people. That is, if the means of control did not stop or even impede people, but did stop, say, dogs, then those means would be irrelevant to human territoriality. For instance, an invisible fence that relies on electrical currents to keep an unleashed dog in the front lawn uses a place to control things, but it does not make a human territory because the current does not stop people. Third, the territorial strategy must be stable rather than ad hoc, and must have an organizing principle. A territorial strategy makes a territory only if rational agents can begin to plan around the relevant in/out of place rules. This does not require complete rigidity of rules, but territories must have a certain degree of stability. The kitchen-exclusion rule discussed above, in other words, is territorial because it is a geographic means of controlling a geographic place, but the rule is ad hoc and so the kitchen does not thereby become a territory.

Another way of stating this is that a bounded place can be a territory only if there is some principle or maxim expressed by the in/out of place rules and spatial flows. A dispatcher for a shipping company may have a territory in the sense that she is to be held responsible for the secure delivery of all packages within a designated area, and hence other dispatchers are forbidden to ship packages to places within that area. The organizing principle is a rational distribution of responsibility.

A territory, then, is a geographical place controlled with a territorial demarcation strategy, where the boundaries are semi-permeable to humans and more or less stable, and the in/out of place rules have an organizing principle. But this conception of territory is still insufficient for our purposes: obviously, if shipping dispatchers have territories, then not all territories are countries. A further necessary condition is that the organizing principle be juridical. This means that at least some of the in/out rules made by at least some of the controllers are rules of law: the in/out rules are the product, at least in part, of a legal system. Legality matters because there must be authoritative in/out rules, and jurisdiction over such rules when they compete. The same place may, after all, be the territory of any number of people – the shipping dispatcher, the newspaper deliverer, the bank loan officer, and the local mob boss, each with his or her own organizing principle. However a territory is a country only if the underlying principle is juridical, and only with respect to that underlying principle. The juridical character of a territory is therefore essential to its being a country.

In sum, a country is in the first instance a juridical territory: a geographic place bounded with borders that are semi-permeable to (among other things) people, and that are structured in a stable fashion by a legal system. To say all this is to say something about scale: the territory must be large enough to be bounded by a legal system. But there is more to say about scale. Suburban subdivisions, after all, can incorporate into juridical territories by our definition, but intuitively, they do not thereby become countries. While there is nothing inherently incorrect about supposing that very small juris-dictions may be countries (and on my theory, some such places may indeed be countries), there is one more necessary condition that we must add.

3.1.2 Resilience

Aristotle held that the *polis* should be sized so as to be self-sufficient.[5] While self-sufficiency may serve as an ideal under certain circum-stances or with respect to certain resources, it is not an appropriate criterion by which to determine which territories are countries. Self-sufficiency is not always attractive. To the contrary, planned interdependence such as the original Franco-German Coal and Steel Union, or more ordinary open-trade policies depending on com-parative advantage, may be valuable for promoting peaceful coex-istence and hence preserving the state in perpetuity. Moreover, the notion of self-sufficiency ignores our utter dependence on ecosystem services, the provision of which is due to processes covering the

---

[5] See Aristotle, *Politics* (I.2.1252b). Ernest Barker writes, "this may be understood to mean the possession of such material resources and such moral incentives and impulses as make a full human development possible, without any dependence on external help, material or moral" (Aristotle 1995, 320 fn).

entire globe.[6] For instance, the Gulf Stream, part of the thermohaline circulation, which transports water around the world, moderating temperatures and modulating the salt content of sea water, raises the temperature of Britain by about 9 degrees Celsius on average and hence completely alters the kind of life that this country can support. Whether the Gulf Stream persists, however, depends in part on the practices of many other countries, in some cases thousands of miles away. Self-sufficiency is a chimera.

Nonetheless, there remain at least two essential insights in Aristotle's self-sufficiency thesis. First, there is some minimal set of material capacities that a state must have in order for its nominal independence to have any worth. A state that lacked any food production capacity, or was dependent on one or two neighbors for all essential products and services, would be on the edge of a precipice even during good times. Admittedly, we must not suppose that material capacities are wholly beyond human agency. Second, the kinds of institutions people set up have an effect on whether their territories will be viable as independent states. For these reasons I would weaken and adapt, but not wholly jettison, Aristotle's self-sufficiency thesis. A state should have attained, or be in a position to attain, a kind of resilience. Resilience is the final necessary condition in the analysis of the concept of a country.

Generally speaking, resilience is a property of systems; it is the capacity to resist shocks and get back to an equilibrium state – "to absorb disturbance and still behave in the same way" (Walker and Salt 2006: 62). Resilience is obviously a relative notion, however, and so we need to specify the kind and degree of disturbance that a territory must be able to absorb.

When is a juridical territory resilient enough to support independent statehood? In order to answer this we need to know what sorts of disturbances states need to withstand, and how serious such disturbances typically are. These questions are inevitably fuzzy. No social system could withstand the firing of the entire US or Russian nuclear arsenal at it; no institutional framework could survive the sort of

---

[6] See Costanza et al. (1997). The dollar figures that Costanza and his colleagues reach are hard to accept but the point stands that ecosystem services and natural capital provide benefits that could be artificially reproduced, if at all, only at prohibitive cost.

climate catastrophe imagined for northern Europe in the movie *The Day After Tomorrow*. We might stipulate that the level of resilience must be sufficient to absorb foreseeable catastrophes that would still be compatible with the existence of human life, in a recognizable form, in a territory. A gradual cessation of the Gulf Stream may be such a catastrophe for Great Britain; the inversion of the Earth's magnetic polarity may not be. But it may be more useful to think less abstractly. In order to be a viable state, a territory must be able to absorb foreseeable crises associated with known or possible environmental and social circumstances. Such upheavals include the various effects of dangerous climate change predicted with some level of probability for the next century – for instance, droughts, floods, intensified storms, loss of snow cover and ice sheets, migration of species toward the poles. Further, such upheavals must include the human responses to those changes: population movements and attendant material need; new or exotic diseases; etc.

To demand resilience of a place is different from demanding resilience of a system. Territorial resilience is second-order resilience: if a particular system within a territory proved not to be resilient – that is, if some event caused a regime shift from one stable state to another, which was less conducive to the livelihoods of the population – then other systems in that territory should be able to absorb the social and ecological consequences of that system's lack of resilience. For instance, the four major hurricanes that hit the Caribbean in 2004 caused a regime-shift from coral-dominated to algal-dominated reefs (Walker and Salt 2006: 64–73). This shift is likely to significantly disrupt tourism. With the loss of tourism comes an economic shock. The social system as a whole must be able to absorb this economic shock, preferably without thereupon undermining other ecological systems on which other aspects of the society depend.

Resilience need not be understood solely in ecological terms. A resilient socio-economic system is one that can absorb the catastrophic loss of several of the largest employers in a region (due to plant closings or outsourcing, for instance) without entering a tailspin of decline (see Cumbler 1989).

The threshold proposed – ability to absorb foreseeable or not-wholly-improbable upheavals due to climate change and other foreseeable social and ecological changes compatible with recognizable human life in a territory – rules out suburban areas of a city, which typically have no control over immigration and may not even have control over law enforcement and lack land devoted to agriculture. In the easily foreseeable (and perhaps inevitable) event of a serious disruption in the supply of oil for agriculture and transportation, suburban living as we know it would become impracticable. The metropolitan area of which the suburb was a part, provided it still had some farmland as well as community gardens and green space susceptible of conversion into farmland, might pass the relevant threshold, but the suburb itself would not. Similarly, arguably the West Bank (i.e. the main occupied Palestinian territory), given its current population and institutions, would arguably not count as resilient. It depends excessively on relations with two rather unfriendly neighbors, and lacks institutions to make it through a very bad harvest year. On the other hand, a territory may be inadequately resilient if it is too large and is operated too efficiently. The wide focus required to take in the whole may obliterate the local knowledge necessary for effective planning and governance, while planners respond to the large size by developing just-in-time management that eliminates redundancy, thereby undermining the ability to foresee or prepare for catastrophes or system disruptions. As the failed, multi-level government response to Hurricane Katrina demonstrated, resilience requires redundancy (see also Walker and Salt 2006: 71). For these reasons, too, a world economy that approached a full realization of comparative advantage, where every territory produced only that which it could produce most cheaply, and traded for everything else, would thereby have undermined the resilience of many constituent territories. Our resilience threshold does, then, rule out territories at the margins. But it is not especially restrictive. Given current levels of knowledge and technology, both Costa Rica and Canada seem to meet the threshold.

Resilience matters to statehood because resilience provides an analysis of the concept of sustainability. Sustainability is famously difficult to define, and there is no need for a precise definition here. What matters is that sustainability is about "the scope, quality, richness, and benignity of human culture, the biosphere and the economic life we make from them, and the distribution of those benefits, both now and over time" (Prugh et al. 2000: 8).

The link between resilience, sustainability, and the concept of a country – a territory that qualifies for statehood – has a number of other virtues. Making resilience a necessary condition of statehood affirms that the state system as a global institution ought to be committed to a division of environmental and moral labor both within and across generations. It is not uncommon for institutional cosmopolitans to cite environmental problems as necessitating supranational jurisdiction (Pogge 2002; Held 1995 and 2004). This is true enough, so far as it goes, but it must be balanced against the serious risk that supranational jurisdiction will, by definition, overwhelm local control. By making resilience a necessary condition of statehood, we can honor the extreme urgency of truly global action on environmental issues without sacrificing our commitment to the idea that for both moral and practical reasons, questions of such magnitude must be subject to genuine democratic decision informed by local knowledge.

It may be argued, though, that it is precisely the state's democratic credentials that prevent genuine action on sustainability, and that transnational organizations such as the European Union and the International Monetary Fund are able to make hard choices, such as sharp limits on emissions or on specific popular practices like air travel, only because of their *democratic deficit*. Thus the democratic character of states should not be romanticized. Nor should it be overstated. Even thoroughly democratic states inevitably exclude currently existing foreigners (and future ones) from domestic decisions, thus ensuring that the interests of these groups will not be given due weight. These are good reasons to insist on some measure of global governance, for instance imposing global emissions caps and perhaps regulating the number of carbon credits available for purchase in a given year. But heavy reliance on global governance of environmental decision-making has a number of dangerous implications for the feasibility of democracy and the very sustainability at which environmental governance aims.

First, the lack of clear boundaries between spheres of decision-making raises a practical dilemma for global governance. As a broader range of issues comes to be seen as having sustainability implications, either supranational institutions' capacity to overrule state legislatures must expand, thereby expanding the democratic deficit, or, if this capacity does not expand, then the supranational institutions' legitimating function of delivering sustainability is defeated. By treating sustainability as a question about resilience to be settled at the time of initial recognition of a state, we may be able to avoid the over-reliance on global governance that sharpens the horns of this practical dilemma. Furthermore, backing off global governance as a sustainability solution is a way of recognizing that sustainability involves not just one single technical decision made at one point in time, but an ongoing series of decisions made at a number of levels, touching on webs of distinct issues. The very range and multifacetedness of these decisions makes it essential that, as far as possible, such decisions be under the auspices of democratically accountable governments. Finally, this approach recognizes that there is no single sustainable solution, appropriate everywhere. There are indefinitely many ways of organizing and running a society in sustainable ways. It would be inappropriate as well as quixotic to suppose that a global environmental agency, or even a global legislature, should or could be put in position to make these decisions for everyone.

An international system – the system of states whose job is, in part, to recognize or refuse to recognize would-be independent states – has a strong interest not just in achieving sustainability but, crucially, also in delegating sustainability-maintaining functions to the individual members of the state system. The sustainability of individual units within the larger state system helps to ensure the sustainability of the whole. At the same time, the resilience of each helps to isolate environmental catastrophes when they do occur. There is a difference, from the standpoint of global stability (among other things) between a crisis that undermines the functioning of one state, and a crisis that renders a whole continent uninhabitable. And when, for instance, a refugee crisis does occur, the resilience of surrounding countries increases the likelihood that the crisis can be contained and the refugees rescued and repatriated safely.

The reasons for resilience or sustainability given so far have taken the perspective of the state system as a whole. But the resilience condition also serves individual states themselves. State populations have an interest in the resilience of their basic social organizations, especially their ways of interacting with their environment. Such systems include those devoted to producing or capturing economic staples such as particular natural resources, access to trade routes and waterways, and climate systems. In the event that these are disrupted, the social systems built on them are at risk of collapse. Thus even beyond the simple economic fact that the loss of a given industry such as tourism or iron smelting can undermine a community, the inability to absorb environmental shocks is a constant peril. Shocks that overwhelm resilience can cause not just ecosystems but arguably also societies to cross thresholds from one kind of system into another, such that it is difficult if not impossible to return. This is surely what happened to indigenous societies in North America in the centuries after European contact. System stability matters not just for individual expectations but for a society's capacity to provide for its members and perform essential state functions.

It may be objected that the requirement of resilience is biased in favor of wealthy regions and against poor ones. Drought and desert-ification are foreseeable catastrophes that might befall parts of central Africa, but many states in this region cannot absorb them because they are already impoverished. Thus the criterion of resilience seems to undermine the legitimacy of such states and others that lack the wherewithal to deal with foreseeable catastrophic events. In response, our doubts about global governance should not be taken to rule out the cosmopolitans' more general notion that the threat of climate change and attendant social and ecological upheavals might provide good reason to alter the political map of the world. Quite apart from who is responsible for the nonresilience of a particular place, if that place lacks resilience in the sense we have specified then the population – human and otherwise – is not well served by insisting on the conservation of states. But I deny that the resilience criterion is, in fact, systematically biased in favor of wealthy states. There is nothing in, say, mass market societies that necessarily increases their resilience. On the contrary, their tendency to rely on highly efficient production suggests that such societies may indeed lack resilience, for efficiency is by definition the lack of a buffer. (One need merely imagine overstretched OECD health-care systems responding to an easily foreseeable avian flu outbreak.) It is true that wealth can be a valuable resource in achieving resilience, but of all external goods wealth is also one of the more perilous from the standpoint of rational planning.

But suppose resilience did turn out to covary with wealth. Even so, this would provide the basis for a deeper understanding of the harm wrought by colonialism and the contemporary global economy: to have undermined the capacity of particular countries to absorb shocks that are in turn often caused by the practices of the wealthy in the first place; that is, to have undermined the viability of states. This would ground a significant justice-based critique of current practices, as well as a deeper justice-based critique of the conditions under which colonial overlords departed from their colonies. Thus the criterion of resilience does not in general favor wealthy states as at first seems. However even where it has negative consequences for impoverished states, these consequences help us better to identify and counteract the particular form of rapacity that colonialism and its descendants have perpetrated on them.

It is still possible that some extant states ought not, by the account developed here, to be such. In this event, we have three mutually compatible, but independent, options. First, we may endorse a "conservation principle" (Christiano 2006: 91), holding that states should be left in place provided they are not engaged in gross injustice or at an advanced stage of breakdown. Second, we may insist that this conservation principle is an accommodation to non-ideal theory – that in ideal theory, such states would, in fact, not be states at all. It may be the case that, in the world as we know it, they ought to maintain statehood for the time being because they are surrounded by corrupt dictatorships, or because altering state boundaries would imperil the already-impoverished segment of the population, or whatever. In such a case we may retreat to a non-ideal theoretic stance to the effect that, in the interests of basic human goods and political stability, outsiders must subsidize their resilience. But in ideal theory, if a territory lacks the physical and human resources required for resilience, then there is good reason in principle to subdivide or to amalgamate with neighboring territories. Finally, we may endorse a transnational institutional framework designed to move territories along a path toward resilience. I would support such a framework, but the current theory does not engage in this task of institutional design.

The notion of a country is partly a normative notion, and the normativity has to do with the desirability of some territory's attaining to statehood. In this event the normative aspect of the concept of a country is provided by an analysis of resilience. Hereafter I shall use *country* in this normative way to mean a juridical territory that has sufficient resilience to make it a legitimate candidate for statehood. I should emphasize that not all legitimate candidates for statehood – not all countries – will ever be states. There is no positive argument here for the thesis that all countries ought to be states. The argument is, rather, better taken as negative – that no territory should be a state unless it is a country.

This states-need-countries thesis is unrelated to a distinct thesis with which it might be confused, namely, the familiar liberal nationalist claim that states need nations. According to nationalists, key state functions – particularly those requiring trust, redistribution, shared burdens, or an articulated "national interest" – are hindered or even impossible if the population lacks the solidarity typically character-istic of national groups (Miller 1995: 90–4). This is a sociological and psychological thesis about the causal conditions for the successful achievement of certain quotidian state functions. In contrast, the claim that states need countries is an ecological thesis, broadly con-strued, about counterfactual conditions for the survival of social systems in case of emergency. A state that lacks resilience is constantly one crisis away from potentially massive shocks to the socio-economic or political system that organizes the territory. Such a state may be extremely wealthy, achieving levels of efficiency that propel economic growth. But the state's very efficiency may put it one major drought, one bad hurricane season, one disease outbreak, one lost resource, or one foreign policy blunder away from catastrophe. In contrast, a state that modulates its practices in the name of resilience and under-standing its environment may dampen economic growth and political power (at least in the near term) while thereby insuring against col-lapse. As we noted at the outset, no institution or social system can absorb just anything; but there are good reasons, especially in a time of ecological emergency threatening "nonlinear threshold effects" (Gardiner 2004: 562), to favor states and a state system that enhance the capacity of our social systems to absorb shocks.

It may be argued that resilience is not necessarily a good thing; when bad systems are resilient they are impervious to improvement (Carpenter et al. 2001: 766). In response I should emphasize that the subject of resilience in the discussion is not a particular cadre of political elites, and nor is the sort of shock imagined a democratic upsurge. The sorts of shock against which countries must be resilient are social and ecological shocks of the sort that threaten to undermine the basic functioning of society, rather than a particular government or party. But it is true that resilience can protect bad regimes as well as good ones. To hold that resilience ought to be a necessary condition of statehood does not mean that it is sufficient for justice.

In this section I have developed and defended an account of coun-tries that is partly normative, but which falls short of ensuring the legitimacy of any state founded on a country so understood. A country is a juridical territory that meets a criterion of resilience. Going forward, at least, I have suggested that only countries ought to qualify for statehood – that is, being a country is a necessary condition for having a legitimate claim to statehood.

3.2 Whose country?

We can now state clearly what a territorial right is a right to: to make a juridical territory. Such a territory may constitute a country by itself, or it may do so only together with other territories. The current section solves the eligibility problem by explicating what sort of group can have such a right. Territorial rights are held in the first instance by what I call *ethnogeographic communities*. The notion of an ethnogeographic community builds on the notion of an ethnogeography – a culturally specific ontology of land. (The term *community* in this notion is not intended in any metaphysically loaded way. It is simply a placeholder for the kind of organized population I shall describe.) The notion of an ethnogeographic community is related to, but departs from, that of a nation as generally understood by liberal nationalists.

3.2.1 Eligibility and liberal nationalism

From a nationalist standpoint, the eligibility problem would seem to solve itself: a nation's "collective identity involves a rhetoric about . . . special relations to a certain territory" (Moore 2001: 6; see also Tan 2000: 110). That is, national identity is bound up with the homeland; without the homeland, the entity is not a nation, and the issue of territorial rights does not arise.

   Support for this nationalist claim to eligibility might be found in a kind of "indispensability" argument: (i) national solidarity is for some reason essential, or at least highly valuable, to improving individual human lives; (ii) to improve lives in this way is a legitimating function of the state; and (iii) territory is for some reason indispensable to political efforts to do so. This general argument contains determinable elements ("for some reason") that any particular instance of the argument must determine. Tamar Meisels (2003: 34) specifies these by appeal to the role of nationality in individual identity. Other

nationalists foreground other phenomena, including moral development and the welfare state (Miller 1995: 65–70).

The nationalist indispensability argument faces fundamental difficulties. First, it seems doubtful that nations are unique in their ability to
achieve any particular legitimating goal, such as moral development or
identity formation, that is ascribed to them. Some non-national groups,
such as subcultures (e.g. the gay community, particular churches)
as well as religious communities (Islam, Judaism, the Church of
Latter-Day Saints, and Catholicism), may constitute "encompassing
cultures" (Margalit and Raz 1990), and play the same role in premise
(i) at least as well as nations. Indeed, Margalit and Raz defend
nationalism on grounds that nations are such encompassing cultures,
and nationalists have not backed off this assertion. But if that is right,
then premise (i) will be true of many types of encompassing group. If
nations are not necessary, however, then the force of (iii) is ques-
tionable. For given the effect of nationally exclusive territorial claims
on all outsiders, not to mention nonmember insiders, the essential
territoriality of nations is a mark against them relative to any other
encompassing culture that does not require exclusive territoriality.
That is, if some good goal G can be achieved at some cost n through
nationalism, or at some lower cost m without nationalism (for
instance, with nonterritorial encompassing cultures), then the cost
differential between m and n, namely exclusive territoriality, becomes
a relevant consideration against nationalism.

The liberal nationalist might reply that group memberships are not
wholly voluntary, and so the fact that other sorts of encompassing
groups can serve the same functions as nations without territorial self-
determination is no argument against nationalism. For the same reason, the fact that other religions than mine can, as a matter of
sociological or psychological fact, perform whatever functions religion performs in my life or community does not constitute any
argument for conversion from, or abolition of, my religion. If some
people turn out to be members of nations, and others to be members
of other encompassing groups, that is all to the good; but the nations
need territory while the other groups may not. And so thesis (iii)
stands, irrespective of the cost differential and the multiplicity of
encompassing groups.

The problem with this reply is that thesis (iii) is in fact false –
nations themselves do not require territory in order to perform their

legitimating functions. For the link to the homeland is not part of the national identity in the right sort of way. On the contrary, as liberal nationalists understand homelands, the territorial aspect of nationalism could be hived off and the nation might perform its functions equally well.

Nationalism is defensible only on account of the role of nations in achieving important individual interests. To make this claim is to be a liberal nationalist rather than an ethno-nationalist. The problem is that precisely because of this liberalism, liberal nationalism is unable to provide a compelling link to land in general – and so its claim to solve the eligibility problem is implausible. Distinguish two ways that some feature may be part of the conception of a type of group: *additively* and *integratively*. An additive link is merely listed among other aspects of the group. An integrative link occurs when the connection to land structures the group and is the keystone of the group's other features. Any feature could be either additive or integrative, depending on the feature and the conception of the group. For instance, "having a distinct language" is only additively, if at all, a feature of nations, since nations (such as Britain and the US) share languages. But having a distinctive language is integratively a feature of linguistic groups.

Applied to nations, this distinction illustrates the problem for liberal nationalism. Liberal nationalists reject an ethnic conception of national membership; appeals to blood and soil are suspect. As a result, for liberal nationalists, the land cannot have structured the group or its members in any very significant way, because then anyone who is not born and raised in a place would be a permanent outsider and the liberal character of the nation will be lost (Meisels 2005: 88). But this otherwise happy commitment to liberalism constitutes a serious problem for eligibility, because the link to land can only ever be an additive part of a liberal nation. And because it is additive, it can be left aside with little harm. One could theorize a politically active, historically self-aware encompassing group identity that had all the characteristics of a nation except exclusive attachment to a particular homeland, and familiar nationalist arguments would seem equally plausible, for all the same reasons; that is, thesis (a) would be equally true. Such an identity is clearly possible; it has been posited and implemented by, for instance, the Jewish Labor *Bund* in prewar eastern Europe (Levin 1977), and may be typical of "unmelted" or "unmeltable" ethnic communities in liberal states (Novak 1972). A variety of other nonterritorial subcultures, including such otherwise quite distinct groups as bikers, the Ku Klux Klan, and the communist movement in the US during the Cold War, seem to have performed many or all of the same legitimating functions for their members that national groups purport to perform. Lack of territorial rights in the homeland as such should not, then, hinder any nation's capacity to achieve everything that nations supposedly do for their members.

The nationalist may, finally, argue that (i*) even if nations as such are not necessary for the legitimating functions, nations are permissible ways of achieving these functions for those who identify with nations; and (iii*) even if territory is not necessary for liberal nations as such to perform their legitimating functions, territory may in fact be necessary (or very helpful) for certain nations to do so; and as long as this is the case, it is at least permissible for these particular nations to seek territorial self-determination as a strategy for achieving the legitimating functions. Thus in circumstances such as these, nations are eligible to seek territorial rights.

The problem with this weaker argument is that it is not nationalist at all, but rather constitutes an endorsement of a kind of permission right to freedom of political association: those who want to associate with a nation may do so, and may (within the limits of others' rights) seek various trappings of this national identity, including the territorial trappings. All the elements that made liberal nationalism a nationalist view then disappear, and what is left is an associative view where nations have no special role in any legitimating functions. This proposal then holds that nations can be eligible because anyone can be eligible.

Liberal nationalism therefore seems not to have solved the eligibility problem. Unfortunately, nationality has thus far been the only real contender for a response to the eligibility problem. In the next subsection I shall develop an account of eligibility, based on ethnogeographic communities, which can serve in theories of territorial rights. I regard this account as a wholesale departure from liberal nationalism, but those who remain committed to the idea of the nation may regard it as an interpretation of the territorial aspect of nationality.

3.2.2 *Ethnogeographic communities*

An ethnogeographic community is a number of persons with 1) densely and pervasively interacting land-use patterns, and 2) a shared ontology of land. Land-use patterns are *densely interacting* when people's uses of land are such as to rely on each another for their possibility or viability; and these interactions are *pervasive* when they structure a whole way of life. Each of these relations is on a continuum. The land-use patterns of Americans in major metropolitan areas densely interact to a high degree, because they share the infrastructure of their lives – a single-family property arrangement, displacement between home and work, heavy reliance on transportation infrastructure, and a landscape heavily devoted to automobiles and their support infrastructure, with retail areas, office parks, and green space designed so as to accommodate automobiles. And this dense interaction is pervasive, since it typically structures the whole day and has a role in nearly every interaction that a given person might have in that day – from the design of housing, to the energy used to maintain the house, the food used to feed the household, the ride to school or work, the source of income, the schedule of the workday, the leisure activities, etc.

An ontology of land is shared either when people all accept and endorse the same conception of land – often because, once shared, it is treated as natural and not open for discussion or revision – or when people live as if they accepted and endorsed that ontology. Not everyone willingly goes along with a dominant ethnogeography; familiar dissident ontologies, such as ecofeminism and agrarianism, exist within the broader Anglo-American ethnogeographic community. In the absence of unanimity or voluntariness, what makes an ethnogeography shared is its power to recruit people into participation with it in their daily lives.[7] For instance, I may adhere to agrarianism, but full participation in urban American society requires material relationships characteristic of the Anglo-American ethnogeography. Even though an ontology is an intellectual construct, then, it is logically possible that a

---

[7] The notion of recruitment here is not intended to deny autonomy, but just to recognize that the choice to live according to the shared ontology of land is not made against a neutral background, but is heavily stacked in favor of one ethnogeography. One often does not experience it as chosen, or optional, even though in an important sense it is.

particular ethnogeography be shared and dominant in a community even if every single person within the ethnogeographic community intellectually rejects it.

The distinctness of the two aspects of ethnogeographic communities may raise flags. Where the first aspect, involving land-use patterns, is material, the second, an ontology of land, is intellectual. Why cobble together such divergent notions? If the two together ground territorial claims, why cannot each aspect individually do so? Further, the inclusion of an intellectual criterion, an ontology of land, raises the specter of claims' being unverifiable or of ethnogeographic communities' being "imagined" (Anderson 2006).

In reply, we have so far said nothing about morally compelling attachments to land, but only about eligibility to assert territorial claims. Even if two different kinds of groups could be eligible, this would not show that the theory itself was incoherent, provided we made identical or complementary demands upon them to demonstrate attachment. But, second, I should emphasize that the divergent criteria serve as individually necessary and jointly sufficient conditions of eligibility. Persons who share an ontology of land but do not feature densely and pervasively interacting patterns of land use are not an ethnogeographic community and are not (taken together) eligible to assert territorial claims. This restriction is required to prevent mere sets of persons, such as the set of all those who accept the Anglo-American ethnogeography, from claiming territory on a par with real groups of people. Finally, third, the two elements of ethnogeographic community are really both material in different ways. This is signaled by the fact that ontologies may be shared in an *as-if* form; in effect, in some cases the shared ontology may amount to nothing more than a story that could be told that would make sense of the patterns of land use within some society. In most cases, to be sure, most members of the ethnogeographic community will have a relatively coherent web of beliefs about land and their relationship to it – for instance, they will believe that land can be owned, that natural resources of all sorts should be exploited in the most efficient way consistent with sustainable profitability, etc. – and these beliefs will tend to be manifest in their legal and economic institutions. Such people may not identify themselves as Anglo-Americans, indeed may never have thought much about land at all; but even so, the Anglo-American ethnogeography may properly be imputed to them as constituting their ontology of land.

At the same time, it is possible to carve out dissident spaces within an ethnogeographic community. A group of agrarians may come together through community-supported agriculture, rendering viable an agrarian lifestyle, establishing increasingly dense relationships between specific places in the city and counterparts in the countryside, and reducing their reliance on oilfield workers. This means that there is a continuum from shared to unshared ethnogeographies, with no sharp dividing line. The dissidents may, after gaining sufficient organization and enough ability to extricate themselves from the dominant land-use patterns, become a distinct ethnogeographic community. Or more likely, some if not all of them will lead ethnogeographic double-lives, integrated into both the dominant and the dissident ethnogeographic communities. In this event the pervasiveness of each pattern of land use will be significant but limited.

It is also possible to impose a new ethnogeographic community from above, including by force. Colonialism and neo-colonialism often work in this way, organizing places and recruiting people into the supply of foodstuffs and raw materials for the metropolis, or changing economic or other relationships to land. This was especially pronounced in the Global South under European colonialism. In the late nineteenth century, at the high point of European colonialism, as Knox and Marston (1998: 80) put it, "Africa, more than any other peripheral region, was given an entirely new geography." Today, globalization involves similar top-down alterations in ethnogeographic organization. Revolutionary governments may do the same thing in the opposite direction. And grassroots groups such as the Landless Movement (MST) in Brazil may attempt to impose a new ethnogeography from below, by broadening access to land and implementing a semi-collectivist orientation to land ownership (Wright and Wolford 2003). Thus ethnogeographic communities are not static.

The members of an ethnogeographic community need not share a primordial identity, political opinions, or even any particular desire to live together. They must, however, be distinguished by densely interacting pervasive patterns of land use and an as-if shared ontology of land. Normally, the pattern of land use and the shared ontology will interact, each affecting the other, and each potentially challenging the other, but over time, they will tend to converge such that the ideology matches the material reality. Whether, in addition to being an ethnogeographic community, a given group also shares an ethnicity or a national identity may be relevant to political choices of a variety of sorts, but is irrelevant to territorial disputes. And if a group of people shares an ethnicity or national identity but does not constitute an ethnogeographic community, it is ineligible to assert a territorial claim. I shall defend these contentions below as well as in Chapter Four.

There is an inherent oddness to positing the existence of a kind of group, of which each of us is a member, but of which we have never previously heard. To be sure, this oddness did not stop those who theorized encompassing cultures, cultural structures, or even cultures, races, and nations in the first place. Like these other concepts, an ethnogeographic community is an analytic construct. It aims to make sense of a certain feature of our societies, namely, links to land and to one another through land. It aims to call out the key difference, from the standpoint of territorial rights, between groups that are eligible to claim distinct territories in order to live apart from other groups, while also explaining what is lacking in groups that have no compelling basis for a territorial claim. Because it is an analytic construct, the ultimate existence and character of ethnogeographic communities is subject to empirical testing that goes beyond the scope of this work. The task for the notion of an ethnogeographic community is to be able to call out real and significant similarities and differences between groups of people; to do so without appeal to race, ethnicity, religion, or nation; and to show that these significant differences and similarities are wrapped up with land.

Whether Quebec is a nation, a distinct society, or just a linguistically distinct province within Canada is a merely symbolic question. For instance, in late 2006 the Quebec wing of the Canadian Liberal Party voted to recognize Quebec as a nation, laying a minefield for the candidates for party leadership (Canadian Broadcasting Company, (CBC) 2006b). The Conservative Prime Minister, however, refused to recognize the nationhood of Quebec (CBC 2006a). Later, he changed his mind, and the nationhood of Quebec "within a united Canada" is now official Conservative doctrine and has been enacted by Parliament (CBC 2006c). Presumably if there were a fact of the matter it would be possible to settle the dispute by appeal to some further information. On the other hand, whether Quebec is a distinct ethnogeographic community from the rest of Canada can, at least in principle, be determined

by appeal to the conception of land embodied in the main institutions
of Quebec society, the patterns of land-use in which Québécois engage,
and the relationship, in each respect, to the rest of Canada. And it is
clear that, whatever was the case prior to the Quiet Revolution of the
late 1960s, Quebec is now not a distinct ethnogeographic community.
According to the 2001 Census, Quebec matches Canadian rates of
urbanization (a roughly 80/20 population split, with Quebec slightly
higher than Canada as a whole), and closely mirrors Anglophone
Ontario in issues such as commuting to work and household organization (Statistics Canada 2002a, 2002b, 2002c, and 2003). Quebec
matches the rest of Canada in the sectoral breakdown of employment
between production of goods and services. Québécois are only half as
likely as other Canadians to move between provinces when they move,
but this is presumably due to the language barrier, and interprovincial
trade and cultural relationships remain dense. As a result my account of
eligibility would say that Québécois currently lack any distinct eligibility to lodge a territorial claim against that of Canada.[8] This quick
test of the analytical construct gives a (fallible and mutable) indication
of how the notion of ethnogeographic community would apply, and
why it would do so more fruitfully than the concept of a nation.

3.2.3 Contrasts

It will be possible to get a better handle on the concept of an ethnogeographic community by contrasting it with related notions in the
literature. Some writers distinguish between *ascriptive* and *associative*
groups. An ascriptive group is one into which members generally feel
themselves thrown; they do not experience themselves as having
chosen their ascriptive-group membership, even though such groups
are not natural. Some examples are genders, races, and ethnicities
(Buchanan 2004: 380–2; Young 1990: 46). An associative group, in
contrast, tends to have its members due to factors that are more

---

[8] This quick consideration of province-wide statistics, focusing on Francophones,
says nothing about smaller groups within the province. In particular it seems
clear that the James Bay Cree and the Kahnawake (Mohawk) are distinct
ethnogeographic communities and do have eligibility to lodge competing
territorial claims against those of Canada and Quebec. See Joffe (1995); Alfred
(1999). See also Chapters Four, Five, and Six below.

widely understood to be conventional, and are often voluntary. Examples include universities, clubs, and neighborhoods.

An ethnogeographic community is a third kind of group, sharing characteristics with both ascriptive and associative groups, but differing from each in crucial ways. As with ascriptive groups, membership of an ethnogeographic community is usually, and at least initially, unchosen, and often feels natural. To discover that one's own ethnogeography is artificial is often to engage in a kind of debunking or unmasking, just as occurs when we discover the artificiality of an ascriptive identity such as gender or race. So an ethnogeographic community is not an associative group. But ethnogeographic communities are structured by concrete relationships that do not depend on ascription, either – they depend, rather, on the shared ontology of land and patterns of land use. Ethnogeographic communities exist even if unrecognized by their members or others. Indeed, failure to recognize the demarcations of ethnogeographic communities risks putting too much weight on ascriptive-group membership. In the case of Nazi Germany's claim to the Sudetenland, for instance, an ascriptive similarity overwhelmed the fact of ethnogeographic difference; in the case of the breakup of Yugoslavia, ascriptive differences overwhelmed ethnogeographic community.

Ethnogeographic communities are also distinct from Rawlsian "Peoples" (Rawls 1999b). A People is simply the socio-political manifestation of a comprehensive conception of the good. Rawls is not interested in respecting nations' rights as such, but in maintaining neutrality among numerous "reasonable" comprehensive conceptions, as well as respecting and tolerating numerous "decent" ones. Peoples and ethnogeographic communities – unlike nations – do not presuppose the existence or value of any sort of cultural identity. But the similarity between Peoples and ethnogeographic communities ends there. Rawls's comprehensive conceptions are primarily religious and/ or ethical views, judged reasonable or not based on moral principles and social practices. Nothing in Rawls's conception of a People requires or indeed even permits the comprehensive conception to include a concrete connection to a particular place; on the contrary, a connection to a particular place will be inadmissible to any international agreement because it cannot be shared across conceptions of the good. Rawls starts from domestic societies with fixed boundaries, and works outward from there. At the same time, he justifies the existence of boundaries by appeal to a property-based account of the value of internalizing externalities and stewardship over natural resources (Rawls 1999b: 39). This means that, no matter how central to a comprehensive conception, no ontology of land other than the Anglo-American is even admissible to the international original position; while the Anglo-American ethnogeography is enshrined within it as a fundamental principle of global political organization.

Rawls's project of toleration, then, comes out as arbitrarily constricted: any religious ideology or theocratic system of social organization is permissible provided it meets some minimal criteria of decency, while no alternative ethnogeography, however reasonable, is admissible. Rawls thus ends up quietly but arbitrarily restricting the zone of toleration to practitioners of the Anglo-American ethnogeography. That he does so is particularly ironic, given that liberal criticism of his view has focused on Rawls's allegedly too-promiscuous toleration of moral and political diversity (Tesón 1998: chap. 4; Tan 2000, chap. 2; Buchanan 2000).

The concept of an ethnogeographic community avoids the liberal nationalists' pitfall of having to treat land additively if it is to keep its commitment to liberalism. An ethnogeographic community is manifestly not an *imagined community*. Ethnogeographic communities are material rather than intentional, and are unencumbered by the psychological baggage of identity. Although an ethnogeographic community is characterized by a shared ontology, as emphasized above, sharing an ontology is about behavior, not intentions. The ontology is manifest in the material organization of the community; whether it is also in the heads of the individual members is not directly relevant. In this respect the ethnogeographic community is not an intentional group at all. There is therefore no risk that the link to land will cause an inexorable shift toward ethno-nationalism. To become a member does not require a process of acculturation (though that is a likely concomitant), but simply participation in the major institutions of a society. In contrast, with respect to membership of a nation, the criteria of success are themselves intentional.

Ease of individual entrance and exit should not give the impression that ethnogeographic communities are ad hoc and constantly shifting. The sense in which an ethnogeographic community is a community is that it embodies an intellectual and material response to the particular environment in which a group has lived over time. But because the ontology of land is also manifest in densely and pervasively interacting land-use practices, the land itself and the ethnogeography are in a constant give-and-take. That is, the group and the land interact in mutually formative ways: the land is as it is, in both its natural and its built features, because *this* group has been there; the group is as it is, in both its ideological and its empirical features, because it has been on *this* land. And since the concept of an ethnogeographic community entails no appeal to ascriptive identities of other sorts, the land-linked character of the community is of its essence. While there may in many actual cases be overlaps between ethnogeographic and ethnic or other bases of identity, the latter are merely accidental to the attachment to land; in such cases it remains the ethnogeographic aspect of the group that makes it eligible to assert territorial claims.

Consider the example of Bedouins in the desert regions of the Middle East and north Africa. Bedouin tribes are distinct from their historically sedentary compatriots, but their distinctiveness has nothing to do with ethnicity, religion, language, beliefs about political destiny, ethnogenesis, or any of the standard hallmarks of national identity. Rather, their distinctiveness has to do with the fact that their way of life is a response to and interaction with the land on which they make their lives. To coerce them to settle and take up sedentary occupations such as manufacturing, oil-drilling, or, just as likely, servicing tourists – even if they were provided with a community of fellow Bedouin transplants and given decent wages and benefits – would be a great imposition and assault on their ability to get by in the world. And the problem would go beyond the mere fact of coercion; it would render their skills worthless and their habits counterproductive.

3.2.4 *Individuation across time and space*

Over time, of course, the settled Bedouins' practices would become accommodated to their new conditions and they would develop a new ethnogeographic community or melt into that of their new neighbors. This raises a problem for a theory that seeks to build political relations on a social-ontological category rather than the other way around: the individuation and persistence conditions of the kind of group in question.[9] When, and where, does one ethnogeographic community end and another begin? Individuation in social ontology is a difficult problem, no matter what sort of group is in question. (Even corporations are hard to individuate, given their odd relationship to natural stockholders, employees, the authority structure, subsidiaries and parents, etc. And corporations are highly articulated legal constructs.) In his account of the concept of a society, David Copp appeals to counterfactual participation: "two temporal stages of a temporally extended population linked by the social relations" – say, England in 1550 and England in 1990 – "are parts of the same society only if a member of one would have been able to fit into the other without serious psychological distortion."[10] A similar strategy for ethnogeographic communities might go some way toward accounting for individuation: if a person from one place or time could make a living, using the skills she already has and relating to land as she already does, in another place or time, then we may say she is in an ethnogeographic community that falls within the same general family. But this is insufficient, because the concept of an ethnogeographic community makes essential reference both to the density of interactions between patterns of land-use in two places, and to the pervasiveness of these dense interactions. The idea of making a living (rather than merely being able to do one thing) serves as a useful proxy for pervasiveness; but we would have to add to this counterfactual conception – at least when applying it synchronically – that one remains implicated in a social and economic structure that touches both places to a high degree. By this criterion, most Canadians are part of the same ethnogeographic community. On the other hand, while Canadians remain distinct from most Americans, they are becoming less so as the two economies become increasingly intertwined and similar. The two communities share ethnogeographies and

---

[9] Ethnogeographic communities are not primordial or prepolitical, but they share with primordial identity notions the requirement that the concept has to be specifiable independently of the political organization that it purports to justify.

[10] Copp (1995: 142). Copp (1995: 133) has an alternative account of how to individuate societies synchronically, namely, that societies are "closed by and large under the key social relationships." An analogous strategy could ground synchronic individuation of ethnogeographic communities, but the strategy I've opted for is defended in the text.

patterns of land use, and these patterns are densely and pervasively interacting. It is easy to move back and forth between the two, using the same skills, and to make a living just as well (or badly) on either side of the border. But these two communities differ only inasmuch as the social and economic institutions that structure them are distinct. As the Canadian economy becomes more like that of the US, the two economies grow together, and the legal and quasi-legal institutions binding them together increase in intensity and effectiveness, the distinctness of the two ethnogeographic communities erodes. If each seeks to remain eligible to lodge independent territorial claims against the other on the basis of territorial rights rather than mere political expediency, the two states will need to nurture their socio-economic differences. (Whether doing so would be a positive development all things considered is a further question.)

Across times we cannot make quite the same use of shared institutions unless we have an independent theory of the persistence conditions of socio-economic structures. But over time we can appeal to an unbroken chain of social reproduction. Two places at different times are the same ethnogeographic community if a person from one could make a living using the skills she already has and relating to the land as she already does, and there is a causal chain of descent between the two communities. Social reproduction does not require human reproduction – the Shakers were, and the Catholic priesthood is, a socially reproducing community because each transmits (or transmitted) its system of social organization, values, etc., from one generation to the next. Thus social reproduction does not import an ethnic element. Conceivably two communities could trade all their infants and each continue, uninterrupted, in perpetuity. An American from 1960, then, is clearly part of the same ethnogeographic community as an American from 2005: she could make a living using the same skills and the same relationship to land, and there is a social-reproduction chain from one time to the next. But, at least in some regions, this is not so with respect to times prior to the New Deal. The Rural Electrification Project, in particular, radically shifted the relationships between people and land. The skills that support life throughout the US in 2005 would have been inadequate for life in much of the country in 1930, and vice versa. Thus despite the unbroken chain of social reproduction, parts of the US today have a new ethnogeographic community.

Both diachronic (temporal) and synchronic (spatial) individuation are crucial for the theory. Appeal to spatial individuation allows us to determine where one claimant ends and another begins. Appeal to temporal individuation allows us to determine when a given claimant's prior attachment to a particular land can and cannot still ground a territorial right. Temporal individuation therefore serves the same function as Jeremy Waldron's doctrine of supersession of historic injustice. Waldron argues that, without rendering the initial injustice of land theft permissible, over time it may become impermissible to reverse a wrongful taking. The key variable is interaction with land in ways that serve everyday life and hence lead people to plan around that particular land. Insofar as, over generations, a new population develops these interactions, while the previous population loses them, the injustice is superseded (Waldron 1992: 19).

A key similarity between my account and Waldron's is that each relies on patterns of land use to determine a community's morally compelling territorial claims. But there are several key differences as well. First, Waldron is a thoroughgoing individualist; the non-existence, down the generations, of the particular victims of injustice renders the injustice historic rather than ongoing. On the view I defend, however, the injustice is historic only if the descendants of the victims have evolved into a new ethnogeographic community, but might still be ongoing if the ethnogeographic community has not evolved in the relevant respects. And if not, then the injustice persists however many generations are denied their claims. My account is therefore collectivist in an important way. Second, though Waldron also treats land use as crucial, he accepts the Anglo-American ethnogeography and so pays attention only to one-way effects, not to bi-directional relationships between people and land. As such, the gradual weakening of a person's claim to land is the result of their slowly coming to plan their lives around some other land, while the thief plans his life around the stolen land. For this reason Waldron proposes that claims to spiritual and religious sites fade more slowly than claims to residential or economic sites. Interestingly enough, Waldron's account here diverges from moral claims to property. If my bicycle is stolen, I almost immediately begin to plan around its absence by buying a new one or walking more. But if, against my expectations, my bike eventually turns up in the hands of the kids down the street – who have begun to use it every day – I am still entitled to get it back. The change in plans is normatively irrelevant. I agree with Waldron that land is different in this respect; but Waldron cannot, whereas my view can, nonarbitrarily distinguish between territory and property in order to capture the relevant difference.

It follows from both Waldron's view and my own that indigenous peoples' territorial claims in settler states such as Australia and the US must confront the harsh and, in its origins, grossly unjust, moral reality that the land from which they were expelled now houses legitimate claimants whose expulsion would itself be an injustice. But my view differs from Waldron's in withholding judgment about whether indigenous claims remain valid – whether the injustice of the theft per se (as opposed to other injustices whose persistence is obvious) is ongoing, rather than historic. This can be determined only with a further theory of attachment to territory and then by applying the theory on a case-by-case basis; it cannot be inferred simply from the passage of time and generations.

An ethnogeographic community is, then, objective and empirical rather than ascriptive, and independent of intentions to associate, and therefore not associative. It does not depend on a primordial or pre-political identity, and it is demarcated by material, not ideological or religious, commonalities among its members. It is an analytical construct susceptible of fuller articulation and nonarbitrary application to real territorial conflicts. It is a concept of a group into which the land is built integratively rather than additively, and hence, an ethnogeographic community is eligible to lodge territorial claims.

We began this section by defining a territorial right as a right to make a territory. We can now flesh that out. A territorial right is a right of an ethnogeographic community to make its ethnogeography concrete and viable; and to do so by using political, legal, economic, and other institutions to bound, shape, and control space, and to be shaped by it in turn, over time.

3.3 Conclusion

Writing about secession, Allen Buchanan (2004: 337) establishes a territorial criterion for the legitimacy of any would-be secessionist: "Unless a theory [of legitimate secession] can provide a plausible account of the validity of the claim to territory by those to whom it ascribes the right to secede, it fails" (emphasis suppressed). In order to develop a "plausible account of the validity of the claim to territory," we need to know first of all what such a claim is a claim to, and what sort of entity is eligible to make it. Those two basic challenges have animated this chapter.

A territorial right is in the first instance a right to manifest an ethnogeography. Initially, such a right says nothing about statehood. Statehood is appropriate only when a territory is able to provide for itself a certain kind of insurance that I have called resilience, following a growing movement among ecologists. Resilience is the ability to absorb shocks and continue to do the same thing. Obviously, resilience comes in degrees, but our stipulated cut-off – ability to absorb foreseeable or not-wholly-improbable upheavals due to climate change and other social and ecological changes compatible with recognizable human life in a territory – though a mouthful, provides a useful threshold, albeit not the last word on the subject. Resilience is key to the normative conception of a country. Statehood is appropriate only if a certain territory is a country. Not every country ought to be a state, but only countries ought to be states.

Only ethnogeographic communities are eligible for territorial rights. In thus resolving the eligibility problem, the concept of ethnogeographic community remains normatively and ontologically individualistic while putting an appropriate emphasis on the way human groups and their environments interact in mutually formative ways. This account of eligibility also supersedes the account offered by liberal nationalists. Nations seem prima facie eligible because the account of a nation usually includes attachment to a homeland. But the specifically liberal commitments of liberal nationalism imply that what is crucial about national attachments is their encompassing character; for liberal nationalists, land is merely an additive feature of nations. But as an additive feature, it cannot be (normally) shown to be a necessary condition of encompassingness and the associated values. At least in many cases, this character can be achieved without territorial rights. The liberal nationalists' inattention to land is understandable, given their opposition to ethno-nationalism, the fear of losing the liberal character of their view. Ethnogeographic communities, in contrast, build in land integratively without opening the door to blood-and-soil ethno-nationalism.

Ethnogeographic communities are integratively connected to land. The shared ontology of land is not just a defining feature of the group, but is an intellectual and material response to the particular environment in which the group has lived over time. But because the ontology of land is also manifest in densely and pervasively interactive land-use practices, the land itself and the ethnogeography are in a constant give-and-take. That is, the group and the land interact in mutually formative ways: the land is as it is, in both its natural and its built features, because *this* group has been there; the group is as it is because it has been on *this* land. And since the concept of an ethnogeographic community entails no appeal to ascriptive identities of other sorts, the terrestrial character of the community is of its essence. While there may in many actual cases be overlaps between ethnogeographic and ethnic or other bases of identity, the latter are merely accidental to the attachment to land; the ethnogeographic aspect of the group makes it eligible to assert territorial claims.

It is, of course, possible for multiple ethnogeographic communities to have affected a particular place, and for multiple places to have affected an ethnogeographic community or its members. So a theory of eligibility, just by itself, does not resolve territorial disputes. Developing, fleshing out, and applying criteria for resolving such conflicts are respectively the subjects of Chapters Four, Five, and Six.

4 | *Plenitude*

At the beginning of this book I introduced four schools of political thought on territory. The *conflict* approach, epitomized by Jacob Levy (2000), eschews general theories of territorial rights – essentially taking groups at their word regarding their interest in particular lands – in favor of a general strategy for resolving territorial conflicts between groups who conceive of land in incompatible ways. The *dissolution* approach, associated with institutional cosmopolitans (Chapter Two above), treats attachment to territory as, at most, a problem to be managed – an atavistic strain found among those who have failed to embrace global citizenship – not an autonomous element of social life worthy of moral consideration in its own right. On this view, the only aspect of territory that justice must consider is its value for markets or conventional political goods such as democratic institutions; special attachments to particular places are to be regulated by justice, not vice versa. Territory is therefore up for bid in a Dworkinian resource auction, or subject to ignorance in an international Original Position (Beitz 1999; Pogge 1994). Aspects of this view are shared by *individualists*, who accept or defend the territorial state as a significant phenomenon worthy of preservation, but either cannot ground special connections to particular lands (Buchanan 2004), or, if they can, then treat them as derivative upon the property rights of individuals (Simmons 2001).

If the arguments of Chapters One and Two succeeded, then each of these approaches to territory fails, and the field is ripe for the fourth, which I called the *attachment* approach. This approach starts from an account of what links particular groups to particular places, and moves more familiar questions of global justice, such as distributive and maybe even retributive justice, into the background. The challenge for this approach is to explain the nature of attachment and show why that sort of attachment commands moral weight.

This challenge poses special problems for attachment theorists. For in many cases, their commitment to the attachment approach is

100

grounded in a kind of particularism born of anti-colonialism, which effectively refuses to subject the claims of any autonomous or quasi-autonomous people to rigorous examination, at least in terms that are not distinctive to the claimant group itself. Such accounts – especially those based on indigeneity or prior settlement – deny that a general theory of territorial rights could be anything but the imposition of an ethnocentric conception onto all peoples. If some place is sacred to some group, who are we to say otherwise? All we can do is hope that these claims fall out such that no two groups end up being indigenous to the same place.

Extant accounts of attachment include those based on indigeneity (Maaka and Fleras 2000), ethnogenesis (Walzer 1983, Gans 2003), longstanding settlement (Miller 2000, Moore 2001, Meisels 2005), and sacredness (acknowledged by many, including Waldron 1992, but honored mostly in the breach).[1] This chapter adopts the attachment approach, but proposes a distinctive attachment criterion – plenitude – that, alone among criteria available in the literature, meets a variety of theoretic desiderata and is applicable both for general theory and as a way of resolving territorial disputes.

4.1 Accounts of attachment

An account of attachment to territory is *backward-looking* if only the past matters; *forward-looking*, if the present and future matter; or *diachronic*, if past, present, and future all matter. And such an account may be *particular*, if it links people(s) to particular places on the basis of some relation between that people and that place, completely independently of any other claim; *universal*, if putative links between people and places are in the first instance irrelevant to the choice of settlement location – that is, relevant only for reasons of implementation or convenience, but not for the initial determination of who ought to be where; or *rooted*, if both particular and universal features matter.

In Table 4.1, the purest forms of the two orientations we have discussed appear, respectively, in the bottom-right and top-left boxes.

---

[1] Such views are particularist about territorial attachment *as such*; they need not be particularist in general. Indeed, on the contrary, Gans and Moore explicitly defend moral cosmopolitanism. Their particularism lies in not treating territorial attachment claims as susceptible of assessment from outside the claimant group.

Table 4.1: *Accounts of attachment*

	Backward-looking	Diachronic	Forward-looking
Particular	Indigeneity; ethnogenesis; prior settlement	Sacredness; long-standing settlement	Current settlement
Rooted		Use; plenitude	
Universal			Efficiency; need; equality

This chapter argues, first, for criteria that inhabit the middle box as opposed to any other, and second, for one criterion that is found there, namely, plenitude. The challenge for plenitude will be to retain what is importantly right about the strategies on the corners, while avoiding their fatal flaws.

4.1.1 Particularist accounts

Let us first consider the temporal axis of Table 4.1. I shall say the most about settlement criteria, which appear in all three boxes in the top row. But I shall also address the other criteria given there. The basic notion of settlement is mere presence in a place. A *prior-settlement* condition asserts that a group's having inhabited some place in the past gives that group a special claim of attachment to that place today. The underlying normative orientation of prior-settlement principles may go in either (or both) of two directions: the significance of the people to the place, or the significance of the place to the people (Gans 2003). Either way, prior-settlement principles face both ontological and epistemological problems. The most common versions of prior settlement posit that groups have special rights in particular territories because of the significance of the group to the territory. Such accounts face the ontological problem of determining what it means for a group to be significant to a territory. The history of expulsions and migrations, and the variety of relationships that go by the name of (e.g.) indigeneity, mean that there will be no consensus about what it even means for a group to be especially significant to a territory (Gans 2003; Waldron 2003), let alone which group has this relationship to the highest degree. This problem could be resolved with a statute of limitations, but this risks rewarding conquest; by appeal to other criteria that are universal and/or forward-looking, such as current settlement or need; or with a more sophisticated account of the sort of use that establishes priority. None of these strategies, however, is backward-looking.

This ontological problem exacerbates (and is in turn exacerbated by) the related epistemological problem of determining which group actually does bear this special relationship to the place. Even if we knew what it meant to bear, to a very high degree, a significant relationship to a place, the drive to establish one group over another as the (or a) primary bearer of such a relationship would lead to games such as competitive archeology.

Proponents of prior settlement might instead adopt the opposite orientation, positing the importance of the territory to the people. One such approach is Gans's (2003: 100) proposed right to "formative territories." Gans holds that each nation is entitled to special rights in one place on earth – presumably the place that is most significant in that nation's history. Gans avoids the specific problem just mentioned, but faces others. The previous orientation raises the specter of competitive archeology. But at least there is some possibility of empirically grounding claims – some clear sense of what must be true about the world for the claim to be valid. But Gans's orientation means that the putative grounding is not susceptible of empirical determination. For suddenly we are talking about interpreting the national memory of a people, as understood through its literature, intellectual production, rhetorical practices, and rituals (Smith 1999). And these things, in addition to being manipulable through the "mass-production" of traditions (Hobsbawm 1992), are subject to disagreement and competition not just between but within groups. There need be no fact of the matter, independent of particular stories or myths at particular times, about which territory actually is the most salient in a particular group's history. That may vary significantly as the group evolves or as different political movements within the group gain the upper hand over time. Gans trades competitive archeology for competitive literary studies.

For example, the events that constituted Jewish ethnogenesis arguably occurred not in the Biblical Land of Israel (as Gans assumes) but in Egypt or Babylon. On the other hand, the multiplicity of Jewish ethnic groups – *mizrahi* Jews, Ashkenazi Jews, Ethiopian Jews, "Anglo-Saxon" Jews, etc. – would permit an interpretation on which each group might have a distinct ethnogenesis event and, hence, homeland. Which of these factors, if any, turns out to be significant in the designation of one or more formative Jewish territories will depend on which political factors are ascendant at the moment of decision.[2] How a given nation conceives of itself at a time determines not just the demographic boundaries of the national group but which events are taken to be formative, and consequently where those events are taken to have occurred. Thus, appeal to the significance of territory to people fails to solve the problem of uniqueness. The same place may be important to multiple groups, and the same group may have links to multiple places, with choices among these places based on arbitrary or highly variable phenomena that ossify temporary political coalitions. Moreover, if, in an effort to solve the uniqueness problem, we did make such arbitrary choices, the formativity principle would fail to solve the normativity problem; for why should a putative link that just happens to be ascendant at a given time command respect from the moral point of view, or from the perspectives of outsiders? If such principles are to have any non-arbitrary implications, they will need either to smuggle in some additional attachment criterion, or to ossify national identities at one particular time and in one particular political formation.

These objections to backward-looking principles may appear less damaging when the aim is not to justify sovereignty but merely special political rights intended to ensure cultural survival. Gans argues that these political rights may, indeed, most often should, be satisfied within larger states that are not the property of the nations whose homelands they encompass. Gans may, then, have a simple reply to the objection that linkages and identities will be multiple or arbitrary: pick one and go with it. That this risks ossifying an identity is a small price to defuse zero-sum territorial conflicts. Because sovereignty is not at issue, there is no need to solve these problems once and for all.

---

[2] Prior to the Holocaust, Zionism commanded the loyalty of only a minority of Jews, and to this day there remain Jewishly identified anti-Zionists, including orthodox Jews, lovers of Yiddish culture, proponents of Jewish–Arab reconciliation, and opponents of ethnic politics. Further, many sentimental or political Zionists are also strongly connected to particular sites outside Israel, such as countless Jewish quarters in the cities of Europe, the Americas, and elsewhere. That these places are not formative in the right way is a contingent political matter, not an inherent feature of the group.

I share the goal of delinking territorial rights from sovereignty. But the proposed solution is still inadequate. First, precisely because of its pragmatism, this approach to national identities and attachments cannot solve the problem of normativity – it cannot show why any given territorial claim should carry any weight for those who are not benefited by it. If Jewish claims to the Biblical Land of Israel can be backed only with a statement to the effect that this was the group identity that happened to be ascendant in 1948; that under different circumstances the Jews might have been just as happy with Poland, Morocco, or even no political homeland at all, then surely Palestinians will be even less inclined to accept Jewish encroachment or special rights. This pragmatic alternative therefore risks not only failing to defuse territorial conflicts, but instead, reinscribing and worsening them. To be sure, part of the problem lies in the conception of the nation, since nations are intellectual and political constructs, unlike ethnogeographic communities, which are material. But the greater problem lies in the backward-looking character of the formativity principle. Ultimately formativity appeals to a conception of past importance – irrespective of who is where now – and such a conception cannot but be subject to the kind of ideological bias and political shifts that stoke, rather than tamp down, territorial disputes, and that inevitably fail both the uniqueness and the normativity tests. Backward-looking conceptions of attachment are therefore unacceptable.

Forward-looking particularist principles, such as current settlement, face a similar problem. Despite appearing as a hard-headed attempt to avoid the murky past, current settlement just places an extremely short statute of limitations on prior claims. There is a certain attraction to saying, for instance, that ethnic cleansing should not be remedied by a further round of ethnic cleansing – especially if the beneficiaries are not directly the perpetrators, and have already set down roots (Meisels 2005: 93). But even if this attraction were decisive, it could be achieved without violating the territorial right of the expelled people, for instance by permitting the illegal settlers to dwell as a peaceful minority group within the state of the returning refugees.[3] Current settlement, however, not only lets the illegal settlers

---

[3] There may, of course, need to be restitutions if the settlers took the best land and are now economically better off than returning victims. But this is compatible with letting them stay.

stay, but gives them exclusive rights to determine the political destiny of the stolen land. Quite apart from whether the putative right of return asserted by the refugees is decisive – as it would be on a solely backward-looking principle – that right surely carries some weight; and thus a purely forward-looking principle cannot be correct. For these reasons a diachronic principle seems best.

Longstanding settlement is such a principle. As defended by authors such as David Miller (2000: 116) and Margaret Moore (2001: 191), it appeals to the fact that the nation has shaped the land in its image, and possibly been shaped by it in turn. For this reason it avoids rewarding recent expulsions: it can distinguish between victims of ethnic cleansing and long-ago dispossessions that are beyond an intuitively plausible statute of limitations. Such a principle may also appeal to specific characteristics of the use that longstanding settlers are making, or intend to make, of the land. It may fit in with their plans in a particular way, and this integration may partly justify the claim (Waldron 1992; Meisels 2005). On the temporal dimension, then, it is clear that a diachronic principle is best.

4.1.2 Beyond particularism

The problem with longstanding settlement is not on the temporal dimension but the spatial dimension of Table 4.1. Particularistic principles, including longstanding settlement, treat territorial claims as though no one else existed – as though land were not scarce and the resources it contains not valuable. Such criteria therefore raise two problems. The first is the distributive problem of the proverbial last water-hole in the desert: even if one's moral claim on the water-hole is spotless, it is morally intolerable to exclude parched wanderers from having a drink (Nozick 1974: 179–80; Lyons 1977). Tamar Meisels (2005), however, argues that universal distributive justice criteria ought to play no role in individual territorial disputes, but are admissible only in broader theories of global justice. For there is something macabre about insisting that, say, the fourteen or so million people who collectively occupy, or claim a right to occupy, the 26,000 square kilometers of Mandatory Palestine be subject to distributive justice criteria while the mere half-million residents of Wyoming may spread out over nearly ten times that amount of land.

Meisels's argument risks proving too much. It is certainly true that the ham-handed application of global distributive justice criteria in a single instance, when no one else is asked to meet these demands, can itself be unjust, failing to treat like cases alike. And moreover, as I argued in Chapter Two, uniform theories of global distributive justice are inapplicable to territory, in part because land has particular value and partly constructs the people who live on it. A theory of distributive justice that treated land as a uniform good to be distributed according to a unitary principle would be mistaken. But there is a difference between appealing to distributive justice and appealing to the sorts of criteria that factor into the theory of distributive justice. Land and its constituent resources and processes have universal value. To acknowledge this value in the account of attachment does not require incorporating a fully fledged theory of distributive justice, but merely requires that the account of attachment reflect the nature of the thing to which a morally significant attachment is asserted. Given that land is, among other things, a scarce resource, access to which is a necessary condition of meeting certain universal human needs, carrying on as though that were not the case – as though only group-specific considerations carried any weight – would be a form of willful blindness.

This last point brings us to the second problem confronting particularistic criteria. Ironically, particularists make no reference to what good land is even for the privileged claimant. The fact of being there (or having been there) does all the moral work. For this reason, particularists do not appeal to any kind or degree of use that the inhabitants may be making of the land at the current time, or any plans they may have for it in the future. On the one hand this may seem like a virtue. As Michael McDonald (1976) and Margaret Moore (2001) have argued, appeal to any specific kind of use – usually smuggled into an efficiency criterion – risks imposing upon all peoples an unshared conception of the good. I argued in Chapter Two that the relevant problem here is universalizing and imposing a particular ethnogeography. Further, efficiency risks obliterating the very idea of territorial entitlement, since there would always be a more efficient potential user (McDonald 1976; Kolers 2000). And other universal criteria, such as need or the equality principles, are incompatible with the idea that attachments to specific places may constrain the application of universal principles such as equality.

These arguments rule out principles that appeal solely to universal criteria, but do not prevent our allowing such criteria some role. That universal criteria should not be absent is apparent from the fact that land is both a universal and a particular good. In Locke, instances of appropriation, though necessitated by the need to survive and flourish, are justified (and delimited) by the fact that they prevent waste and do no harm to those thereby excluded. Locke's approach, then, respects the basic idea that private or particular appropriation should answer to universal concerns. Whatever we conclude about Locke's larger approach, he is right to attend to both universal and particular goods.

4.2 Diachronic and rooted criteria

One could accommodate universal considerations in a number of ways. Meisels, for instance, grants that each nation may have its own conception of the good, thereby undermining an unqualified efficiency criterion. But she argues that a thin theory of use is indeed common to all people(s), and that this thin theory constitutes a universal element by which to assess territorial claims. Meisels thus defends a *rooted* criterion of attachment. It imposes a universal constraint – use – on particular relationships, respecting that land is both a universal and a particular good. Moreover, her criterion is *diachronic*, because it appeals to use as a test of ongoing relationships.

Meisels's criterion, I shall argue, is flawed for two main reasons. First, though rooted, her formulation is rooted in the wrong way, and therefore fails adequately to accommodate either the particular or the universal element of rootedness. I shall propose an alternative conception of rootedness that meets both demands. This first problem, though of the first importance to accounts of attachment, is perhaps not fatal to Meisels's use criterion. What is fatal is that use criteria impose a minimum but not a maximum. Any criterion that takes seriously the (universal) demands of contemporary outsiders and the (forward-looking) demands of future people must impose not just a minimum amount or form of use, but a maximum. We need, in other words, a sustainability element. In the remainder of this section I shall explicate these critiques of Meisels's use criterion; the next section develops a more attractive alternative.

4.2.1 *Understanding rootedness*

Meisels's thin theory of use includes uses of land for "goods such as food, water, natural resources, shelter, and various other means of subsistence" (2005: 67). Land that is not in use (so understood) "might bring entitlement into question" (*Ibid.*: 69). But this list is both too broad and too narrow. It is too broad because, even though the list is justified by the role that the various goods play in subsistence, these goods also play a role in allowing states such as the US and Canada to "ingross as much as [they] will" (Locke 1988: II.31). Indeed, the behavior of these and other states and their members constitutes abuse of those resources, reducing their value both to their claimants and to any others who might care about them, and sharply reducing the resilience of the territories themselves as well as their underlying ecological and social systems. A better criterion would thus be narrower inasmuch as it would require sustainable use.

However, Meisels's list is in another way too narrow, since there may be many uses for land other than the economic and anthropocentric ones that Meisels lists. For instance, despite their many environmental crimes, the US and Canada also maintain wilderness areas and wildlife corridors such as the Yellowstone to Yukon ecoregion, which stretches from Wyoming through the Yukon territory to the Alaskan border (see Figure 4.1). To charge that such lands are not in use in the ways Meisels mentions – though in many cases true – misses the point.

Meisels recognizes this problem. As she sees it, the difficulty lies in overcoming the cultural bias that has befuddled universalists.

It is admittedly extremely difficult to construct a non-culturally biased account of what constitutes 'non-use' of land to an extent which calls its inhabitants' claim to it into question. I have in mind a situation in which a portion of land is, while not totally unpopulated, nonetheless neglected by its local inhabitants (2005: 70).

Meisels's strategy to avoid imposition of a criterion of use is to lower the bar almost to the floor, in hopes of ensuring that everyone can jump over it. But this then counts as use many forms of desolation that beset Anglo-American cultures, such as the proliferation of white elephants, brownfields, ghost towns, abandoned mines, and the like. The attempt to universalize the criterion of use by lowering the bar

Fig. 4.1: The Yellowstone-to-Yukon ecoregion, USA–Canada. Designed by D. J. Biddle, University of Louisville Center for Geographic Information Systems.

ignores the fact that conceptions of neglect are also culturally particular. Meisels's strategy is ultimately a form of what James Tully (1995) refers to as "Esperanto constitutionalism": acknowledging diversity in principle but failing to find the flexible perspective that would permit real accommodation of it.

From an Anglo-American perspective, indigenous forms of use may indeed be neglectful, and vice-versa. The trick is not to try to commensurate – to find a lowest common denominator between culturally particular conceptions of use – but to learn what counts as use and what counts as neglect from each perspective. An attachment criterion should be rooted in this way: to acknowledge that a conception of use must itself be derived from the ethnogeography of the community whose use is in question. We do not need a universal criterion of use; we need a universally fair way to test particular criteria of use. For instance, if the Anglo-American ethnogeography venerates resource extraction and a market in land, then the test of use for Anglo-Americans should be whether they are extracting resources and maintaining markets in land. In contrast, if the Woodlands Anishinabe (Ojibwa or Chippewa) venerate sustainable forestry, then sustainably managed forests are the hallmark of use for Woodlands Anishinabe communities (Callicott 1997: 126–30). The bar is not lowered, but – to continue the high-jump metaphor – moved to a different pair of uprights. It is still possible to fail to jump over, but not simply due to miscommunication about the nature of the challenge.

This refocused cultural sensitivity supports a use criterion that is rooted in the right way. But it does not help us solve the problem of sustainability. This is no surprise, for use is essentially a minimal criterion – non-neglect – while sustainability imposes a maximum of sorts. For this reason I depart from use altogether. Instead, I shall defend a criterion of *plenitude*. Plenitude is the only criterion that is both diachronic and rooted in the right way. In its rootedness it follows the strategy I have just outlined for cultural sensitivity, while incorporating a sustainability aspect. Further, as we shall see, plenitude also links groups to particular territories, thereby solving the uniqueness problem. And due to these elements – diachronicity, rootedness, uniqueness, and sustainability – plenitude is the one attachment criterion that solves the normativity problem. It thus completes our resolution of the three claimant challenges from the framework developed in Chapter One.

4.3 Plenitude

Plenitude has a long history in both liberal and illiberal political thought. But if it is nothing new, plenitude may also seem to be an idea well lost. European expansionists justified settlement in the Americas and elsewhere by arguing that the land was antecedently empty (Tully 1994: chap. 5). Their ensuing behavior made this a self-fulfilling prophecy (Jennings 1976; Crosby 1993). Early Zionists repeated this process (Meisels 2005: 64; Morris 2004). In the other direction, US opponents of immigration claim, in almost as many words, that their country cannot hold more people (FAIR 2002).

But while plenitude has – at best – a checkered history, the normative premise on which it is based is not the problem. Rather, expansionists and imperialists have interpreted the normative premise in ethnogeographically specific ways, coupled such interpretations with false empirical claims, and imposed on others an unshared conception of plenitude. In this section I hope to recapture what is attractive about plenitude by positing and defending a conception that is diachronic and rooted in the right way, and which resolves the problems of attachment (including uniqueness) and normativity.

4.3.1 *Sketching the notion*

What is plenitude? The obvious fallbacks have to do with population density, a constructed environment, and carrying capacity. But these proposals carry no normative significance. If a territory is at or beyond its carrying capacity, this may be due to excessive consumption; for carrying capacity is a relationship not between the land and the number of people, but between the land and the demands the population makes on it. Unless the standard of living is at a minimal level of comfort, and is attained highly efficiently, the appeal to carrying capacity on its own would serve more as a critique of the extant population than as a justification for its claim. Moreover, constructed environments are compatible with emptiness. Empty places are not necessarily mere space. Rather, they may be vacant, desolate, burned-out, or abandoned. White elephants, brownfields, and ghost towns are all empty, despite the fact that they are built-up areas and there may be a small number of people living or working there. Similarly, a town that has suffered severe bombing in wartime might be filled with rubble and wreckage. All the same physical stuff (and more) goes into the rubble and wreckage as went into the town or city. But there are no more buildings, gardens, shops, etc. There is only rubble.

On the other hand, the failure to meet any of the obvious fallbacks is not clearly a failure of plenitude. The Yellowstone-to-Yukon ecoregion is full, but not densely populated (by humans), not at carrying capacity, and not heavily built up. The obvious fallbacks are nonstarters.

Consider, instead, some examples that bring out three features essential to a better account of plenitude. Suppose a city-dweller travels through Henry County, Kentucky on his way from Louisville to Cincinnati to visit friends. He sees endless expanses, occasionally interrupted by cows, horses, and barns that, for all he knows, may be unused or even fake. Most of the expanses are yellow or green, but he cannot identify the crops, if any, under cultivation. He does not even know if there is a difference between hay and straw. He sees very few people. At one point he passes a clearing with three large crosses, and nearby, a large sign listing the Ten Commandments. When he reaches his destination his hosts ask, "How was the drive?" He replies, "Uneventful. The countryside is pretty much empty, except for the crosses and the Commandments." His host follows up: "But isn't Henry County beautiful?" And he replies, "Except for the signs, I couldn't tell where one county ended and another began."

In contrast, consider Wendell Berry's response to his "native hill" – rural Henry County, Kentucky – upon returning there from New York:

It is, I saw, inexhaustible in its history, in the details of its life, in its possibilities. I walked over it, looking, listening, smelling, touching, alive to it as never before. I listened to the talk of my kinsmen and neighbors as I never had done, alert to their knowledge of the place, and to the qualities and energies of their speech. I began more seriously than ever to learn the names of things – the wild plants and animals, the natural processes, the local places – and to articulate my observations and memories. My language increased and strengthened, and sent my mind into the place like a live root system ... I came to see myself as growing out of the earth like the other native animals and plants. I saw my body and my daily motions as brief coherences and articulations of the energy of the place, which would fall back into it like leaves in the autumn (Berry 2002: 7).

Berry's description suggests at least three key aspects of plenitude. First is *diversity*: a place is full not when we fill it with things, but when it is both internally and externally diverse. A place is internally diverse to the extent that its elements are distinct one from another; it is externally diverse when the place itself is distinct from other places. Diversity is closely linked to the account of geographic places we used in Chapter Three. To make a place out of mere space is to bound it, to subject it to in/out of place rules, and to control, to some degree, the flows within and across its borders. Plenitude extends this bounding and controlling. Second, it is clear that diversity, be it internal or external, is *observer-relative*: our city-dwelling traveler sees emptiness where Berry sees plants, animals, processes, and places that he understands. And where Berry can see the limit of his native hill, our traveler cannot. Thus diversity is as much a property of the observer as it is of the geographical place itself.

Third, diversity is a *variable*. It is enhanced when the observer embarks on a project of knowing and responding to the place; it is diminished when entropy sets in or a single species subjugates all others. Henry County is full for Wendell Berry, but empty for our city-dwelling traveler. And what makes a rubble-filled war zone empty is not a lack of medium-sized physical objects, since that is precisely what is there: rubble. What makes it empty is the lack of internal diversity. To describe it as rubble-filled is to call attention to precisely this feature – the dearth of *qualitatively distinguishable* things. To be sure, as time passes, a community of sorts might emerge, scratching out a living amidst the rubble. These people might eventually fill the place. They could then recognize a variety of sorts of things, and through their activities increase that variety. And so the people who have filled the place thereby develop a significant attachment to it, even as it remains empty for anyone who would call it rubble-filled.

To generalize: plenitude is both an empirical property of places and a project upon which one or more persons may embark. In the former sense, plenitude is the objective fullness of a place from a perspective, whereas in the latter sense it is a stance that one adopts with respect to a place, a decision to enhance its plenitude. To enhance plenitude there is no need to increase the number of different things, or even different kinds of things, present in the place, but only to set out to know the kinds of things that are there, and to help ensure that they are able to stay and flourish there. These projects may involve increasing the number of things or kinds of things in the place, but they may also involve reducing it: for example, getting rid of the kudzu to protect the biodiversity of a forest.

4.3.2 Empirical plenitude

Empirical plenitude is a high degree of internal and external diversity. This property is both objective and relative. It is observer-relative, or more precisely, ethnogeographically relative. In order to see a place as internally diverse one must presuppose an ethnogeography that recognizes a multiplicity of kinds of things there. In order to see it as externally diverse (distinct from other places) one must presuppose an ethnogeography that recognizes some difference between the things there and those in a contiguous territory, or between the arrangements of things in each. This ethnogeographic relativism of plenitude is crucial to achieving rootedness in the right way – that is, cultural sensitivity without simply lowering the bar.

But the relativism here may seem to bring back particularism, and with a vengeance, thereby undermining the universalistic elements of rooted criteria (which require that empirical plenitude is a universally testable fact about a place). To impute existence to something is to include that thing in one's ontology; with a different ontology one might see different things, or nothing at all, in the same place. But this is compatible with a given ontology's itself being subject to both internal and external assessment.

Ethnogeographic relativism about plenitude crucially does not entail subjectivism. To the contrary: to say that it is true, relative to E, that p, is to say that in the ontology of E, p is objectively true. It is not to say that the truth of p is up to those who use E, and that for them, as it were, sincerity is the criterion of truth. That would be subjectivism. By analogy, for theists who believe that God is all-knowing, all-powerful, and all-good, the problem of evil objectively poses a serious challenge. This challenge is "theologically relative": if one rejected that particular account of God, the problem would dissolve. But the challenge does not go away simply because theists can sincerely claim to believe in God without having confronted the problem; it demands an answer. Similarly, plenitude is ethnogeographically relative, but for this reason it is possible to demand of any community that its members show (objectively) that the land is full by their own lights. Further, it is possible even for outsiders to assess whether they have successfully shown this. The conflation of relativism with subjectivism and the notion that internal assessments must lack critical bite may reflect an assumption that (nonwestern) systems of thought are simple and thus lack the internal resources to subject their own commitments to rigorous testing. Ethnogeographic relativism does not make this mistake, but rather presupposes that each ethnogeography will contain such resources and thereby be able to subject its adherents' plenitude claims to demanding standards of evidence.

In addition to internal criteria, relativism is compatible with assessment by appeal to external criteria, such as independent moral and logical norms, as well as empirical generalizations. The only genuinely relativistic aspect may be understood as a limited application of Quinean ontological relativity: for a certain range of cases, existence claims are true or false only in light of an ontology (Quine 1969). There is no ontology-free perspective, nor is there any single privileged ontology. But this claim entails neither the failure of inter-translatability between ethnogeographies, nor even the "scheme-world dualism" pilloried by Donald Davidson (1983). It remains possible to assess whole ontologies as well as their proper subsets for coherence, attractiveness, plausibility, moral worth, etc.[4] The ethnogeographic relativity of plenitude points us to a source of assessment tools and sets guidelines for the fair evaluation of claims.

To avoid imposing a single ethnogeography when assessing claims of plenitude, we must use the two-level strategy developed earlier for rooted criteria. The claimant group must affirm that some place is full. Its plenitude may be apparent only given the claimant's ethnogeography, but the group must nonetheless corroborate the affirmation by appeal to some account of the demands of plenitude, given that ethnogeography. This alleged achievement of plenitude would then be susceptible of objective empirical assessment by both international fact-finding teams and internal skeptics. (Returning to the high-jump metaphor: the jumper herself informs the judge which pair of uprights will be in play; she lacks full control over how high the bar will be set; and whether or not her jump is successful is an objective fact assessable as easily by others as by the jumper herself.) Wendell Berry's agrarian ethnogeography, for instance, would entail that his land should be sustaining multiple uses, such as produce for food, timber for building, pasturage for livestock, trails for recreation, etc. In the

---

[4] Haack (1996) deflates Quinean ontological relativity, finding that it is not especially deep. I follow Haack's analysis here.

event that outsiders wanted to test Berry's claim, they could watch him work; examine his ability to name the various species of plants and animals in the region; ask him to lead them around the region's trails. These achievements would be irrelevant to testing the plenitude of, say, industrial sites controlled by endorsers of the Anglo-American ethnogeography. But these achievements would be empirical evidence of the plenitude of Henry County, Kentucky, given an agrarian ethnogeography. The ethnogeography itself, and its conception of plenitude, are not put in question; what is tested is the extent to which the ethnogeographic community satisfies its own criteria.

4.3.3 Intentional plenitude

Intentional plenitude exists when the claimant is engaged in a project of enhancing and/or maintaining the empirical plenitude of the place. To remain full the place need not be left untouched; on the contrary, since all places are subject to spatial flows both internally and across their boundaries, maintaining a place as full is rather a matter of equilibrium. A community or state adopts a project of enhancing plenitude by, for instance, remaining committed to enhancing resilience and preventing dereliction, disuse, and permanent vacancy. Also characteristic of such an attitude is the project of developing a deeper understanding of and appreciation for the diversity of the place – for instance, investigating animal and plant species, avoiding interference with predation patterns, etc.

Berry's native hill is full for him and other members of his agrarian ethnogeographic community. The empirical plenitude of the place consists in its internal variety and external diversity; its intentional plenitude consists in his making a project of enhancing his understanding and appreciation of the variety, and maintaining it thus. Like empirical plenitude, intentional plenitude is objectively testable in that Berry and those among whom he lives could demonstrate their ongoing commitment by, for instance, drawing freehand maps of the main market areas or routes to farms in the area; and more importantly, they could apply their skills to the land so as to produce food and other goods, while improving the soil from one year to the next. By demonstrating the plenitude of the land, Berry demonstrates that the agrarian ethnogeographic community of rural Kentucky passes the first crucial step in achieving territorial rights.

I do not mean to privilege cultivation or to suggest that only agrarians can attain plenitude. Urban plenitude is demonstrated in similar ways every day by city dwellers, at least in many cities. Nor need plenitude involve a positive attitude to a place. One could loathe a place or its people, but not thereby lose one's right to it, provided that the loathing did not preclude intentional plenitude. Indeed, I have focused on agrarian, as opposed to urban, plenitude, only because the two diverge sharply, and the idea that areas with high population densities might be full is uncontroversial.

To say cities are full for their inhabitants, or that Henry County is full for agrarians, is ultimately to say something about mental states. Even empirical plenitude, since it is ethnogeographically relative, is a relation between a place and a belief-set. Thus one way of enhancing the empirical plenitude of a place is to learn more about it. Indeed, plenitude does not demand that we fill the place up with new things or kinds of things. Sometimes, the lack of plenitude is due not to ethnogeography but to ignorance. For instance, our city-dweller who crossed Henry County might be embarrassed by his ignorance, and on the return trip, stop to examine whether part of Henry County might be a good place to build an auto plant or a factory outlet store. He would then set out to determine the driving distance to urban areas, the accessibility of major highways, railway lines, and infrastructure, the topography and availability of land for sale, etc. In learning all these things he embarks on a project of enhancing the plenitude (by his own lights) of the place. He may continue with this project, for instance by setting out to purchase land, acquire building permits, etc. Eventually, he could demonstrate empirical plenitude by (for instance) rattling off figures, and intentional plenitude by coming up with a business plan.[5] (Note that he could not use this plenitude to support a territorial claim, since an individual does not constitute an ethnogeographic community, and he thus fails the eligibility test.)

It may seem ironic, and even to constitute a potential objection, that both empirical and intentional plenitude are ultimately facts about mental states. For the initial account of ethnogeographic communities was explicitly materialist, and this was held to be a virtue; but now

---

[5] This example raises the question of whether plenitude is a scalar, maximal, or threshold notion. I shall propose a rough threshold below.

that materialism seems to have been lost. The irony can be defused. Unlike eligibility, which is a status, attachment is an achievement. If the requisite status were ideal rather than material, this would raise a range of challenges (and moral hazards) regarding membership and identity criteria, and would obscure the land's significance to the group. These problems were evident in the contrast between ethnogeographic communities and liberal nations. On the other hand, the requisite achievements must at bottom be ideal for two reasons. First, while these achievements of knowledge and aims are empirical relative to the ontology of the group in question – the particular ethnogeography – they need not meet the challenge of accuracy with respect to an alternative, unshared, ethnogeography. Second, these achievements are, after all, achievements of knowledge and aims. Even when they involve transformations of the material world, they are the result of intentional decisions and actions. Empirical plenitude might conceivably occur unintentionally or by accident, but such plenitude is still ethnogeographically relative, and thus makes essential reference to the intellectual construct of an ontology of land.

Plenitude is, then, divided between an empirical element and an intentional element, each of which is empirically testable and each of which is normally necessary for a fully fledged territorial claim, but each of which is also at bottom ideal.

To foreshadow Chapter Five, recall the status quo axis on which territorial claims may differ (see Chapter One). A viable theory of territorial rights must have something equally plausible to say about conservative, revisionist, and radical claims. I have so far articulated plenitude in conservative terms, except for the case of the city-dweller with designs on Henry County. But an easy shift permits us to account for revisionist and radical claims. Radical claims occur when a group that neither inhabits nor controls a territory asserts a claim to be able to do both of these. What's crucial in this case is demonstrating empirical emptiness and intentional plenitude. That is, the radical claimant must show that the place is currently empirically empty, but that the claimant has a project of filling it, one way or another. Lest this sound too much like Locke on America, I should emphasize that such claims will be both testable and, more importantly, rebuttable: the people, if any, who are already there or who already control the place will have the opportunity to demonstrate both empirical and intentional plenitude. The problem is not with plenitude as such but with the imposition of an exclusively Anglo-American criterion.[6]

Revisionist claims come in four types: (i) those where controllers want to settle; (ii) those where residents want control; (iii) those where controllers want to disengage, and (iv) those where residents want to depart. In order to articulate a claim (which may or may not suffice to justify political changes), controllers who want to settle must demonstrate empirical emptiness and intentional plenitude in the same way as radical claimants. On the other hand, revisionist claims of type (ii), lodged by residents who want control, are conservative with respect to plenitude and seek only to alter political relationships. So the first two forms of revisionist claims resemble radical and conservative claims, respectively. And controllers or residents who want to depart must ensure that their departure would not lead to a wholesale emptying-out, for instance by ethnic cleansing or genocide. I will discuss competing territorial claims in Chapter Five. I include this digression here simply to avoid giving the impression that my account can Comprehend only conservative claims.

4.3.4 Plenitude or settlement?

It may be objected that plenitude is just a dressed-up version of settlement, and thus there is no need to posit a new and confusing concept. Meisels understands settlement as including both a narrow conception, of "human residence in a territory," as well as "a fruitful relationship with the land, which consists primarily of building on it and shaping its landscape . . . not only the presence of individuals on a piece of land but also . . . a permanent physical infrastructure" (Meisels 2005: 79). Plenitude may take this form, but it may also take other forms; indeed, it may take the form of preventing or sharply restricting human encroachment in order to keep an ecosystem – be it directly economically productive or otherwise – intact.[7] Settlement

---

[6] For further explanation and defense of this claim see 4.4 below.
[7] This reply may raise a further objection in terms of need and urgency. I shall deal with this below. Also, this is not to endorse "the exclusion of human inhabitants for the protection of the purity of the natural environment enclosed in park boundaries" (Heyd 2005: 230). The point is just that reducing or even eliminating the human footprint may be the best strategy for plenitude in some places.

criteria can support claims based on permanent physical infrastructure, but plenitude can support both these sorts of claims and other
claims based on, say, ecosystem preservation. An even more extended
conception of settlement might include other types of relationships to
land – for instance, by saying that some group identifies itself as
intertwined with the environment, such that it imprints itself on the
landscape by preserving biodiversity (Heyd 2005: 229). This may be
more plausible, but then the term "settlement" has become simply a
technical term that bears little relation to the standard meaning of the
term. Settlement is then merely a dressed-down version of plenitude.
In this event, I need not insist on rejecting the term "settlement," but
then, there is nothing gained (and some clarity lost) in using it.

Moreover – and more importantly – it is possible to settle one place
in a way that expresses alienation from another place. Arguably (see
Chapter Six below), part of the preservation of Palestinian claims has
to do with the organization of life in exile around a village-map
geography: "[t]he inscription of a Galilean landscape in the camps"
(Peteet 2005: 110–12, discussing Lebanon in particular). When settlers
seek to build a new life in a new place, their activities may have the
meaning that Meisels suggests. But when part of the settlers' aim is to
recreate their home and thereby make concrete their alienation from it,
settlement may have exactly the opposite valence, materially asserting
a claim to a place that is manifestly not settled by the claimants, who
are exiled, but by others the legitimacy of whose claim is challenged
by the existence of an inverted mirror some miles away. The concept
of settlement simply cannot encompass this settlement-in-exile.

Meisels (2005: 94) admits as much by biting the bullet of "moral
hazard" in her account of settlement. The moral hazard arises because
she opposes displacements that have not yet happened, but defends (as
irreversible from a moral point of view) displacements that already
have happened – when the incursion and settlement is a fait accompli.
There is thus an incentive for any would-be ethnic cleanser to just go
ahead and cleanse (and settle), and see where the moral chips fall at
the end of the day. As I shall explain at greater length in Chapters Five
and Six, plenitude reduces or eliminates this moral hazard. Settlements that make concrete alienation – that reproduce the map and
social relations of the lost homeland – serve to maintain empirical and
intentional plenitude over time. Refugees who do this are on a par
with people living under occupation, because they have empirical

plenitude but no political control. To be sure, plenitude-in-exile cannot likely be maintained in perpetuity, and is never the whole story (see Peteet 2005). But it is surely possible to maintain it for at least one or two generations.

This point also underscores another virtue of plenitude as a criterion of attachment. Theorists of territorial rights inevitably confront the issue of a statute of limitations, since most if not all the Earth's land area has been subject to conquest and displacement at some point or other (Waldron 1992; Miller 2000: 116; Moore 2001: 191–3; Meisels 2005: 94). Statutes of limitations raise a crucial difficulty for the very idea of territorial rights. New settlers are likely to become entrenched long before their exiled predecessors have lost their yearning for home or have found a new home elsewhere. The exiles will likely still "deserve" repatriation after (possibly long after) their dispossessors start to "deserve" to be left alone. To reverse the dispossession would then require repeating it. Thus any statute of limitations must err on the side either of entrenching the crime or of repeating it in reverse. While reverse-repetition may seem the obvious choice given the wrongfulness of the initial dispossession, this will typically involve uprooting many people who were not responsible for the policy and not even ideologically committed to the dispossession, but merely needed someplace to live. They may even have been underprivileged pawns of a nationalist elite or government using them as a vanguard. Or they may be victims of a prior displacement that is now irrevers-ible.[8] To reverse one displacement without continuing to put the dominoes back up, so to speak, all the way back to the very beginning, in effect picks one set of victims over another. It is therefore simply not obvious that reverse-repetition is the morally superior choice. At best we may say that there is a default in its favor; but the theory will still have to choose, and the deep problem is not avoided.

The plenitude criterion, in contrast, makes the cut-off, as it were, not just a temporal question but a spatial one as well. As long as empirical plenitude with respect to the lost homeland persists, the claim persists – and is type-ii revisionist (residents who want control) rather than radical – even though the dispossessed people are phys-ically elsewhere. Only after the empirical plenitude dissipates does the

---

[8] Fisk (2002: 31) powerfully discusses the tragic case of Palestinian exile David Damiani and Jewish Auschwitz survivor Shlomo Green.

claim become radical; but as we shall see in Chapter Five, even radical claims can have some force. So the issue of a statute of limitations is not an arbitrary cut-off imposed in an effort to prevent chaos, it emerges from the practices of the people involved. To be sure, there remains the problem that the new settlers are likely to be ensconced long before the expelled have lost their empirical plenitude and, hence, right of return. What the account here does is permit a clear distinction between a right of return and a mere desire to return. Further, because we are discussing territorial rights as such, and not rights to full-blown territorial sovereignty, we avoid, or at least keep a lid on, the fatal idea that one side must be chosen *over* the other, one group recognized as sovereign and the other expelled or subjugated. Territorial rights short of sovereignty open up a range of possible solutions that do not presuppose that only one group can be in a given place at a time; as Gans (2003) puts it, the state can accord special rights to nations without itself becoming the property of any one nation. I shall discuss these issues at much greater length in Chapters Five and Six.

The discussion in this subsection has presupposed the coherence of plenitude; at issue is merely its distinctiveness. I have shown that plenitude is distinct from settlement, and where the two overlap, it is plenitude that does the work. Ultimately, of course, the section as a whole has been more interested in coherence than distinctiveness. I have laid out the basic idea, including empirical and intentional plenitude, and explained how it is both rooted in the right way and capable of setting a maximum based on sustainability, not just a minimum based on use or settlement. Further, it meets a number of other challenges, including the challenge of uniqueness and that of speaking to claims at a variety of places on the status quo axis. The question remains whether plenitude solves the problem of normativity – whether it is attractive from a moral point of view. The next subsection makes the moral case for plenitude.

4.4 The ethics of plenitude

We now know that plenitude is a meaningful notion that we can apply to territorial disputes, if we want it. But should we want it? What moral argument can be given for thinking that plenitude is the best basis for discerning normatively significant territorial attachments, and for grounding standing based on those attachments?

Concomitantly, can plenitude solve the problem of normativity? Can people excluded by some group's successful showing of plenitude in a territory recognize plenitude as a normatively significant basis for their exclusion?

This final section of the chapter constitutes a moral argument for plenitude as a criterion of attachment that can help to resolve territorial disputes. Plenitude can be accepted by each side as a threshold that must be met as well as a source of compelling claims from competitors. Properly deployed, plenitude achieves what Jacob Levy (2000: 213) argued was a crucial aim for accounts of attachment to territory: to respect each while reflecting none. The section offers three distinct arguments for the plenitude criterion. The first argues that the criterion is already widely shared; disagreement has to do with the imposition of particular ethnogeographies, rather than with the criterion itself. The second argument links plenitude to state legitimacy, arguing that plenitude encompasses a number of the state's legitimating functions, and failures of plenitude are hallmarks of state failure. The third argument appeals to sustainability, arguing that plenitude links political philosophy with ecology in a way that is fruitful and urgent – and that is especially appropriate in consideration of territorial rights. If successful, these arguments show that plenitude is indeed attractive from a moral point of view, as well as from the points of view of competing territorial claimants. Plenitude therefore meets the normativity requirement.

4.4.1 *Actual acceptance*

We noted earlier that plenitude has a long and checkered history in the polemical writings of imperialists and expansionists. Even if the intervening discussion has laid the groundwork for a superior interpretation of plenitude, then, this principle may seem an unlikely basis for mutually acceptable resolutions of territorial disputes. Thus in this first leg of the normative argument I shall show that, so far from being an unshared principle doomed to irrelevance, plenitude is in fact a shared principle, endorsed by both sides in real territorial disputes. This fact does not constitute an independent normative argument from a philosophical standpoint – everyone may agree on an error – but it does support the view that plenitude may be relevant and even have a leg up on other attachment criteria.

European colonialists appealed to the purported emptiness of the New World to justify displacing indigenous peoples. Further, one reason for the continued plight of indigenous peoples in the Americas is precisely that traditional uses are regarded as waste, such that governments pursue development of natural resources even on remaining indigenous lands. Similarly, the roots of the Israeli–Palestinian dispute lie partly in the failure of Zionists to regard Arab Palestinians as genuinely inhabiting the territory, discussing them instead in much the same way that Locke and his descendants discussed indigenous Americans. In each of these cases, of course, the appeal to plenitude was dubious at best; in each of these cases there were people within the dispossessing cultures – Roger Williams and Ahad Ha'am, for instance – who insisted that the imputations of emptiness were false, but who for the most part went unheeded (Jennings 1976; Ben-Porat 2006: 70).

From a theoretic standpoint it is crucial to see, not that the empirical claim was false, but that even from the perspective of the dispossessed, empirical falsehood is taken to be the core problem. Defenders of indigenous rights, for instance, manifestly do not deny the normative premise:

(P1) For any land L, a newcomer's unilateral claim to L is valid only if L is antecedently empty.

Rather, they deny the empirical premise:

(P2) This particular land L_i is antecedently empty,

when applied to most parts of the Americas (Jennings 1976; Alfred 1999). Similarly, nearly every historically minded articulation or defense of Palestinian claims emphasizes the population size, demographic breakdown, and land ownership distribution prior to the UN Partition of 1947 (e.g. Drysdale and Blake 1985: 270–6; Khalidi 1992; Beinin and Hajjar 2000: 1). All parties accept that plenitude or emptiness is normatively significant, arguing only about whether it is accurately imputed to these specific places prior to European or Zionist encroachment, respectively.

Disputes among competing territorial claimants thus typically do not involve debate over the notion of plenitude itself, but rather, over whether plenitude is satisfied in a given case. Despite being on the receiving end of dubious plenitude-based arguments for radical territorial claims, indigenous peoples, Palestinians, and others have not shunned plenitude but embraced it, turning it around to affirm the prior plenitude of the disputed places. This fact of actual acceptance by both sides in two bloody territorial disputes obviously does not constitute a significant moral argument for the plenitude criterion, but it does provide reasonable grounds for thinking that plenitude is the sort of notion we are looking for in a criterion of attachment, and can be the object of agreement. If we understand normativity in contractualist terms, where justification is understood in terms of something like reasonable acceptability to those affected, then the fact of actual agreement lends the plenitude criterion an initial degree of plausibility.

It follows that plenitude can do, and in real-life conflicts often does do, the moral work we need from an account of attachment: it has the particularity to connect specific groups to land, but also the universality to be compelling across cultural lines. Moreover, plenitude meets this demand more plausibly than other criteria. Ethnogenesis or national formation may explain some group's intentional plenitude claim – why they focus on that place rather than another – but without the plenitude, the ethnogenesis is morally inert. Need, too, becomes plausible as a specifically territorial claim only with intentional plenitude. A need-claim unaccompanied by intentional plenitude seems excessively short-term; it might ground material aid, but not territorial rights. For instance, if a people subject to famine can plausibly claim that empirical plenitude has been destroyed by drought and war, while intentional plenitude remains intact, then their territorial claim is as strong as ever; the appeal to need justifies aid and support in reestablishing their communities and farms, but need by itself does not link them to a particular territory. On the other side, if Australians desperate to justify the White Australia Policy profess a need for the Outback (Walzer 1983), and yet demonstrate no intentional plenitude, the need claim is worthless.[9] Thus in claims of need, plenitude does the territorially significant work.

---

[9] Walzer might agree; but because for him the scope of need is subject to "shared understandings," outsiders are incapable of assessing any group's need claims. Walzer is particularist in this respect: if Australians can articulate a shared conception of need according to which they need the outback, their claim must be valid. In contrast, by being rooted instead of particularist, my account gets the right answer here. Even if the Australians worked up an extravagant conception of need, they nonetheless would have to back it up with empirically testable plenitude.

Settlement criteria are particularist; they thus cannot answer to the legitimate expectation that territorial claims respect the universal value of land, not just its value to insiders. In addition, settlement criteria cannot, while plenitude can, support the claims of nomadic peoples to their sites of seasonal settlement or pasturage. For continuously occupying a place with one's body or house is not the only way to fill it. Finally, use – the only other diachronic and rooted criterion – cannot distinguish between sustainable and unsustainable uses (see section 4.4.3 below). Thus plenitude seems to be the most plausible criterion for territorial claims, explaining the intuitive appeal of some criteria and helping us to discern the implausibility of others.

4.4.2 State legitimacy

According to Rawls's "liberal principle of legitimacy":

[O]ur exercise of political power is fully proper only when it is exercised in accordance with a constitution the essentials of which all citizens as free and equal may reasonably be expected to endorse in the light of principles and ideals acceptable to their common human reason (Rawls 1993: 137).

Rawls's formulation has earned many liberal critics, but it successfully captures a core element of the liberal notion of political legitimacy – namely, that legitimacy is ultimately about the conditions under which it is permissible for the state to coerce individuals. I want to suggest that legitimacy is also about how place-making institutions structure life and plan for the future in the territories they govern. The argument to this conclusion is in two parts, moving from the concrete to the abstract. First, many standard legitimating functions of states – provision of opportunities, security, equal respect, etc. – have crucial place-related aspects, and understanding these aspects helps in understanding the nature of the functions the state is asked to perform. Second, state legitimacy is bound up with land- and environmental-management functions that protect people and increase the chances that the social order will survive in perpetuity. A liberal conception of legitimacy that considers only the justification of state coercion on persons thus may be incorrect; but even if it is roughly correct, it is less perspicuous than an account that also considers land-use practices.

One of the most significant ways that coercive state institutions act upon individuals is by making and altering the places where those individuals live and work. Intentional plenitude therefore characterizes much of the state's behavior, and failures of plenitude call state legitimacy into question. For instance, vacant lots and burned-out buildings, as well as rural areas left bare (if not done as part of a long-term soil-conservation project), constitute a dereliction of plenitude. In the case of rural areas, this dereliction undermines the legitimacy of enforcing private property or any other putative state interest in the place. In urban areas, disinvestment in the city and the disappearance of public services and private businesses contribute to social breakdown and turn police patrols into occupying armies (Daniels 2000: 247, 259). Indeed, the view of law enforcement as military occupation reflects several place-based problems. First, the government designates certain areas of the city as having no valuable social function, nor any potential to serve one – for instance, by being an economic engine or a destination-tourism site. Second, the government and the private sector disinvest in that section. Third, the population of that section is portrayed as a problem that must be controlled by crackdowns on crime. Fourth, police are drawn from outside the area they patrol, and attempt to enforce order by preventing people from engaging in quotidian activities, through the imposition of curfews and the assumption that every person who lives in the area is probably a criminal (Daniels 2000: 244). Finally, desperate city planners forcibly disperse the population through so-called renewal strategies that demolish housing, disregard grassroots organizing, and thereby create internally displaced persons whose fate is somebody else's problem (Imbroscio 2006).

In such cases it is perhaps more accurate to say that, at the root of the problem lies, not emptiness itself, but a disagreement between state and citizens regarding the plenitude of the place. The state sees rubble and its human equivalent; the residents do not. The state's capacity to act on its ignorance – empirical emptiness – and eventually impose its version of intentional plenitude by razing and replacing housing has the same normative character as an occupier's power to do so in disputed territory. The very fact that the state does not recognize the people who live in such regions as engaging in productive activities is evidence that the state's claim to legitimate control of the place is dubious; the residents' claims to "ownership" of the city have a point (Blomley 2003). The power of such disagreements to undermine legitimacy is evident also in land disputes in Brazil, where the

Landless Movement (MST) works in part by forcing the government to live by its own rules about land ownership: insisting on regular, if not continuous, cultivation of rural land and opposing efforts to clear the Amazon rainforest (Wright and Wolford 2003: 24). To be sure, neither the metropolitan regime described above, nor the Brazilian government of the 1980s and 1990s, would pass muster as legitimate in the eyes of liberal political philosophy. The point, however, is that the clearest articulation of the problem makes essential reference to the effects of these policies not just on the individuals, but on their communities and the places where they live. At this most concrete level, then, plenitude may not offer a new conception of legitimacy, but it brings certain elements of legitimacy into better focus.

More abstractly, legitimacy involves the management of places, even when there are no direct, immediate, or certain impacts on humans. One such function, perhaps the overarching one, is managing places and resources to help ensure the survival and flourishing of just institutions in perpetuity. Doing so requires an attitude of nurture or stewardship regarding places, ecosystems, and natural processes, quite apart from simply avoiding undue coercion of individuals. Current and future individuals, including those inside or outside the state's borders, have an interest in the way the state manages these assets. A state that was devoted to extracting the maximum amount of wealth from the ground, even at the cost of radical unsustainability, would be committing a grave political crime even if no individuals were unduly coerced, and even if all currently living people shared in the bounty. A state whose institutions operated at peak efficiency, leaving no room for a bad harvest or a significant drop in aquifers would be playing Russian roulette with its residents' lives and basic interests.

Individuals have a compelling claim that the state not engage in this kind of environmental brinkmanship. And yet the liberal conception of legitimacy, understood in terms of coercion of individuals, cannot bring these state obligations into focus. What is required instead is to understand the state as having some place-based obligations, which may be explained in terms of intentional and empirical plenitude. Among these place-based obligations is the intelligent spatial distribution of economic and other activities, such that development is sustainable and tends not to leave wastelands, brownfields, or ghost towns. We have condemnatory names for policies that fail to meet these place-based obligations: slash-and-burn, strip mining, clear-cutting – each of which connotes emptying-out in one form or another.

Intentional plenitude does not require the state to ensure that, for any given spot, someone lives there, so that neighboring states or secessionists do not get any ideas. Rather, intentional plenitude requires husbandry of population, resources, and territory to increase the likelihood of maintaining and improving its institutions into the indefinite future, even as social, ecological, and political conditions change. State legitimacy is bound up with resilience. This is as it should be, since, as we saw in Chapter Three, resilience is what makes the difference between a mere territory and a country, and only countries are eligible for statehood. By parity of reasoning, maintaining resilience should constitute one of the state's legitimating functions.

4.4.3 Resilience and sustainability

Locke's defense of a plenitude criterion develops from his requirement that goods removed from common not spoil. That Locke and others misapplied this requirement is one of the great travesties in the history of philosophy. But this misapplication does not undermine the basic idea that if the goods I claim spoil while in my possession, my claim is worthless. On the contrary, in a time of ecological emergency the justification for some such requirement is as great as ever. The challenge is to implement it without the same narrowness displayed by Locke and his followers – that is without imposing a single ethnogeography on all. I shall argue that plenitude uniquely meets this challenge. This may seem implausible on its face, because plenitude seems like a maximalist notion, which would almost by definition undermine limitations on use and hence encourage (or require) unsustainability. Here I want to defend plenitude precisely on the grounds that it uniquely links state legitimacy to sustainability or resilience.

In developing the theory of ethnogeographic communities I belabored the point that people and land interact in mutually formative ways: the people are as they are partly because of where they are (were), and the land is as it is partly because of who is (was) there. One essential aspect of plenitude is its unabashed commitment to the bi-directional character of human–environmental interactions. This aspect – which I shall develop further in a moment – defends plenitude against the charge of unsustainability, but it may raise another concern, specifically about the Anglo-American ethnogeography.

Intentional plenitude entails a commitment to maintaining empirical plenitude in perpetuity. Plans to use a place for a limited time only – because the plan is time-limited, or the use is destructive – may be perfectly legitimate so far as they go, but they are not admissible grounds for territorial claims. On the contrary, they presuppose such claims, held either by the users or by others from whom the users rent. Plenitude on the other hand requires perpetuity; and hence plenitude dovetails with resilience. A putatively full country is one that, at least, gives every indication of being resilient. Thus plenitude avoids the charge of unsustainability because intentional plenitude is incompatible with what we might call, analogously, *intentional exhaustion* – the intention to use up a place and be done with it. Indeed, if any kind of use maps onto the Lockean concern with waste, it is not nomadism but the kind of intentional exhaustion characteristic of unsustainable use.

This requirement also helps to define the threshold between emptiness and plenitude. We noted earlier that plenitude gives the appearance of being a maximal notion but on closer inspection seems to be scalar. This raises a problem. If plenitude is scalar, then we can make sense of the project of enhancing plenitude; but if for that reason it is possible to judge that some place is more full than another, that fact would seem to be relevant to territorial disputes. On the other hand, if plenitude is a threshold notion, it may collapse into some form of use criterion. But on the third hand (so to speak), if plenitude is maximal, we risk finding that most territories are not full and have no prospect of becoming so, in which case no territorial claim is valid.

I shall resolve the problem by arguing that plenitude is indeed scalar, but our theoretic purposes require a threshold. There is, in practice at least, no maximum – no point at which a place is completely full. As plenitude approaches the top end of the scale we should expect the slope to decline into an asymptote. Given this model of plenitude, the key challenge is to set a threshold that is politically applicable and that, being rooted in the right way, does not merely set the bar at any particular level for everyone. Rather, in order to maintain the right sort of rootedness, we must set the threshold in three steps. First, in the case of empirical plenitude, the threshold is set partly by the existence of feedback: that the people and the land are, in fact, mutually formed. Effects are unidirectional rather than mutual when people have somehow affected or been affected by land, but the two have not interacted. For instance, we might imagine a mountain that plays some role in popular mythology, and hence influences the people, while remaining sublimely uninfluenced by them; or, in the other direction, we might imagine a mountain's being left alone for its entire history, then for one summer demolished by a coal company, and then left to its somewhat shorter self. These examples describe non-mutual effects. Further, feedback must be not just mutual, but also mutually formative. Effects are merely incidental rather than formative when they do not alter any significant feature of the object, or when they last a very short time. Thus mutually formative interactions between people and land occur when the land shapes the character of the people – for instance, when their dwellings, cuisine, and eventually social relations and kinship patterns develop over time due to features of their environment such as climate, soil, and so on; and the people in turn shape the character of the land, for instance, causing forests and grasslands to grow or shrink, undertaking significant urbanization, etc. Effects are mutually formative when the significant effects of one on the other then feed back onto the first – for instance, a major waterway attracts settlement, the damming of the river reduces the threat of floods, which permits more intensive construction but reduces soil fertility, which encourages suburban development of erstwhile farmland, which causes political and cultural changes, and so on.

Beyond feedback, the second step for setting a threshold of plenitude is knowledge. When the ethnogeographic community or its members can demonstrate an appropriate kind of knowledge about a place – again, knowledge that is subject to empirical testing – they have attained empirical plenitude. For instance, if medieval Europeans could affirm the existence of some place south of the Mediterranean Sea, with some people in it, this would not have constituted plenitude. If they could affirm the existence of such a place with, say, information about its basic topography, villages, religious establishments, and economic activities, they would have demonstrated plenitude. Obviously the precise cut-off remains fuzzy. If in addition to some sketchy knowledge of topography, demography, religion, and economics, the medieval Europeans had affirmed the existence of a variety of man-eating monsters and abominable snowmen, we might or might not accept their claim of empirical plenitude; that would depend on the canons of evidence we applied (see Krugman 1997: 1). But the need to specify canons of evidence in political argument is a problem that every political theory faces, and at which most simply gesture, on the assumption that such canons can be specified independently of the theory itself. For our purposes we can admit that such canons are as yet unspecified, but insist that we do not need to specify them here in order to understand the notion of knowledge as applied here. Thus empirical plenitude requires feedback plus knowledge.

The final step in setting a cut-off for plenitude has to do with intentional plenitude. Intentional plenitude has to do with projects for maintaining and enhancing empirical plenitude into the indefinite future. Thus intentional plenitude is a progressive notion. We may capture this by appeal to Rawls's "Aristotelian Principle," according to which,

> human beings take more pleasure in doing something as they become more proficient at it, and of two activities they do equally well, they prefer the one calling on a larger repertoire of more intricate and subtle discriminations (Rawls 1999a: 374).

Applied to intentional plenitude, the idea would be that a place is full if the group's plans for it are both a) reasonably well specified, and b) subject to increasing complexity, understanding, or specificity over time. Intentional plenitude will include a progressive element, a project for improving the place and the understanding of it.

Admittedly, the thresholds for both empirical and intentional plenitude remain fuzzy. For empirical plenitude, the canons of evidence in the relevant knowledge claims remain to be specified. For intentional plenitude, the degree of specificity and the rate of progress over time are unclear. These are genuine gaps, but again, ones that are shared with most if not all political theories. To say this about political theories is not to criticize them, but to plead innocence by association. We have left open some genuine questions of evidentiary canons and projects, but these questions can be reasonably well closed in practice – indeed only in practice. They are not susceptible of final settlement in the abstract.

Even if I am granted this indulgence, the account of the appropriate threshold raises a further question. Plenitude demands mutual formation, and evidence thereof. But as we have repeatedly noted, the Anglo-American ethnogeography treats land as purely passive; its adherents are unlikely to be able to demonstrate their attachment unless they reconceive their relationship to land. It follows that even when Anglo-American ethnogeographic communities have attained plenitude as a matter of fact, they will not be able to demonstrate that they have done so – they will not be able to win a challenge to their territorial rights without altering their ethnogeography. And so the theory appears to build in a kind of reverse cultural insensitivity: it can accept the claims of anyone except Anglo-Americans. The question is whether this putative insensitivity is a problem for the theory.

It is not a problem for the theory because the rejection of mutual formativity in the Anglo-American ethnogeography is a symptom of a genuine and serious problem in that ethnogeography: the inability to recognize the value of places, ecosystem services, and land for any-thing but economic exploitation. This inability generates squalor in the face of abundance and emptiness in the face of need. It is hardly unique in this; what is distinctive is that the dereliction is in fact part and parcel of the system's success, in its own terms: in 2006, even as 16 million US housing units sat unoccupied (US Census 2006: Table 9) and owning third homes trickled down to the ranks of the merely "economically comfortable" (Umberger 2006), hundreds of thou-sands of people remained homeless.[10] Dereliction and abandonment are common themes in American history, from the Upper Peninsula of Michigan to the Midwestern rust belt, to the Oklahoma dust bowl and more recent massive topsoil losses, and countless ghost towns in former farming communities depleted of their human population. In each case these losses occurred precisely because economic product-ivity rose. Indeed, given the Anglo-American ethnogeography, the growth, decline, and eventual abandonment of small towns seems to be an evolutionary process that governments are all but powerless to stop (Forth 2000; Keneley 2004). Insofar as intentional plenitude is a progressive notion that involves a project of coming better to know and more intelligently to use places, and to do so in perpetuity, Americans have historically demonstrated little intentional plenitude. The issue goes beyond an inability to explicitly make a claim to this effect; the claim would be false even if it could be made. If environ-mental conditions are forgiving or population pressure is low, then

---

[10] USICH (2007) estimates some 155,000 "chronically homeless" persons; National Alliance to End Homelessness (2007) estimates some 744,000 total homeless persons in the US.

inattention or ignorance may not undermine resilience. But when people are not so lucky – the environment is under stress – sustainability requires understanding one's own place in a web of systems, and accommodating one's quotidian practices to this understanding (Heyd 2005; Walker and Salt 2006).

The inability of Anglo-American ethnogeographic communities to articulate their intentional plenitude is thus a symptom of their inability to achieve intentional plenitude. The close link between this particular inability and the impossibility of sustainability suggests that the putative cultural insensitivity here is the fault not of the theory but of the ethnogeography. The theory is merely noticing what the facts about global climate, the collapse of fisheries, and other ecological catastrophes have forced us to notice. If the account of plenitude I have offered here is plausible, then, many if not most Anglo-American assertions of attachment to territory will remain empty (so to speak), unless Anglo-American ethnogeographic communities recast their territorial claims in ways that generate intentional as well as empirical plenitude.

In short, the Anglo-American ethnogeography treats land as wholly passive and merely a commodity. As a result it cannot recognize the ways that land is active in shaping people. In turn, that ethnogeography lacks intentional plenitude, because there is no reason, apart from its ability to attract investment, that any piece of land would matter. The land matters only as long as the investment is attracted. And a lack of intentional plenitude – the project of maintaining a place as full even after the strategic importance of its economic keystone has declined, for instance – means a lack of the right sort of attachment to ground a territorial claim. Hence the Anglo-American ethnogeography is typically incompatible with territorial rights. This is, though, a mutable fact, and some places have indeed overcome it, through green spaces, community farms, infill, the reclamation of white elephants and brownfields, responsible forestry, wildlife refuges or migratory-bird rest areas, etc.[11] Thus if Anglo-American countries are to succeed in grounding territorial claims, they must rethink their

---

[11] To the extent they have done so, it is partly because of the existence in certain areas of dissident ethnogeographies, but it is no doubt also due to a large dose of nimbyism, where comfortable people deny to others what they demand for themselves.

relationship to land so as to make possible true claims of intentional plenitude.

I have argued that there is a close link between plenitude and sustainability or resilience, and that this close link supports plenitude as a criterion of attachment to territory. In this respect plenitude is uniquely attractive, since no other criterion on offer can endogenously include a close link between ecological and political principles.

4.4.4 The return of settlement?

Proponents of a settlement criterion, however, may find here an objection to plenitude. Distinguish between two senses of ecological: one having to do with environmentalism as a practice, and the other having to do with a deeper philosophical concern for the inherent value of natural phenomena such as ecosystems. We may call the former the *sustainability* sense of ecological, and the latter the *ecocentric* sense of ecological. The objection then goes as follows. Insofar as territorial attachments must meet a Lockean "nonwaste" criterion, this may be achieved with a criterion that is ecological in the sustainability sense; call it *sustainable settlement* or *sustainable use*. In contrast, plenitude goes beyond this and insists on an account that is ecological in the ecocentric sense. And this not only goes beyond the needed degree of ecology, it misses a crucial point: that any account of attachment ought to give pride of place to human settlement, and perhaps some minimal material base to support it (such as culturally appropriate food sources). Whatever else people may do with land, they inhabit it, and this matters more than any other form of attachment. Further, if some ethnogeographic community's conception of plenitude involves expelling other people to create an ecoreserve in the name of ecology in the ecocentric sense, the theory developed here seems to regard them as filling the place, and that seems like a terrible mistake.

Chapter Five provides a full account of territorial disputes, and Chapter Six applies the theory in a systematic way to a real-world case. But in the interim there are some things we can say. First, insofar as settlement and subsistence are in some sense basic, they are also going to be core aspects of any ethnogeography. Thus the claim that some place is empirically empty is hard to defend if people live there – every ethnogeography is able to recognize human settlement as such. It would be even harder to defend the claim of emptiness if the claimant's aim were to settle that place with its own population. For in this event the place is already full in the very same way that the claimant intends to fill it. Therefore colonizing inhabited places is one of the hardest things to defend.

But perhaps, then, we do not need plenitude at all. For if human settlement and subsistence take pride of place, then what work does plenitude uniquely do? First, it is crucial to distinguish between saying that human settlement and subsistence are *core elements* of any ethno-geography, and saying they have *pride of place*. The latter locution connotes a hierarchy of needs whereby we get to paintings, pastries, and parklands only after our bellies are full. On the contrary, these things are part and parcel of the filling of our bellies. Cuisine, kinship, dress, and housing are among the most culturally variable aspects of human life, full of adornment and self-expression that are indivisible from the material core of these activities (Wiredu 1996). And this is so even (or indeed, especially) under straitened economic conditions, when people cannot afford to purchase entertainment or self-expression opportun-ities separate from their work. It is by understanding humans as place-makers that we can understand why and how they need territorial rights in the first place. Second, for these reasons, human settlement and subsistence do not have pride of place – or to put it in our terms, they are not the only core elements of any ethnogeography. They are joined in the core by other practices and patterns of land use that we cannot specify due to their variety.

To conclude, let us put the discussion more precisely into the terms of the framework developed in Chapter One. Plenitude demonstrates the close link between eligibility and attachment. Ethnogeographic communities, which are eligible to assert territorial claims, can legit-imate their assertions of attachment to particular territories by dem-onstrating that the fullness of the territory has been formative in their own identity, and their projects have been formative of the place itself. The fact that plenitude is appealed to by both sides in numerous extremely divisive territorial conflicts, and that it captures much of the same intuitive ground held by criteria such as use and settlement, while also building in a strong component of environmental sustainability, suggests that plenitude also meets the normativity problem. That is, a demonstration of plenitude carries weight that any party to a dispute can affirm. Further, both empirical and intentional plenitude are empirically testable in objective ways, so the assertion of plenitude is not subjective. Finally, plenitude also meets the demand of uniqueness, since it will connect particular groups to particular places, rather than to any number of places. As we saw above, ethnogenesis might link Jews to Palestine, Babylon, the Sinai Peninsula, or to the condition of being diasporic. Plenitude will choose among these by simply not caring where the ethnogenesis occurred, and asking only which place the claimants have filled or plan to fill. In contrast, even the use criterion is susceptible of unacceptable multiplicity. In the age of imperialism and neocolonialism, the US can claim to be using export-processing zones in numerous countries in Latin America, Southeast Asia, and elsewhere. One of the core functions of imperialism is to transform economic geographies. Whether colonialist claims (be they classical, neo-, or internal) can ever be credited from the standpoint of plenitude seems dubious at best; where they can, plenitude has a process (sketched very briefly above in the Henry County example, and discussed at much greater length in Chapter Five below) whereby these claims may be tested and applied. Thus ethnogeographic communities' claims of empirical and intentional plenitude meet the demands of eligibility, attachment, uniqueness, and normativity.

Chapter Five will show how the plenitude criterion applies to the three axes on which claims may fall – status quo, epistemological, and worldview. The current chapter has developed and defended an attachment approach to territory based on plenitude which, as a rooted and diachronic criterion, uniquely meets all the desiderata of attachment criteria. Further, because it is both objective and ethno-geographically relative, plenitude is culturally sensitive in the right way. What remains to be seen is whether the account of territorial claimants that we have developed in the past two chapters is useful when applied to claims and to the resolution of territorial disputes.

5 | *Territorial disputes*

Plenitude is objective in two senses. First the criteria of plenitude – the two aspects, empirical and intentional – are laid down by the theory, not by the claimant. Second and whether the claimed place is, in fact, full in the relevant sense is objectively assessable. But as we've noted before, plenitude also has an essential relative aspect, for it is claimants' ethnogeographies that determine in what plenitude consists in any particular place. This relativity underlies territorial disputes, and is one of the key features of the problem of territory that have made it so difficult for political theorists even to see a viable way forward in developing normative criteria for resolving territorial conflicts. Chapter Five continues the progress toward a full theory of territorial rights by explicating how the plenitude criterion works in practice, and thereby taking us to the point of being able to understand how claims work on their own. Understanding how to resolve competing claims is the core task of Chapter Six.

5.1 Applying the plenitude criterion

The best way to demonstrate the relative aspect of plenitude is to illustrate it. Recall the discussion of Wendell Berry's agrarian ethnogeography, and his demonstration of the plenitude of his native hill, which we discussed in Chapter Four. To be an agrarian it is neither necessary nor sufficient to be engaged in an agricultural lifestyle; to wit, the US food system in general applies the Anglo-American ethnogeography to the production of food (Berry 1977; Pollan 2006: Part I). Moreover, an agrarian ethnogeography is distinct from the larger social or moral philosophy of agrarianism inasmuch as the latter contends that "agriculture is an honorable (and virtuous) way of life," often in contrast to urban life (Montmarquet 1985: 5). The agrarian ethnogeography as such need make no claims about the absolute or relative virtue represented by an agricultural lifestyle, or about specific virtues and vices associated with rural and urban living. Rather, the agrarian ethnogeography differs from the Anglo-American in the following respects. First, agrarianism denies the two central tenets of the Anglo-American ethnogeography, regarding human interactions with land as bi-directional (rather than unidirectional), and regarding land as having non-economic as well as economic value. Relatedly, agrarianism denies, whereas the Anglo-American ethnogeography affirms, that land is reducible without remainder into its constituent elements; for the agrarian, emergent properties such as fertility depend on the integrity of the land and its processes. Further, an agrarian ethnogeography holds that productively and sustainably working the land significantly contributes to human flourishing. Though some agrarians, such as Thomas Jefferson, have held that working the land was a necessary condition of a good human life (as well as good citizenship and various other virtues), there need be no claim of necessity or sufficiency (Wunderlich 2000). Thus, like the Anglo-American, the agrarian ethnogeography may be held by residents of city or countryside; the agrarian urbanite may seek more or deeper personal interactions with land, for instance by gardening, but this is neither necessary nor sufficient for endorsing an agrarian ethnogeography.

The agrarian plenitude of Wendell Berry's native hill does not imply that it would be full to someone with the Anglo-American ethnogeography; provided that the Anglo-American had revised her ethnogeography to permit the requisite bi-directional relationship to land, such a person could demonstrate plenitude by offering, for instance, a detailed account of property values, the market value of natural capital and ecosystem services, commodity prices, investment in capital goods, etc., in that place. Such a claim of plenitude might be empirically tested by demanding evidence of financial flows and economic activity, as described for instance through GIS models, sales receipts, or environmental audits.

To lodge a competing claim (though not, as we'll see, necessarily to win), such an Anglo-American would not need to demonstrate that the land was empty in Berry's sense, but only that it was full in the sense that the Anglo-American proposed. This was the strategy of Locke and his followers who appealed to the alleged emptiness of the North American continent prior to European arrival. These Europeans did not claim that no one lived in North America; on the contrary, Locke's works are full of references to "Indians" and "Americans" (Locke

1988; Tully 1994: chap. 5). What Locke meant was that the land had not been brought under market relationships:

[Y]et there are still *great Tracts of Ground* to be found, which (the Inhabitants thereof not having joyned with the rest of Mankind, in the consent of the Use of their common Money) *lie waste*, and are more than the People, who dwell on it, do, or can make use of, and so still lie in common. Tho' this can scarce happen amongst that part of Mankind, that have consented to the Use of Money (Locke 1988: II, V, 45).

As before, then, plenitude directs us to allow claimants to appeal to a conception of plenitude consonant with their own ethnogeography, bearing in mind that whether the relevant territories count as full in that sense is not up to them, but is an empirical matter.

It would be possible not to respect the ethnogeographic relativity of plenitude, for instance by decreeing that there is one and only one way that land can be full, be it agrarian, Anglo-American, or whatever. But such an absolutist account cannot avoid imposing a single ethnogeography on all claimants. Intentional plenitude demands of claimants that, however they understand land, their ethnogeography recognize the bi-directional character of human–environmental relationships. This is the limit of imposition compatible with finding a criterion that is both *objective*, that is, useful as a normative principle across communities with incompatible ethnogeographies, and *vernacular*, that is, articulable in the ontology and language of each claimant, rather than solely in diplomatic language or in some purely notional language such as that of public reason. We meet claimants on their own terms, but demand that those terms not be isolated from reality.[1]

The next few sections address the assessment of various sorts of claims along the status quo axis; section 5.5 addresses the epistemic

---

[1] Does public reason deserve a better run for its money? I laid it out in not quite so many words in Chapter One above. Public reason in Rawls's sense makes no demands of the ontology, epistemology, or larger value system of various groups, beyond commitment to the two principles of justice and the liberal principle of legitimacy (and the Anglo-American ethnogeography, though that sneaks in unremarked). But this minimalism gives up on the possibility of – and ignores the need for – outside access to the epistemic standards and ontological commitments of other cultures. If groups A and B each claim land *L*, we need to assess the merits of their competing claims by appeal to the epistemic standards appropriate to each. Each group may set the terms of assessment, but outsiders must be able to get into a position to determine whether those terms are met.

Table 5.1: *Along the status quo axis*

Kind of claim	Must show	If claim fails
1. Conservative	Empirical and intentional plenitude	Invalid, but probationary claim persists if empirical plenitude is demonstrated
2i. Revisionist: controllers want to inhabit	Empirical emptiness (but lack of retrospective emptying-out), intentional plenitude	Invalid, but no automatic loss of control: see 2iii
2ii. Revisionist: inhabitants want to control	Intentional plenitude; empirical plenitude (or imposed empirical emptiness)	Citizenship and other moral rights persist
2iii. Revisionist: controllers want to disengage	Intentional emptiness, and no risk that departure will precipitate empirical emptiness by the lights of the remaining inhabitants	Must stay until orderly transfer is possible
2iv. Revisionist: inhabitants want to abandon	As 2iii	Must stay until threat of empirical emptiness is resolved
3i. Radical: foreigners want to immigrate and control	Empirical emptiness, intentional plenitude	Invalid
3ii. Radical: resident controllers want to abandon	As 2iii	As 2ii

and worldview axes. Successful claims do not in themselves guarantee that the claimant gains the right to sovereignty in a territory, since a given territory may be subject to multiple competing successful claims, in which case multiple territorial rights must be respected in a particular place; or it may not be a country, in which case statehood is unjustified. The discussion here is thus simplified inasmuch as it treats claims in isolation and its conclusions are limited to the achievement of standing in any settlement. The assessment of competing claims begins only after standing is established for multiple groups in the same place.

5.2 Conservative claims

Valid claims are fundamentally all alike – they require demonstrations of plenitude or lack thereof – but manifest themselves differently depending on the type of claim in question. Conservative claims, which defend the territorial status quo, are simplest, since empirical and intentional plenitude are individually necessary conditions for the success of the claim. Such assertions must be translatable into arguments of the following form:

1. Plenitude is necessary and sufficient for valid territorial claims
2_C. Plenitude exists when F obtains (where F is specified by the claimant's ethnogeography)
3_C. The empirical F-plenitude of territory T_1 can be demonstrated by [empirical indicators of F-plenitude]
4_C. The intentional F-plenitude of T_1 is demonstrated by [projects, policies, plans, etc., indicating intentional F-plenitude]
5_C. Therefore F obtains in territory T_1 (2_C, 3_C, 4_C)
6_C. Therefore we [the ethnogeographic community claiming T_1] have a valid (morally compelling) territorial claim in T_1 (1, 2_C, 5_C).

The truth of premise 1 follows from the theory so far. What we must evaluate is the conclusion 6_C based on premises 2_C through 5_C. Consider the Australian state's claim to the entirety of Australia, circa 1945 (i.e. during the White Australia Policy and well before recognition of indigenous peoples' land rights). Assume that the Anglo-Australians would complete the argument using the Anglo-American (AA) ethnogeography:

$2_C{}^{Aus}$. AA-plenitude exists when constituent land is brought under market relationships, generating significant sustained economic activity.
$3_C{}^{Aus}$. The empirical AA-plenitude of Australia can be demonstrated by a catalogue of assessed property values, a list of property transactions, and GDP growth.
$4_C{}^{Aus}$. The intentional AA-plenitude of Australia is demonstrated in development projects of which private land tenure and markets in land are essential aspects, and in low economic rents[2] taken by landowners.

---

[2] Economic rent is "a payment received by the owner of a factor of production over and above the minimum price necessary to obtain that factor's services" (Casler 1992: 245).

5_C^{Aus}. Therefore, AA-plenitude obtains in Australia (3_C^{Aus}, 4_C^{Aus}).

6_C^{Aus}. Therefore the Anglo-Australians have a valid territorial claim in all of Australia (1, 2_C^{Aus}, 5_C^{Aus}).

This illustration is necessarily simplified. Nonetheless, we may comment on it adequately to show how the theory would evaluate conservative claims. First, premise 2_C^{Aus} is merely an explication of AA-plenitude, but this is strictly speaking erroneous: recall that the unreconstructed Anglo-American ethnogeography is incompatible with intentional plenitude. Thus let us reinterpret plenitude in what we might call an *Anglo-ecological* sense:

$2*_C^{Aus}$. AE-plenitude exists when constituent land is brought under market relationships subject to full payment for ecosystem services and natural capital and the internalization of negative ecological externalities, generating sustainable economic activity.[3]

Whether or not we use the Anglo-ecological standard, Australia circa 1945 is not full in the required sense. Both 3_C^{Aus} and 4_C^{Aus} are false. As of 1996, 16% of the land area of Australia was given over to "minimal use," while another 56% was devoted to livestock grazing, much of it on native vegetation that could not sustain the practice (Australian Government 2007). Ironically, the uses to which the Anglo-Australians have put their country violate the very Lockean land-use orthodoxy that supported their designation of Australia as *terra nullius* and indigenous America as waste. Much other land was not subject to market relationships; some of this (13% of land area) was designated for Aboriginal uses and so explicitly forsworn by the Anglo-Australians. Further, in 1945 the government was engaged in a project of forcibly emptying Aboriginal communities through the removal of children. It may be true that plenitude obtained in eastern, southern, and southwestern coastal sections – the "neo-Europes" (Crosby 1993). But the plausibility of the southern coastal claim does not extend to the whole. Therefore premise 5_C^{Aus} is false, and hence, so is 6_C^{Aus}. The Anglo-Australian claim to the entire continent, then, is invalid.

What follows from the failure of a conservative claim? The answer depends on whether the claimants lack empirical plenitude,

---

[3] The other premises may have to change slightly in light of this change, but the premises as written should suffice for the example.

intentional plenitude, or both. Consider first a failure of empirical plenitude alone. Empirical emptiness eliminates the claim's conservative character. It becomes a type-i revisionist claim, that is, a claim to fill a place that is currently controlled but empty (relative to an ethnogeography). And this sort of revisionist claim – empirical emptiness, intentional plenitude – has the same structure as a type-i radical claim. It is as though the claimant were not there at all. So failures of empirical plenitude within conservative claims are extremely serious. What can be said in defense of this strong result? First, lacking empirical plenitude in a regularly populated place is hard to imagine. So the strong result does not undermine the territorial integrity of states in their populated or attended-to areas. Even if, for some strange reason, that could happen, territorial rights do not carry rights to expel resident populations. At most what would be conferred would be rights tantamount to eminent domain: a right to impose limited fair-price buyouts for important state interests. Changes in territorial rights alone do not derogate any basic right of any citizen. Further, we would not expect to see a state's conservative claim fail, for its entire territory, when confronted by international challengers. Rather, such failures might occur in three sorts of cases: when a state administers some peripheral place for historically contingent reasons – for instance, the overseas possessions of erstwhile empires – and faces a revisionist claim from a native population that wants territorial rights there; when a state is trying to prevent a radical claim in the form of encroachment upon a derelict or unsettled part of its territory; or when internal challengers such as land-reformers or indigenous groups lay claim to extensive lands that the state has left unattended. In these three sorts of cases, the strong result for failed conservative claims to empirical plenitude seems to get the right answer.

For instance, the strong result would justify agrarian reform programs. Portugal supported its initial sixteenth-century claim to Brazil by granting massive tracts of land to feudal lords who rarely cultivated more than a small part of their land. The system descended from this has left huge unoccupied or uncultivated estates in a country with millions of landless peasants. Conservative claims lodged by the state on the landlords' behalf are appropriately rejected as groundless: the places are empty by the lights of the ethnogeography to which the landowners and the state subscribe (Wright and Wolford 2003). Similarly, in much of the inland western US, massive government-owned lands are disused except for grazing (sometimes illegal) by privately owned cattle herds.[4] Now suppose an Apache tribe sought to take control of some Bureau of Land Management (BLM) land subject to seasonal grazing but unpopulated by humans. If the lands are well managed – the government prevents overgrazing, enforces the quantity, range, and date limits of ranchers' grazing permits, ensures that grazing is not increasing the likelihood and severity of forest fires in neighboring forests, etc. – then a conservative claim of empirical plenitude would be successful. But in the event, it seems that, in many places, such conservative claims will be unsuccessful. It is still possible that the US government will pass a test of intentional plenitude in these places, so there may be room for a revisionist claim here. But the failure of conservative claims of empirical plenitude in the sort of case we've just discussed could pave the way for significant restitutions of land to Native American nations, even without having to resolve some of the hardest questions about the supersession of historical injustices or the nature of indigeneity. Thus the strong result of failures of empirical plenitude in conservative claims may seem initially implausible, but due attention to the circumstances in which such failures are likely to occur lends plausibility to that result.

Failures of intentional plenitude are less severe. Even if intentional plenitude is absent, the place is empirically full. So any competing claim of emptiness would be rebuttable. The difficulty would rest in parrying the intentional (and possibly also empirical) plenitude of a competing claimant. The question is whether the lack of intentional plenitude leaves the claimant with an utterly invalid territorial claim. Here is where the conservative character of the claim becomes crucial. Whereas lacking intentional plenitude undermines type-i and -ii revisionist claims, it should not have the same effect on conservative claims. Governments that achieve empirical plenitude but lack intentional plenitude may instead be given some period of time – the duration of which may vary depending on other circumstances – in which to develop intentional plenitude. Such a probationary territorial

---

[4] Between Bureau of Land Management (BLM) and US Forest Service holdings, approximately 250 million acres are open for permit grazing. This grazing permits ranchers to increase the size of their herds, but it also increases the incidence and severity of environmental problems. Many such costs are externalized onto private citizens, other government entities, and the land itself. See Moskowitz and Romaniello (2002: 6–7, 17–18).

right would grant, say, a ten-year window in which to achieve intentional plenitude.

What can be said in defense of this result? That is, granting the plausibility of the conclusion, how can our theory license it? First, that a claim is conservative means that it is lodged by the state or some other juridical body that currently governs the territory in question. That the territory is empirically full means that the state or other entity is in fact performing essential jurisdictional functions familiar from mainstream justifications of the state. For instance, it is keeping the peace, prosecuting criminals, underwriting property law, providing certain benefits to the residents, etc. The loss of intentional plenitude, while empirical plenitude obtains, means that the state lacks any commitment to maintain or enhance plenitude in that place. But it does not mean that the array of human and environmental interests served by the state have disappeared or can take care of themselves. Thus a conservative claim that lacks intentional plenitude does not license open season on the territory. By using intentional emptiness as a basis for downgrading, rather than rejecting outright, the territorial claim, the theory creates an incentive for intentional plenitude. While we will have more to say about incentives below, this is an important initial point about the incentives built into the theory: for all the reasons that plenitude is valuable, an incentive structure that rewards plenitude is, other things equal, also valuable. And downgrading conservative claims that lack intentional plenitude creates such an incentive.

5.3 Radical claims

Earlier we discussed the Anglo-Australian claim to the outback, finding it (in truncated and simplified form) wanting. But now suppose that, "driven by famine in the densely populated lands of southeast Asia," a number of boatloads of refugees sought to set up an autonomous territory in Australia, despite the objections of the Australian government.[5] The example is perhaps odd, since refugees would be more likely to request asylum than to set up a territory. But it is surely imaginable – especially in cases where no country will accept them. Such boat people would then have a strong interest and an intuitively

---

[5] The example is adapted from Walzer (1983: 46).

reasonable claim to be able to settle empty land elsewhere. Such a claim would be a type-i radical claim in our taxonomy.

Type-i radical claims are the conclusions of valid arguments that can be translated into the following form:

1. Plenitude is necessary and sufficient for a valid territorial claim.
2_R. Empty places are available to be claimed by ethnogeographic communities with intentional plenitude regarding such places.
3_R. Plenitude exists when G obtains (where G is specified by appeal to the claimant's ethnogeography).
4_R. The empirical emptiness of territory T_1 can be demonstrated by appeal to the absence of [features indicating empirical G-plenitude].
5_R. The intentional plenitude of T_1 can be demonstrated by appeal to [plans, projects, skills indicating intentional G-plenitude with respect to T_1].
6_R. Therefore we have a valid claim to T_1.

Premises 1 and 2_R follow from the theory as laid out so far. Regarding 3_R, let us suppose that the ethnogeography of the refugees is largely agrarian, with irrigated agriculture, especially cultivation of rice, making up the single biggest use. The refugees thus propose to develop farming cooperatives in a tropical zone of Australia's Northern Territory, to practice sustainable farming methods and build a main coastal city that would serve as a trading port. The refugees would then fill in the argument above as follows (with appropriate imaginary specifications for the sake of illustration):

3_R^{REF}. Plenitude exists when smallholders practice cooperative, sustainable rice farming to attain subsistence plus a surplus, and use the surplus to maintain at least one market/port city.
4_R^{REF}. The empirical emptiness of some section S of Australia's Northern Territory can be seen in the facts that the current agricultural output of S is zero and there are no significant port cities in the region.
5_R^{REF}. The intentional plenitude of S can be seen in the fact that the claimants have democratically approved a set of proposals, with implementation strategies (including a division of labor), for establishing plenitude as defined in 3_R^{REF} above.
6_R^{REF}. Therefore we have a valid claim to S.

Supposing that the empirical claims in 4_R^{REF} and 5_R^{REF} are true, the argument succeeds in establishing a type-i radical claim to S. But more must be said. First, the Australians may rebut; second, not every such claimant is a refugee group, and so we must determine what role that status plays in this argument.

Suppose the Anglo-Australians seek to rebut the refugees' claim. They may choose among three possible angles. They may counter with a conservative claim to S; challenge the reality of the refugees' intentional plenitude with respect to S; or charge that the radical claim actually constitutes impermissible expansionism. Let me elaborate on these three strategies briefly below; the third strategy covers the further question about the role of refugee status.

Consider first a conservative rebuttal. We have already seen the prospects for conservative claims: if S lacks Anglo-ecological empirical plenitude, then the conservative claim fails; Australia's claim is then on a par with that of the refugees. If S lacks (only) intentional plenitude, then mere empirical plenitude generates a *probationary* territorial right. If, on the other hand, S meets both empirical and intentional plenitude by Anglo-ecological criteria, then both the Australians and the refugees have valid territorial claims. How to deal with competing valid claims is the subject of Chapter Six below.

But suppose the Australians chose the second strategy, namely, challenging the refugees' intentional plenitude. It is essential to the admissibility of collective intentions such as intentional plenitude that they be empirically demonstrable. If it simply one day dawned on one of the leaders of the refugees to settle the Northern Territory as New Java, but this idea lacked any paper trail or development through various stages of collective planning, then it does not qualify as an intention of this community. On the other hand, if, as 5_R^{REF} connotes, the refugees can show the existence of a paper trail replete with the sorts of land assignments, job descriptions, and other plans that would be necessary for getting started in their new home, they can demonstrate intentional plenitude.[6]

---

[6] To be sure, as refugees they are not likely to have highly developed political institutions, let alone a printing press. What is needed in practice to ascertain the genuineness of the intentions appealed to in 5_R^{REF} must be determined by appropriate international organizations.

Finally, suppose the Australians tried the third rebuttal strategy, namely, to charge that the refugees' claim constitutes impermissible expansionism. At this point premise 1 becomes more than a mere axiomatic starting point. Some groups that assert radical claims already have territorial rights somewhere else, and the specification of a plenitude criterion that is not merely sufficient but necessary for valid territorial claims commits such communities to a view that applies in both their base territory and the claimed territory. Thus the validity of a radical claim depends on whether the claimants have a base territory and, if so, whether that territory is full by their own standards. The refugees in our example claim to lack a base territory, and if they are genuinely refugees, this claim is true. Whether they are genuinely refugees must, of course, be determinable by a body such as the United Nations High Commission for Refugees, which would assess the claim to refugee status based on familiar standards. Presumably, diasporic claimants – those who make radical claims from a situation of expulsion or scattering, rather than expansionism – would also lack a base territory, and so their claim would survive as well.

But if the radical claimant does indeed have a base territory, then in lodging their radical claim they run the risk of impugning their conservative claim to their territorial base. If it turned out that the putative refugees were in fact agents of a clandestine Indonesian effort to colonize Australia, the plenitude of Indonesia itself would be a crucial consideration in the assessment of territorial rights. Similarly, nineteenth-century US expansionism based on the Manifest Destiny to control the entire continent of North America required radical claims to Indian lands. Such claims are not absurd on their face, but it is essential to the validity of such claims to determine whether the base territory of the US was full. To test claims this way is simply to take the claimants at their word: if they hold, as premise 1 requires them to, that some criterion is necessary for valid territorial claims, then consistency demands that they respect that criterion in every territory they claim. If they succeed in demonstrating plenitude in their territorial base, then their claim is serious: their base territories are full, and expansion is one way of avoiding excessive scarcity or ecosystem deterioration. But if the radical claimants fail this test – that is, the US or Indonesia is not full by their own criteria – they must choose: drop the conservative claim, drop the radical claim, or revise the criterion of plenitude.

This consistency test builds into the theory a further bias in favour of conservative claims and against type-i radical ones. The theory permits, but discourages, expansion. The value of discouraging expansion is obvious, but there is also value in permitting it. In the first place, if a base territory genuinely is full and a rapidly expanding population – or a stable population that has learned something new and dangerous about its effect on the environment – genuinely needs more or different territory, this need can be respected through a peaceful process rather than through military expansion or colonialism. Second, the process as described exerts pressure for consistency and coherence, spurring rethinking and improvement of relationships to land when expansionists have allowed greed or unplanned social change to undermine the plenitude of their base territory.

It may be observed that the Anglo-Australians are not the only ones who might have a competing interest in the disposition of the Northern Territory; indeed, the local indigenous population may object to both the Anglo-Australian and the refugees' claims. The presence of indigenous people may affect the dispute in either or both of two ways. First, they might be non-controlling inhabitants, in which case their claim is revisionist (see section 5.4 below). Alternatively, suppose the region is, as the British initially claimed of Australia, *terra nullius*; then it is not a juridical territory. There may be people there, but they (by hypothesis) have not used territorial strategies to bound and control the land, or organized it with a legal system. In this case – granting the newcomers' intentional plenitude and the plenitude of their territorial base – encroachment is permissible. Crucially, though, the newcomers are nonetheless required to assert and justify a radical claim; they may not simply hold a land rush.

There are several reasons to reject land rushes, even on unclaimed land. First, there is nothing inherently good about settling, bounding, and developing land. Unclaimed lands may perform essential ecosystem services or harbor animal and plant populations that are better off undisturbed. Requiring radical claims (as opposed to land rushes) offers some protection against the environmental devastation that humans have so often visited on new-found lands. Second, for the same reasons, the requirement that claimants achieve plenitude in their territorial base protects not just the target territory but the home territory. Finally, requiring that all claims go through a regularized process protects public order in the international system. This is one core function of the framework for territorial rights with which we have been working since the first chapter.

These three considerations also show us how to deal with type-ii radical claims, those where resident controllers seek to abandon a territory. Just as the theory rejects land rushes, it also rejects unaccountable land abandonments. For the reasons just mentioned – public order, leaving environmental devastation in their wake, and protecting both previous and future territories – it is essential that those who want to abandon territories be accountable for the condition in which they leave them. In practice, this means that the resident controllers have no ongoing plans regarding the territory – it is intentionally empty – but that their departure will not precipitate empirical emptiness for anyone who remains. To be sure, applying this prescription requires an account of social causation that goes beyond the scope of this work. If the resident controllers abandon the territory and two remaining groups then go to battle over the remnants, whom to blame will depend on the prior relationships among groups, etc. In the archetypal post-colonial scenario, where the colonists depart after sowing strife, much fault surely lies with the colonists; departure under such circumstances, with such foreseeable consequences, is impermissible. But other cases are different. Apart from the general determination – the departure must not engender empirical emptiness for remaining populations – the practical implications must be determined on a case-by-case basis.

It may be objected, however, that the theory has got things backwards, permitting expansionism but looking askance at the departure of imperialists. The objection fails. Inasmuch as expansionism names a political ideology of territorial expansion, such as Manifest Destiny, the theory rejects expansionism outright. Radical claimants on the Andrew Jackson model lack intentional plenitude in the target territories and also derogate from others' empirical plenitude there. So far from permitting expansionism, the theory unequivocally rejects it, admittedly in an unfamiliar vocabulary. Similarly, the theory has no objection to imperial departures, but is opposed to colonists who skulk away from a mess that they have made, presumably after the empire becomes burdensome to the metropolis. That they are obligated to clean up their mess is the most obvious moral position imaginable. This need not involve staying on as administrators of the territory, but does require a real plan rather than willy-nilly abandonment.

5.4 Revisionist claims

It remains to consider revisionist claims – claims for a change in either control or habitation, but not both. Revisionist arguments take any of four forms, depending on the claimant's status.

5.4.1 Type i: controllers seek to settle

A controller who seeks to settle is analogous to a type-i radical claimant. But we may plausibly put a further burden on the revisionist. If the lack of plenitude in the target territory is due to the policies of the controller, this emptiness cannot support a revisionist claim. That is, a territory may be empty because previously subject by this very controller to ethnic cleansing or some other form of emptying-out, such as undermining the economic base of the territory. In this event it would be perverse to grant territorial rights. So a controller making a revisionist claim for rights to settle must demonstrate not only (prospective) intentional plenitude, but also the retrospective lack of emptying. When revisionist claims of this sort fail, the controllers lack the right to settle. They do not automatically lose the right to control; that depends on whether they face a competing claim, as well as other considerations mentioned in the next sections.

5.4.2 Type ii: inhabitants seek to control

Inhabitants seeking to control – any ethnogeographic community under the sovereignty or occupation of another group, such as the indigenous people in the Australian example above, or Palestinians in the West Bank and Gaza – are in a position similar to conservative claimants, and so their revisionist arguments are akin to conservative ones. But where conservative claims must demonstrate both empirical and intentional plenitude, type-ii revisionist claims face a slightly lower bar that mirrors the higher bar faced by type-i claims: type-ii revisionists who lack empirical plenitude may still show that this failure is due to emptying-out policies that were imposed upon them, such as restrictions on land use, the refusal to grant building permits, a coercive residential-schools system, ethnic cleansing, cantonization, unilateral abrogation of treaties, etc. That is, for type-ii revisionist claims, lack of plenitude may in fact constitute a harm visited on the claimants, rather than their own dereliction, and the theory must not exacerbate such harms by blaming them on their victims.

To apply this result, recall the account of individuating ethnogeographic communities. If this very ethnogeographic community suffered this treatment, the conclusion applies; if it was a predecessor, the conclusion does not. The new ethnogeographic community may still make a revisionist claim (if it remains in the territory) or a radical one (if it has been expelled and lost empirical plenitude), but in such cases, since the previous emptying-out did not constitute a harm against this very group – indeed, if the group is there, the emptying-out may have contributed to the group's creation – then it cannot avail itself of the lower bar described here.

This result may seem odd or retrograde, both because it seems to treat diasporic claims as merely radical rather than revisionist, and because it seems to put a sunset date on the grievances of populations under foreign rule. Take these challenges in order. Our result does not prevent diasporic groups from claiming historical homelands; the historical link may legitimately motivate the group to assert a radical claim, and may be part of the reason that the diasporic group develops plans and projects constituting intentional plenitude in that particular place to begin with. So in this sense the historical link may indirectly contribute to justifying the claim, insofar as it motivates the group to develop a well-justified claim. But the indirectness is crucial. Such motivations cannot themselves directly justify the claim. It is the actions taken, or plans developed, on the basis of those (or other) motivations that can justify the claim. And in this light the result seems plausible. The mere fact of an historical link, be it to a place deemed sacred or a region held at the apogee of a former empire, carries no weight as against claims of groups that have achieved plenitude in the place.

Recall Chaim Gans's (2003: 99) defense of a limited right to "formative territories," sites "that have primacy in the history of the national group." To restate this in our terms: a formative territory is the site where a particular ethnogeographic community arose. Rights to formative territories may indeed exist as type-ii revisionist claims when the following circumstances obtain: i) the community is alienated from the place, and ii) that very community had filled the place prior to iii) an imposed emptying-out alienated the community. The lower bar we are discussing implies only that the claim remains revisionist rather than radical, even though the group is now exiled. But the application of this lowered bar is limited to cases where the displaced ethnogeographic community has not evolved into a new one. The putatively retrograde result under consideration here applies only to successor communities, that is, new communities that emerge out of displaced ones after the initial exile. And it seems clear that the historical-rights principle should not apply to successor communities, even diasporic ones with no sovereign state of their own. Suppose that, after being forcibly resettled in Oklahoma from Georgia, the Cherokee underwent a change in land-use practices and ethnogeography, and this change was sufficient to reconstitute the group as a new ethnogeographic community. For the descendant-Cherokee, Georgia is not the formative territory at all, but an ancestral territory; Oklahoma is the formative territory. The Cherokee may nonetheless enter radical claims to Georgia, but again, it is then the projects and plans – the intentional plenitude – that would justify the claim, rather than the historical link. By emphasizing the intentional plenitude, this answer bases claims on action, rather than status, and creates a strong incentive for claimant groups actually to develop plans for sustainable land use even before arriving in or gaining control of the claimed place.

Let us turn, then, to the second challenge raised above, namely, that the result here places a sunset date on the claims of occupied groups. Numerous theorists have assumed that territorial grievances must be subject to some statute of limitations, but this would seem to apply only to peoples who have been expelled – not those who remain in place under foreign rule. What could be the argument for thinking that their rights to the land on which they have dwelt continuously could evaporate?[7]

Let us first clarify the counter-intuitive result in question. That result places a sunset date, not on the possibility of asserting revisionist claims, for resident non-controllers are always eligible to lodge a type-ii revisionist claim to the land on which they live, provided they continue

---

[7] Locke, for one, famously asks, "Who doubts but the Grecian Christians descendants of the ancient possessors of that Country may justly cast off the Turkish yoke which they have so long groaned under when ever they have a power to do it?" (Locke 1988: II, sec. 192) Current international law on self-determination for overseas colonized peoples seems to agree with Locke.

to be an ethnogeographic community at all. Rather, our result places a sunset date on that group's ability to appeal to an historical emptying-out to justify lowering the bar for their claim. Thereafter, they are required to demonstrate empirical plenitude; they can no longer absolve themselves of this demand by showing that, in the past, they suffered an emptying-out imposed by their rulers. Further, the objection must assume that the historical emptying-out did not consist in expulsion of the entire population or even a vast majority of it, but rather something else – for instance, reorganization of land-use patterns around the needs of empire. And it must also assume that there has been genuine ethnogeographic change: the community that initially suffered conquest (EC_1) is an ancestor of, but not identical to, the community that now seeks to make a revisionist claim (EC_2). So my conclusion is not that the "Grecian Christians" may not "justly cast off the Turkish yoke"; rather the claim is that their argument for doing so – their revisionist territorial claim – faces the same demands as any other revisionist claim.[8] The justification is as follows.

First, for reasons discussed in Chapters Two and Four, it is essential to separate the claims of ethnogeographic communities from those of ethnic groups or nations. Members of EC_2 may be descended from multiple ethnic groups, or from merely some members of an older ethnic group that still survives elsewhere; these descent relationships, though, are irrelevant. This can be seen clearly in cases where the relationship to outside groups has been thought to undermine the revisionist claim. For instance, even if the infamous assertions that "there are no Palestinians" (because the people calling themselves such are recent immigrants to the region) and that "the Palestinians already have a state, and it is called Jordan" (because the majority of Jordanians are ethnically Palestinian) were true, they would still be irrelevant to the validity of Palestinian claims to the West Bank. The validity of those claims rests on the practices and plans of the resident population itself. But if descent relationships do not raise any issue for the Palestinians' revisionist claim, it is because the putative facts in

---

[8] Strictly speaking: *qua* Christians or *qua* (ethnic) "Grecians," they have no territorial rights whatsoever. It is only *qua* a particular ethnogeographic community that they "may justly cast off the Turkish yoke" (*qua* Turkish). This position would reject the ethnicity-based population transfers that occurred between Turkey and Greece after World War I.

question are about the wrong thing – about an ethnic group or nation, rather than an ethnogeographic community.

Second, an ethnogeographic community may arise because of the fact of occupation – the occupation may involve a reorganization of the geography and concomitant creation of a new ethnogeographic community. If the farmers and herders who inhabit some occupied region are descended from traders and craftspeople who were forced out of these sectors by the colonizers; and over time the farmers and herders developed an agrarian ethnogeography, it is possible to affirm their right to the territory on the basis of a revisionist claim, but it seems odd to then say that they ought to have a leg up in their claim because their ancestors had a different way of life. What matters is what the current claimants plan to do with it, not what their ancestors did with it or why they stopped. It might be possible to regard coerced ethnogeographic change as an egregious form of emptying-out – *ethnogeographic genocide*. In this event, while we would not give the new ethnogeographic community a leg up in its claim, we could hold this change against the occupiers, making their revisionist claim that much more difficult. The problem here is to explain exactly why causing ethnogeographic change would be a form of emptying-out; it is not the same as ethnic cleansing, where people are expelled. Rather, a conception of plenitude is caused to dissolve and be replaced by another. The intentional plenitude attached to the dissolved conception then also dissolves. But plenitude might be maintained by the conceptions of both the occupiers and of the new ethnogeographic community that arises in place of the destroyed one. So unless we were to accord value to ethnogeographic survival as such – a position I have not defended – it is hard to see why this change would be relevant. The result then remains counterintuitive: if a new ethnogeographic community is forged in the crucible of occupation by an outside power, that community is considered autochthonous and not given credit for being descended from a previous community that was destroyed.

There is an analogy here with modernization. We rarely suppose that massive demographic shifts, in and of themselves, constitute wrongs done to (or benefits conferred on) the descendants of those shifts, at least a few generations on. From 1900 to 1990, the percentage of the US population that was "rural" dropped from 60.4 per cent to 24.8 per cent of total population as the US became an urban society.[9] The shift consisted of millions of upheavals in millions of individual lives, upon which supervened a major change in the character of the country. But even Jeffersonian agrarians would be hard-pressed to suppose that any city-dweller is wronged by the very fact of being an urbanite descended from rural ancestors.[10] If there is a wrong here it is from either or both of two sources: there may have been valuable cultural or environmental phenomena lost to the people or the world due to the change; or the change may have left the descendants in a state of unjust domination. On the former the theory is silent, and remains neutral on whether and when cultural losses justify remediation or constitute wrongs done to descendants. The latter is more challenging. Coerced ethnogeographic change may, rather than create a new ethnogeographic community, render the community a mere vestige or appendage of a larger ethnogeography, thereby depriving its members of skills essential to the development of intentional plenitude. For instance, through decades of subjugation, a population may have been shunted into one sector of the economy, or left with extremely high unemployment rates, and have lost the architectural, ecological, and bureaucratic skills that are essential to the development of intentional plenitude.

Our theory seems perverse inasmuch as it implies that such a group simply lacks the capacity to assert valid territorial claims. If it is not an ethnogeographic community it is ineligible; if it is unable to develop intentional plenitude, its claims are invalid. Is this a problem for the theory? I think not: other sorts of accommodation may be appropriate, including familiar forms of redistribution and relief from oppression, but a territorial resolution to this problem is more likely a recipe for failure, at least in the near term.[11]

---

[9] United States Census (1995). The actual number of rural residents rose by about 33 per cent (from 45 million to 60 million) over the 90-year period, compared with an overall population increase upwards of 200 per cent (76 million to 248 million).

[10] Which is not to deny that the very people who are forced to give up their rural livelihood and start over in the city suffer a wrong. To settle this question would require, not least, a more precise conception of force. I leave this aside, since my concern is with multigenerational change.

[11] Cairns (2005) at least hints at a similar conclusion, arguing that the tiny populations of many First Nations bands, as well as their lack of bureaucratic capacity, constitute major challenges to the idea of territorial political independence for First Nations in, or alongside, Canada.

This result is perhaps stark, but seems to be a virtue of the theory inasmuch as it takes a dynamic attitude toward claimants and intentional plenitude. Sumantra Bose (2007) endorses phased implementations of territorial conflict resolutions on the grounds that these may build confidence between the parties over time. We may add to this consideration a further one: phased implementations permit claimants to develop intentional plenitude (and its underlying skills) over time. The interim period provides opportunities to flesh out aspects of intentional plenitude that oppressed communities are initially able to articulate only in rougher form. In other sorts of cases, such as that of landless peasants in Brazil and elsewhere, it seems undeniable that an immediate shift to independent control of their own territory would be an inappropriate response to the grievance. Land occupations aimed at forcing reform and allowing permanent settlement typically fail unless the residents are organized by the Landless People's Movement or a rural union – organizations that have the skills for achieving plenitude. Even then, the settlements require credit and infrastructure support from the government (Wright and Wolford 2003). The point is not that the grievances of subjugated and landless peoples are not serious, or not about land; they are both. The point is that when the aggrieved parties do not form an ethnogeographic community, or lack the capacity to achieve and maintain plenitude, using immediate grants of full territorial rights as a way to redress the grievance is a recipe for failure. That our theory can respect the territorial character of the grievance, while also having non-arbitrary grounds for rejecting (immediate) territorial sovereignty as a solution, is a mark in favor of our theory.

This long digression has been aimed at rendering plausible a deceptively minor implication of the theory: that in cases of ethnogeographic change due to outside control, where an ethnogeographic community goes out of existence and a new one (or a vestige of one) arises in its place, the latter ought not to get a leg up in its revisionist claim on grounds of being descended from the people whose community suffered conquest and ethnogeographic destruction. The obvious answer from this perspective – that the wrong was done to one group, the claim made by another group – seems to violate strong intuitions that the residents of unjustly conquered territory maintain a permanent right to throw off their rulers and return to the status quo ante. When the ethnogeographic community remains the same, they do. But in the event of ethnogeographic change, although the new community has a perfectly legitimate opportunity to assert type-ii revisionist claims, the fact of prior emptying-out no longer serves directly to buttress that claim. And in the event that oppression has made the group incapable of achieving or maintaining plenitude, or has made it not an ethnogeographic community at all, there is an array of wrongs here but the appropriate remedy in the near term is not territorial sovereignty. I believe that this result is more plausible than other contenders, such as permitting unilateral secession as a remedy for persistent injustice.

5.4.3 Types iii and iv: abandonment

Sometimes, controllers seek to depart or cede territory to others. Why not just allow them to leave unilaterally? The risk is that their departure is an attempt to externalize environmental or communal problems that they (culpably) caused or exacerbated. For instance, Britain pursued partition in Palestine and India as part of a blame-worthy strategy of "divide and quit" (Ben-Porat 2006: 103). For reasons of order as well as justice the theory insists that all territorial changes – even in instances of cession or departure – be couched in demonstrations of plenitude. Type-iii revisionist claims are, then, similar to the radical abandonment claims discussed above.

The controller that seeks to depart must show that its departure will not engender emptiness from the standpoint of remaining populations or other stakeholders: it must not leave the territory uninhabitable due to environmental destruction; must not have engendered massive strife through divide-and-rule tactics;[12] must not leave the local population without the infrastructure or institutional capacity to set up a functioning economy and state. Thus a controller who seeks to leave can be required to contribute to plenitude (by the criteria of the remaining community) – for instance, by helping to clean up environmental problems, to build trust and cooperation across ethnic lines, or to build state capacity in the territory. It may, of course, be the case that

---

[12] Ethnic strife engenders emptiness both because rival ethnic groups seek to eliminate each other and because intentional plenitude is crowded out by the conflict.

the departing controller lacks the trust of the remaining population, in which case the mediation of an international body or another state may be required. This does not absolve the departing controller of its obligations; it merely affects how those obligations can be discharged.[13]

Finally, type-iv revisionist claims are those lodged by resident non-controllers who seek to depart. This sort of case covers large-scale evacuations, for instance by diaspora nationalists who achieve a dream of statehood in a homeland. While resident non-controllers typically have much less power than controllers, resident or otherwise, a similar standard applies to type-iv as to type-iii claims. If the residents have laid waste the environment or fomented conflict among remaining populations, their departure is impermissible. This requirement protects future territories from similar treatment, and rewards comity and sustainability.

5.4.4 Secession

Secession may seem to be orthogonal to the status quo axis as discussed here. Some secessionist claims seem to be neither revisionist nor conservative. They seek to alter the political status of the territory, so they are not conservative; but if the claimants already have partial political control of the territory – for instance by controlling provinces within a federal system – they do not seem to fit any of the forms of revisionism.

Some kinds of secession are straightforwardly revisionist. Even secessionists who have a separate province or (nominal) state of their own may plausibly regard their territory as, for all intents and purposes, occupied by a foreign power if they have no effective control of their economy, foreign affairs, immigration or emigration policies, etc.

---

[13] These results apply to the US situation (as of this writing) in Iraq. To simply leave would constitute a serious risk of massively exacerbating the crimes that the US has already committed. It goes without saying that the war was criminal and the occupation should end; but any US departure that does not include restitution and some plan for stopping ethnic cleansing (or worse) would be grossly immoral. It does not follow that the US itself – an untrusted and untrustworthy actor in the region – ought to be the one doing the work here. But the work must be done, and ensuring that it is done is a US obligation.

The peoples of the various Warsaw Pact states until 1989 – and still more, those of the Baltic states and the various SSRs incorporated into the USSR itself – as well as the Québécois in Canada prior to the Quiet Revolution, could plausibly view themselves as under occupation. In other cases this seems less appropriate. The Québécois in twenty-first-century Canada are among the most self-determining people in the world. We cannot regard them as under occupation, since they share equally (indeed, as first among equals) in the exercise of territorial rights in Quebec. Nonetheless, it remains best to treat Québécois secessionism as revisionist: they are trying to alter the allocation of territorial rights, making themselves the unique holders of such rights in a territory. Similarly, a claim emanating from a particular state of the United States would also be revisionist. For this reason our theory could apply in such cases. But there is an important caveat: if the would-be secessionists do not constitute an ethnogeographic community, then they are ineligible to assert territorial rights-claims. While there were distinct regional ethnogeographic communities in the US until about the 1950s, these seem mostly to have dissolved for a variety of reasons, intentional and otherwise. But the country could sectionalize again, and if it did, the various ethnogeographic communities would be eligible to assert revisionist claims.[14] If they do constitute an ethnogeographic community – or at the end of a years-long project of turning themselves into one – they could assert a type-ii revisionist claim (section 5.4.2).

But not all would-be secessionists control a province within a federal system. Some are pervasively integrated into a larger population of non-secessionists. Suppose that Anglo-Canadian Catholics entered a claim to secede; this would be a revisionist claim but the claimant would not count as an ethnogeographic community. The group may, of course, suffer other forms of injustice, but these are not territorial injustices; they do not have a territorial remedy. Finally, what about when the would-be secessionists constitute a tiny, but culturally distinct, group within a larger state, such as the ultra-Orthodox Jews of

---

[14] Lest this come across as a defense of the Confederacy, recall that nothing follows yet about political sovereignty or the conditions under which independent statehood would be granted as against a conservative claim emanating from Washington, DC. The point is only that the theory would cover this sort of claim and recognize the claimants as eligible to assert it.

Kiryas Joel in New York, or the Hutterites in Canada? In each of these cases I would argue that the claimants count as an ethnogeographic community and the secessionist claim counts as revisionist. Whether the appropriate resolution of their rights is to create a state is a different question, of a sort to be dealt with in Chapter Six. Thus the issue of secession falls under the rubric of revisionist claims.

5.5 Epistemological and worldview axes

The status quo axis considers the relationship between the claim asserted and the current political status of the target territory. But claims (and theories) may be assessed on two other axes. We must address these axes, but we do not need to dwell on them to the same extent.

5.5.1 *Worldview axis*

The worldview axis involves the importance of the territory to the claimant. Some claims, such as the Israeli and Palestinian claims to Jerusalem, are to *central* places, while others, such as the Lebanese claim to Sheba'a Farms or the Canadian claim to Hans Island, though perhaps significant, are *marginal*. Previous theories of territorial rights, particularly nationalist ones, have identified centrality with sacredness or significance. For reasons discussed already, I deny that such notions provide a useful mark of centrality. The plenitude criterion, in contrast, does so. A claim is central to the extent that the place claimed is the focus of intentional plenitude on the part of the claimant. Claims of sacredness are well and good, but if they are not backed by intentional plenitude then they are inert, at least for territorial claims. (They may generate special access rights – for instance, all Muslims have access rights to Mecca – but these carry no straightforward territorial implications.) It is crucial to remember, of course, that plenitude does not require human settlement; a graveyard or holy site may indeed be subject to intentional plenitude even if no person lives there.[15]

---

[15] What to do if some graveyard is voluntarily left derelict by the community whose ancestors are buried there? In this event it is hard to see that they still have a territorial claim to it. It does not follow that the ancestors ought to be dug up and moved (though that might not be off the table altogether).

In contrast, claims are marginal to the extent that the claimed place is not the focus of intentional plenitude on the part of the claimant. This may occur either because the claimant does not care about or lacks capacity to pay attention to the place, or because the state is actively engaged in emptying it out. For example, at the time of its founding in 1867, Canada could not legitimately claim the vast hinterlands to the north of the main regions of European settlement. When a state claims land that is, from that state's perspective, mere space, its claim is groundless. It is possible to imagine that the state would assume administration of the region in the absence of any competing claims (for instance, in order to prevent land rushes), but such lands cannot be the legitimate objects of territorial rights. We may render a similar verdict on the US claim to much of the inland west, as well as Appalachia, in the years prior to World War II. The state was mostly uninterested in these places, limiting its concern to various emptying-out projects and leaving ghost towns or dereliction when the emptying was complete. Such claims have no legitimate territorial basis. (Probationary claims may be justified, as discussed in 5.1 above, if the territories are characterized by empirical plenitude.)

In the middle of this continuum between central and marginal lies a wide range of places to which the claimant pays at least minimal attention. In the event of territorial disputes over these lands, the hope would be to devise arbitration or mediating institutions that could not just measure degrees of plenitude but also determine the nature of the competing ethnogeographic links to the place. Ideally, such institutions would be able to use their understanding of these links in order to divide the territory in creative ways that accommodate as much as possible of each side's claim. As noted in Chapter One, it is rare that competing claims are so fully incompatible as to force evacuation of particular buildings or city blocks by particular people. Territorial claims are claims for jurisdiction, and jurisdiction may be divided in numerous ways.

5.5.2 Epistemological axis

The discussion of the worldview axis presupposes that claims are commensurable, and hence not opaque. The epistemological axis covers claims along a continuum from opaque ones that make no sense to, or are utterly unable to garner the respect of, outsiders, to transparent ones that are completely interpretable and seem reason-able to outsiders. Transparent claims are easy, but a theory of terri-torial rights must deal also with opaque claims and those at various degrees of translucency.

One way to deal with opaque claims is simply to treat each group's assertions about its attachment to territory as decisive. This is a par-ticularist strategy (Chapter Four above). One might, alternatively, back up the mere-assertion standard with a "revealed preference" theory based on what the group is willing to sell at what price. This is Levy's (2000) strategy (Chapter One above). Neither strategy makes any attempt to commensurate the content of claims; in effect, no group owes any other group any account of what makes the claimed territory special. Sincerity is the criterion of truth. Another strategy, adopted by Meisels (2005) in her interpretation of the use criterion, is to try to translate every claim into a lowest common denominator (Chapter Four above). More or less everyone can see the significance of use, so this is a transparent criterion; and by lowering the bar for what counts as use, Meisels effectively defines as use anything that anyone might say is their way of using a place, provided it is not very clearly a form of neglect. I have already argued at length against these strategies.

The plenitude criterion uses a third strategy for rendering all claims transparent: to require that all claims entail specific, falsifiable, empirical propositions. The strategy is not to translate claims into transparent language, but to make them susceptible of empirical tests that are transparent. Two groups may claim that completely different gods have promised them the same place; the current theory will be unimpressed unless the gods' promises and, more importantly, the ways that the people have acted in the light of those promises, entail conclusions that are transparent because empirically testable. The wide variety of opaque conceptions of use, sacredness, etc. has no bearing on the theory.

5.6 Concluding considerations for plenitude

It is now possible to claim with some justification that the theory developed here meets all the basic desiderata of a theory of territorial rights, as laid out in the framework articulated and defended in Chapter One. The framework demands that theories of territory speak equally plausibly about claims no matter where they fall on the status quo axis, the worldview axis, and the epistemological axis. Our theory clearly meets this demand. First, on the status quo axis, we saw how the criterion of plenitude operates in conservative, radical, and revisionist contexts. Plenitude also makes sense of the worldview axis – whether the territory claimed is central or marginal – without appeal to slippery notions such as sacredness. An ethnogeographic community determines the relative centrality of various tracts of land not by appeal to a national myth or sacred history, but by intentional plenitude. The centrality or marginality of a specific place can be read off the intentions of the community, but sacredness as such has no direct role in this theory. The epistemological axis is covered by the requirement of empirical testability. Even as opacity is permitted in the conception of plenitude itself – we do not demand that the community adopt anyone's conception of plenitude but its own – the demand for empirical testability renders all claims at bottom transparent. Thus we satisfy all positions on the epistemological axis by permitting opacity in one context but requiring transparency from the perspective of competing claimants in another.

Chapter One also discussed three further challenges for theories of territory, namely, determining claimants' eligibility, articulating criteria of attachment (including uniqueness), and showing how these criteria could be normative. The eligibility of ethnogeographic communities was defended in Chapter Three. Plenitude – both empirical and intentional – serves as our criterion of attachment. We achieve normativity by ruling out appeals to sacredness or national myths, and replacing them with plenitude as a normative criterion of attachment. The value of this move, as defended in Chapter Four, is that plenitude – albeit, subject to differing conceptions – is widely, if not universally, regarded as a normative basis for territorial claims. Expansionists such as Locke and his followers have long asserted plenitude to support their claims, and those who defend against such expansion have challenged, not the normativity of plenitude itself, but the empirical claim that the land in question was empty. These people have also agreed that plenitude must be objectively testable; they have merely denied that the only legitimate test was in government-issued deeds to land (Pinder 1999). Moreover, plenitude is an ingredient in state legitimacy, and connects territorial rights to stewardship and sustainability. We have thus met the theoretic desiderata laid out in Chapter One.

Let us conclude this chapter by mentioning some final normative considerations. First, as we saw, nothing hinges on any alleged primordial identities such as nationality or ethnicity. The very primordial character of these identities tends to make appeal to them unimpressive to outsiders, and so unhelpful in resolving competing claims. Instead, we've found a procedural criterion for such claims: a reliance on empirical facts. But the relevant empirical facts and their truth-conditions are determined by the claimant's own ethnogeography. The claimant cannot legitimately complain if its claims are evaluated for accuracy and consistency; but it would be unfair to evaluate the accuracy in terms alien to the claimant.

Second, the requirement on ethnogeographies that, in order to be legitimate, they countenance mutually formative interactions between people and land serves as only a minimal qualification for claimants. It does rule out both the Anglo-American ethnogeography, which regards land as wholly passive and merely instrumentally valuable, and some versions of ecological holism, which departs from the Anglo-American ethnogeography in regarding land as intrinsically valuable, but nonetheless remains compatible with the passivity of land. But the bi-directionality criterion is open to such alternative ethnogeographies as the Anglo-ecological one discussed above, and those that embody ecological considerations more generally, such as agrarianism, urbanism, ecofeminism, and certain nonwestern views. The bi-directionality requirement ensures that concern for territorial rights moves in the direction of productive human interactions with nature, and prioritizes increased plenitude over territorial change in cases where communities claim to need more land than they control. In other words, the theory offered here discourages radical claims without ruling them out altogether, and supports sound ecological practices by encouraging recognition, in whatever way, of the active role that land plays in human life.

Further, the theory makes sense of the widely held intuition that there must be some sort of statute of limitations on past injustices, while at the same time we must avoid generating a perverse incentive for rapacious governments to cleanse first and ask questions later. It is tempting, when thinking about territory – especially from the perspective of a North American who fears displacement by restitutions – to assert that all claims are tainted at some point in the past, and so there must be a statute of limitations. Sometimes this is explained by appeal to the innocence of the current generation (Moore 2001), sometimes by the moral significance of quotidian use and planning (Waldron 1992). The problem with this is its arbitrariness. On the one hand, when a debt is owed, it is at least as plausible to suppose that it accrues interest, rather than depreciates, over time. More importantly, statutes of limitations are not their own justification, but rather follow from some normatively significant facts attached to the passage of time. But what could such normatively significant facts be? If they are imposed from outside – namely, "the people who stole your land have built cities on it by now" – they run sharply foul of a normativity requirement. But if they appeal to the practices and intentions of the victims – namely, "the place is no longer empirically or intentionally full to us" – then such criteria make sense. This explains Jeremy Waldron's otherwise odd appeal to the extended duration of claims to sacred sites. Sacred sites such as capital cities and burial grounds may remain full because an expelled community remembers who is buried there, or the layout of the streets, and intends to go back to tend the grave sites and rebuild the city. Waldron's use criterion cannot explain this, because sacred sites are often the sites least labored upon and least significant to the daily lives of individuals.

How does this gloss on a statute of limitations, combined with the rejection of primordial identities and mere sacredness, affect diaspora nationalisms? Consider for a moment Zionist claims to British Mandatory Palestine.[16] Intuitively, whatever we want to say about the Jewish claim to Palestine, it is stronger than a Jewish claim to East Africa would have been, had the Zionists accepted the British Uganda Programme (Ben-Porat 2006: 63). It might seem as though the theory here could not explain that strength. But I would suggest that it can. First, the Zionists' intentional plenitude was much greater for Palestine than for East Africa. The Zionists had no intentions regarding East Africa one way or the other. Second, one characteristic of (self-conscious) diaspora communities may be that the lost homeland remains in some respects empirically full: they continue to know the geography, including both empirical and sacred geography; they may pay tithes to maintain religious sites and cemeteries; and they may

---

[16] I discuss this issue in detail in Chapter Six.

maintain links to a remainder group who are descended from the minority who avoided expulsion, or who returned when the opportunity arose. Whether in the case of the Jews, or specifically, Zionist Jews, these forms of attachment existed is unclear. While there was surely a remainder group in Palestine for the entire period of exile, it is also true that the keepers of the religious customs and the sacred geography were least likely to be Zionists, and vice-versa (Boyarin and Boyarin 2002).

It should hardly be surprising if, in the intervening 1800 years, Palestine ceased to be empirically full for the exiled Jews. Further, one element of a diaspora community may be precisely that the relationship to land is understood in terms of alienation.[17] In this event, whether the diaspora community ever attains empirical and intentional plenitude in the ancient homeland would simply be the result of happenstance, including how they are treated in "host" countries. In the case of Jews, prior to the rise of Nazism, Zionism represented a small minority position, and had no foothold at all outside Europe. In this respect the plenitude of Palestine for most Jews was indeed the result of external events. But this does nothing to change the fact of intentional plenitude; recall that the motivations for intentional plenitude serve no justificatory function, although they may explain why the group undertakes the justificatory intentional plenitude in the first place. I would conclude that in the case of the Jews the link to Palestine as opposed to Uganda (circa 1880) was mostly, but not completely, a matter of mere nationalism and sacredness, which I reject as bases for territorial claims. Further, the majority of Jews became invested in the intentional plenitude of Palestine – that is, became Zionists – only because of external conditions, primarily oppression in eastern Europe, the Nazi genocide, and expulsion from other home countries. But these motivations neither improve nor impugn the intentional plenitude that they motivate. A Jewish claim to Palestine should appeal to intentional plenitude, not the ancient covenant.

Finally, it is worth noting that the plenitude criterion suggests a new way to understand the difference between property and territory. The conceptual analysis of territory in Chapter Three emphasized the distinction: territory is a bounded geographical place that has an

---

[17] I am grateful to Aaron Jaffe for this suggestion.

organizing principle. A territory is juridical when the organizing principle is provided by a legal system. But for its boundedness, territory is unlike property.

But plenitude adds a further point of contrast, at least at a symbolic level, and that is the underlying conception of value.[18] Property gains value as its scarcity relative to demand increases. Scarcity, then, is the operative notion. In contrast, the value of territory to claimants has nothing to do with scarcity, but with plenitude, which may be understood as a form of abundance. When Wendell Berry lies down on his native hill and recognizes scores of distinct species of flora and fauna, and the interactions among them that constitute an ecosystem, he makes no reference whatsoever to scarcity. To the contrary, it is the teeming abundance of life, and his role in it, that is the source of value. More generally, when ethnogeographic communities claim territory on the basis of plenitude, they do not assert that territory is a particularly valuable commodity or that it is getting scarce as population increases. Rather, they express their engagement with the abundance of life and possibility in the place. Scarcity comes up, if at all, only in the appeals of radical claimants who express frustration that they lack a base territory, or that their base territory is overfull and risks degradation as a result.

The past two chapters have provided a theory of valid territorial claims. Those who have such claims thereby achieve standing in territorial-dispute resolutions. But there is more to territorial disputes than moral weight and standing; we still need a way to implement the conclusions reached here and institutionalize peaceful mechanisms for asserting, supporting, evaluating, and enforcing territorial claims. These are problems for Chapter Six.

[18] I am grateful to Aaron Jaffe for this point, too.

6 | *Implementation*

We have seen the plenitude criterion in action. Now we must see how it works when multiple ethnogeographic communities assert territorial claims in the same place. To carry this out, we must work at both abstract and concrete levels. Section 6.1 discusses institutional forms in general, taking on two challenges that confront any theory of global order that proposes to change the rules of the game. Section 6.2 sketches dispute types and their appropriate resolutions. I lay out the theory's implications for each dispute type, and argue that these implications tend to confirm the theory. Section 6.3 applies the theory systematically to the Israeli–Palestinian dispute. Finally, by way of conclusion, section 6.4 gestures at some aspects of indigenous-rights disputes to suggest that the theory would be promising if applied in that context as well.

Even the concrete sections are inevitably rather sketchy, relying on what is ultimately a mere fraction of all the empirical studies and analyses of complex and contested subjects. I believe that the empirical foundation of the discussions is adequate, but in the event that the empirical work is incorrect or incomplete, the reader may take section 6.3 as an elaborate thought-experiment informed by real situations. This is sufficient to test the theory. Any attempt in a work of political philosophy to make specific proposals for the resolution of real conflicts is bound to be sketchy at best. (It is sketchy enough in the empirical social sciences.) Even engaged, empirically informed philosophy can say relatively little on this level, since philosophers do not make much, or still less systematic, use of empirical studies or even empirical theory, and anyway, there is widespread disagreement about what sorts of empirical work would even be relevant to the case. The overall purpose of the chapter is to develop the theory by applying it, and to defend it by arguing that its application provides attractive solutions for difficult problems. If the facts as I represent them here depart from reality – I have made every effort to ensure that they do not – then what matters from a theoretic perspective is whether the theory does justice to the facts as represented here.

6.1 Two aspects of global order

The objective of this section is to address two challenges that must confront any proposal for reforming international institutions. The first is ensuring that governance will take place at scales that are both manageable and effective. The second is the conservation principle – the idea that states as we know them perform crucial morally necessary functions, and do so better than transnational institutions are likely to do any time in the near future; thus departures from states as we know them should not be undertaken lightly.

6.1.1 Scale

The diversity of ethnogeographies suggests that an important general principle for international institutional design would be what David Held (2004: 99–101) calls a "principle of inclusiveness and subsidiarity." Subsidiarity is the familiar idea that governance functions should be "as close to the people as possible." This is usually interpreted to mean that they should be at the smallest geographic scale compatible with giving a voice to each person appropriately affected by some phenomenon (Pogge 2002; Slaughter 2004; Föllesdall 2006). On this view, certain functions, such as allocating costs due to climate change, must be at the global scale because they affect everyone, while others, such as planning and zoning, should be local. This interpretation of subsidiarity assumes that there is only one variable in the equation, namely, the scale of the governance function – say, the jurisdiction over which a given legislature enacts law. The problem of "right-sizing the state" (O'Leary 2001) then simply requires tinkering with jurisdictions. But there is a second variable, namely, the scale of the governed phenomenon itself (Held 2004; Kolers 2006). In at least many cases, phenomena themselves – such as economies and basic structures, as well as certain environmental impacts – may be made larger or smaller through human agency. Held's principle may be interpreted as aiming to mutually accommodate the scales of phenomenon and function. But this then leaves open the scale at which we should aim when doing so. The principles articulated and defended in this book suggest that right-sizing should aim at convergence around the scale of a country (Chapter Three).[1] As a general rule governance and governed phenomena should match up with countries: if some territory is not a country (for instance because it lacks resilience), there is reason to initiate a right-sizing effort by adjusting the scope of the governance structure or the governed phenomena, either larger or smaller.

This right-sizing would become most clearly relevant when some group asserted a valid revisionist or radical territorial claim; if, despite being characterized by plenitude, the claimed territory lacked resilience (or by hiving it off the secessionists would leave the remainder less than resilient), then the claim should be accommodated through some means other than independent statehood. Theorists of secession typically have to build into their theories an epicycle to prevent secessions that would make either the new state or the remainder state ungovernable. The current theory gets the same result without the epicycle, because resilience is a necessary feature of countries, and being a country is a necessary condition of a legitimate claim to statehood.

Resilience is not only a necessary feature of countries, but a plausible moral goal for the global-institutional system. In the face of a climate emergency, resilience takes on an importance comparable to that of the cardinal goals of justice and peace (Buchanan 2004); or put differently, even if we admit only two cardinal goals – or only one, peace (Kukathas 2006) – resilience may take on primary urgency among all the means pursued in their name.

6.1.2 *The conservation principle*

A theory that countenances territorial revisions might be challenged on grounds of what Thomas Christiano (2006: 91) calls the "conservation principle": "there is a strong presumption in favor of the boundaries of democratic states remaining as they are." Christiano offers two arguments for conservation. First, liberal democratic states, unlike any extant or foreseeable global governance bodies, "satisfy certain essential prerequisites of legitimacy . . . understood as treating persons publicly as equals in the political society" (2006: 93). They do this

---

[1] Strictly speaking, this is a scale-type, not a particular scale, since not all countries are similarly sized in geographic terms.

through responsible legislatures, constraints on executive authority, and independent judiciaries. In contrast, transnational bodies lack this kind of legitimacy and will not have it in the foreseeable future. Christiano draws two inferences from this argument. First, international law and institutions currently have little if any "capacity to render justice on most of the important issues that human beings face" (97). Second, there must be a strong bias against secession, and even against "grant[ing] legitimacy to the seceding parties through grants of recognition or through the declarations of world bodies," because "secession must take place outside of any system of settled law, and the only way to establish justice is through settled law" (97).

Christiano's second argument for the conservation principle is that the modern state constitutes a "common world" for its citizens: "all or nearly all the individuals' fundamental interests are intertwined" (97). In contrast with other sorts of organizations whether smaller or larger than the modern state, "individuals have roughly equal stakes ... as a result of the idea that all or nearly all of their fundamental interests are at stake for each person" (98). And Christiano argues that the principle of equality makes sense only in a context where everyone has roughly equal stakes in the organization. Because our theory allows challenges to states' territorial integrity and presumably does so through the adjudication of a global body which is sure to be less responsive than liberal democratic states; and because our theory threatens to dismember the common worlds that ground political equality, the conservation principle constitutes a major objection.

The first argument for the conservation principle applies only to liberal democracies. While some illiberal or nonliberal states may meet the normative descriptions that Christiano offers, most do not. (Liberal democracies themselves contain significant pockets of illiberalism, especially regarding ethnogeographic dissidents such as indigenous peoples.) Perhaps the majority of the global population live under illiberal conditions. For these people, international institutions, if the people had access to them, may well be more responsive than domestic ones, or at least offer some counterweight to the power of the illiberal state. More generally, Christiano emphasizes that representative democracy and minimal justice are two of the greatest achievements humans have ever managed, and it would be perverse not to protect them where they exist. True enough, but these achievements are nonetheless fully compatible with, and arguably even promote, catastrophic global climate change – which threatens to be among the worst things we have ever done (Vincent 1998; Gardiner 2004). If we can contribute to global resilience through a willingness to countenance challenges to existing states, then provided that meeting the theory's demands would not undermine foundational moral commitments, the current theory may be an appropriate check on the climatic side-effects of liberal institutions.

Christiano's second argument for the conservation principle applies mainly to unitary states without ethnogeographically distinct minorities. States with minority ethnogeographic communities in their midst do not provide a common world in which each has a roughly equal stake. On the contrary, insofar as the worlds of the two ethnogeographic communities intersect, the main effect will be that the members of the dissident community will be forced to accommodate the majority. This is likely to occur even in cases where the state officially recognizes the minority ethnogeography. For instance, since *Mabo and Others* v. *Queensland* (1992), Australia has recognized Aboriginal title. But when a major court decision came down admitting Aboriginal title to a section of Western Australia including Perth (*Bennell* v. *State of Western Australia*), it was the victorious Aboriginal plaintiffs who had to back-pedal to assure the public that "no one's going to lose their backyard" (*The Guardian* 2006). Realistically, whatever accommodation Australia makes will oblige the Aboriginal community to accommodate the settler society in nearly every respect.

Christiano (2006: 99) agrees that the presence of persistent minorities or groups that are publicly treated as inferiors undercuts the state's immunity from challenge precisely because the state fails to create a common world in which each person has a roughly equal stake. Some form of conservation principle is attractive inasmuch as the international system ought to default toward solutions that protect as many people as possible from upheaval. Our theory does not reverse this default; indeed this form of conservation principle is all but entailed by the plenitude criterion and its attendant preference for conservative claims. I conclude that a limited conservation principle is attractive, but also compatible with and indeed implied by the theory; but the theory rejects a stronger conservation principle that protects states against challenge even from persistent ethnogeographic dissidents whose systems are more resilient than those of the states they challenge.

6.2 Competing claims

Implementing territorial rights would require transnational institutions with at least four types of functions. First, institutions would be required to screen out ineligible claimants: only ethnogeographic communities are eligible to lodge territorial claims. Second, the same or another institution would be required to adjudicate eligible claimants' assertions of empirical and/or intentional plenitude in claimed territories, and use these to determine appropriate results for the claims. Third, an institution would be required to implement and enforce the judgments of the first two stages. In the event of multiple valid claims to the same place, a fourth function, that of brokering agreements – moving from general, theoretically appropriate results, to a viable, implementable resolution – would also be required.

In sketching the workings of these institutions, I shall in each instance first suppose that two competing eligible assertions are both valid, and then address invalidity in various permutations. In each case, I shall state and defend the results reached by the theory. This section attempts to cover all bases, and thus poses the risk that the reader will get bogged down. Readers who are more interested in direct application to a real case may prefer to use Table 6.2 to choose which subsections are of most interest, or skip ahead to section 6.3.

Suppose, then, that two eligible groups lodge competing assertions for the same territory. That is, two distinct ethnogeographic communities attempt to show (with respective nuances and modulations as laid out in Chapter Five) empirical and intentional plenitude with respect to the same place. This is a territorial conflict. What is the right solution in each case?

Table 6.1 shows a number of distinct solutions to disputes where both claims are valid. In some cases, such as type-2 disputes, one particular solution has the benefit of intuitive obviousness. In such cases the theory will have to justify and qualify the right result nonetheless. Such cases serve as tests: if it can't get those right, the theory is in trouble. In other cases, no solution is intuitively obvious. Here, the test of the theory is whether it provides plausible and attractive solutions to previously unsolved problems. The next nine subsections address the numbered boxes in Table 6.1. Each subsection addresses invalid claims after discussing valid ones.

Table 6.1: *Resolving competing valid claims**

	Cons.	Revisionist i (controllers want to settle)	Revisionist ii (inhabitants want control)	Revisionist iii (controllers want to disengage)	Radical i (arrival)
Conservative			1. Territorial autonomy arrangement		2. Conservative
Revisionist i			3. Territorial autonomy arrangement		4. Joint
Revisionist ii	= 1	= 3	5. Joint	6. Rev. ii.	7. Rev. ii.
Revisionist iii	= 2	= 4	= 6		8. Radical i
Radical i	= 2	= 4	= 7	= 8	9. Joint

*Table excludes abandonment claims (type-iv revisionist and type-ii radical), which add nothing of interest.

Table 6.2: *Idealized examples of dispute-types*

Type*	Idealized example
1	Secession from liberal state
2	Refugee example from Chapter Five
3	Quebec vs. James Bay Cree regarding dam project
4	Rare
5	Competing groups under empire – e.g. Jews and Palestinians under Mandate
6	Consensual secession or decolonization – e.g. Canada in 1867
7	Palestinians vs. European Jewish immigrants, circa 1910
8	Rare
9	Competing newcomers – e.g. UK and Spain at Vancouver Island, circa 1790

*Types refer to numbers on Table 6.1

6.2.1 Type 1: conservative vs. revisionist (ii)

Suppose a state controls a region settled by its citizens, but some residents of the region seek greater control of it. This sort of case is familiar from theories of secession: a group within a state wants, for whatever reason, to go its own way. Primary right theories of secession, be they choice theories (e.g. Wellman 2005) or ascriptive-group theories (Margalit and Raz 1990; Miller 2000), would at least be sympathetic to the revisionist claim. Remedial-right-only theories (Buchanan 2004) would sympathize with the conservative claim.

By hypothesis, each side has demonstrated empirical and intentional plenitude, and the controllers have shown additionally that they did not previously cause emptiness. This assumption implies that the revisionists would be in the sort of situation raised by the conservation principle: that of a persistent minority community within a legitimate state. The validity of the revisionists' claim obligates the state to enter good-faith negotiations toward a consensual territorial autonomy regime short of secession. This result is similar to, but importantly distinct from, Buchanan's take on the problem of persistent or permanent minorities. When persistent minorities have not suffered systematic injustice, Buchanan rejects unilateral secession but endorses either consensual secession or domestic autonomy arrangements. I agree that a persistent minority ethnogeographic community within a legitimate state has no right to unilateral secession; the state's territorial claim remains valid. But my theory is even more skeptical of secession than Buchanan's: if the disputed territory, taken on its own, is not a country, then even consensual secession is inappropriate. Some arrangement short of statehood is required.

Sometimes type-ii revisionist claims are lodged by groups that oppose the state's basic justice functions. For instance, the Northern League in Italy and the Confederate States of America in the nineteenth century seem unworthy of our support. The Northern League represents, as Buchanan (2004: 399n) puts it, "a tax revolt utilizing secessionist rhetoric with an undeniable odor of racist nationalism." And of course, the Confederacy epitomized racist nationalism. Let us suppose that in each case the claimants are ethnogeographically distinct. Even so, our theory rejects secession for the reasons just mentioned. But perhaps it will be objected that we have reached the right answer for the wrong reasons: the reason to forbid illiberal secessions is based in justice, not in technicalities of territorial rights. I have argued at length, however, that territorial rights are founded in justice, enhanced by due consideration of ecology. The objection presupposes a distinction I have rejected.

Indeed, against tax-revolt secessionism, we may adduce a further principle grounded in the plenitude criterion. Tax-revolt secession occurs when a wealthy section seeks to secede in order to keep more of its economic output for itself. The wealth of wealthy sections may reflect strategic decisions of the central government regarding which sections to develop in which ways. In this event, the state may deserve partial credit for plenitude. It may therefore retain rights in the territory of the secessionists that it would not have if its practices had had no effect or the opposite effect. Exactly how to honor these residual rights while also respecting the legitimate interest of an ethnogeographic minority in being able to implement its own visions of plenitude depends on the case.

Now consider invalid claims within a type-1 dispute. A persistent minority community with an invalid territorial claim would have no right to secede or demand territorial autonomy. On the other hand, suppose the revisionist claim were valid, while the state's were invalid due to a lack of intentional plenitude only. Then the dispute starts the clock ticking on a probationary period for the state. This is significant, but does not initiate precipitous political consequences. The real difficulties occur when the state fails to achieve even empirical plenitude. If it has achieved intentional but not empirical plenitude, then its claim is in effect a type-i revisionist claim (section 6.2.2 below). If the state lacks both empirical and intentional plenitude in the disputed territory, then its claim is straightforwardly invalid and the revisionist claim carries the day. If the disputed territory is a country, and secession would not leave the remainder state less than a country, then unilateral secession is justifiable. If either or both territories are not countries, then internal territorial autonomy arrangements are required.

The conservationist may object to a proposal on which even a just liberal state might lose its territorial integrity simply because it lacked plenitude in a disputed territory. In reply I should clarify the implications for secession. A state that maintains plenitude is immune to unilateral secession; thus the theory entails a remedial-right-only theory of unilateral secession. The difference between my view and Buchanan's remedial–right-only theory is not whether the right to unilateral secession is remedial but what it remedies. Here, secession may remedy an ongoing lack of both empirical and intentional plenitude. The lack must be ongoing; mere brief lapses would presumably maintain at least one form of plenitude. The lack must be of both types, because the most that could result from a lack of empirical plenitude alone would be intra-state territorial autonomy, not secession (section 6.2.2). And if intentional plenitude lapsed, the state would still have its probationary period. Further, given the close link between plenitude and state legitimacy, it is at best unlikely that a legitimate state could so drastically fail to maintain plenitude. I cannot here recapitulate the arguments for the plenitude criterion. But if those arguments were plausible, then it is also plausible that long-term failures of plenitude override territorial integrity. The objection is therefore correct to point out the logical possibility that just liberal states could be subject to unilateral secession. But the objection is incorrect in claiming that, under the rare circumstances in which this could occur, it would be a morally retrograde result. In particular, it is hard to see that some section of territory within a just liberal state could be both continuously derelict and necessary for the survival or justice of the liberal democracy.

6.2.2 Type 2: conservative vs. radical

This sort of conflict pits a settled community against newcomers or prospective newcomers who hope to attain territorial rights despite having no antecedent empirical plenitude in the place and possibly no prior link at all. This form covers a variety of sorts of disputes familiar from recent history, including diaspora claims, colonialism, and the southeast Asian refugees that we imagined arriving in Australia in Chapter Five.

Validity of the radical claim, recall, means not just that the claimants have attained intentional plenitude but that their territorial base, if they have one, is full. Even in such circumstances, however, there is normally no justification for undermining the territorial integrity of an existing legitimate state; the radical claim may be satisfied somewhere else. Those making the radical claim may disprefer such a result, but when the target territory is full, this diversion of territorial aspirations is superior to partition.

This diversionary strategy would not work, however, if every viable place in the world were already full. In this event, which solution is best depends on whether the group making the radical claim has a territorial base. If so, then the plenitude of the entire world implies that the plenitude of the territorial base in particular cannot justify the expansion as it otherwise would. For in this respect the claimant is simply being asked to make do under the same circumstances as everyone else.

The same answer will not be satisfactory for groups that lack a territorial base. Statehood can be very important for oppressed groups, given the extant state system. Given the counterfactual assumption of universal plenitude – every viable territory is already full – what can we say to a diaspora group that needs a state? Recall the relativity of plenitude and the mutability of ethnogeographies. Conditions of environmental stress are engines of ethnogeographic evolution: communities alter landholding regimes, agricultural practices, residency patterns, transportation, and other aspects of their collective and private lives. As these practices shift, the criterion of plenitude in each place may also shift. This fact has two important implications. First, the possibility of universal plenitude may be a merely conceptual one. In reality, scarcity would engender ethnogeographic change long before every place was genuinely full. Nonetheless, even taking the example seriously, given the fact of ethnogeographic mutability, we can treat the pressure created by diaspora groups' political aspirations as a kind of environmental stress, spurring ethnogeographic evolution in both the diaspora community and one or more target communities. But which communities should be subject to this pressure? While the diaspora community might have special ties to a particular place, it seems more appropriate that the target of this artefactual environmental pressure should be one or more states whose behavior has caused the crisis that leads the diaspora group to need territory in the first place. In the case of a refugee crisis, we may hold responsible those who caused the refugee crisis; in the case of an oppressed diaspora community, we may hold the oppressors responsible. There is a certain punitive aspect to this, but on the assumption of universal plenitude, this putative punishment may be merely an acceleration of inevitable processes – i.e. of ethnogeographic adaptation to scarcity. In this respect, such a change might eventually benefit both communities, as they respond early to environmental pressures that are sure to affect everyone. So while the context of universal plenitude may be a mere conceptual possibility, and while this sort of case would stress the limits of any theory of territorial rights, the theory implies a plausible solution.

Now consider invalidity. When conservative claimants lack intentional plenitude they are put on probation. So again, the serious challenge arises when conservative claimants lack empirical plenitude. A lack of empirical plenitude alone would put the conservative claim on a par with a type-i revisionist claim and turn the current case into a type-4 dispute (section 6.2.4 below). A lack of both forms of plenitude would indeed justify unilateral settlement by the newcomers.

Most likely, the territory will be full in some places and empty in others, in which case the newcomers' territorial aspirations should focus on the empty parts. But then two problems arise. First, empty sections may be noncontiguous. Contiguity may not be a formally necessary condition of statehood, but the fact that noncontiguity carries a high risk of failure suggests that we should not endorse it wholeheartedly. We must remember that the theory does not just allocate empty places willy-nilly; it demands intentional plenitude. The claimant could conceivably aim at noncontiguous pieces of territory, developing intentional plenitude in each place. There is nothing necessarily wrong with a checkerboard state, so such claims, bizarre though they be, should be evaluated on a case-by-case basis. Given the track record, it is unlikely that such a state could be resilient enough to justify statehood, but there is also no basis for ruling it out in principle. Second, partition might leave either the newcomers' or the prior inhabitants' territory in a state of nonresilience and thus not countries. In this event the theory prefers that the newcomers go elsewhere; but if that is impracticable, then the theory requires both territorial and political compromise.

6.2.3 Type 3: revisionist (i) vs. revisionist (ii)

This sort of case occurs when controllers wish to settle, use, or otherwise fill someplace currently inhabited only by others, while the residents desire greater territorial autonomy. For instance, the government of Quebec seeks to use the James Bay area for a hydropower project, while the James Bay Cree respond with a demand that their sovereignty be recognized. Recall that the validity of the former claim requires not just intentional plenitude in the claimed territory, but two other achievements: empirical plenitude in the entirety of the territorial base (the state itself), and, crucially, retrospective lack of emptying-out.

In the case of mutual validity the inhabitants lack the moral priority that they would have under occupancy or use criteria such as those that we discussed in Chapter Four. But they do have empirical plenitude; a valid type-ii revisionist claim thus resembles a valid conservative claim. The controllers would then be required to focus their intentional plenitude on parts of the territory that were not already full.[2] The appropriate response to mutual validity would be some form of accommodation between claimants, limited to these previously empty places.

Claims in type-3 cases may be invalid in numerous ways. The controllers' claim may fail due to empirical or intentional emptiness of part or all of the territorial base, retrospective emptying-out of the target territory, or a failure of intentional plenitude in the target

---

[2] Type-i revisionist claims therefore face three extra requirements over mere plenitude: lack of prior emptying-out to the detriment of their opponents; plenitude in the territorial base; and restriction to empty parts of the target territory.

territory. In any of these cases the type-i revisionist claim is invalid and, facing a valid type-ii revisionist claim, fails. On the other hand, the residents' claim might also fail. Suppose that the inhabitants lack only empirical plenitude in part of the territory, and that this is not due to the imposition of emptiness by the controllers. In this event, the two claimants are in identical positions: intentional plenitude with empirical emptiness. The standoff can be adjudicated only in the concrete, by appeal to the effect of various resolutions on the other parts of the claim: whether granting some part to one side would make the other side's territory more difficult to govern, undermine resilience, or whatever. The type-ii claim may also fail because of a lack of intentional plenitude. In this event we may treat the inhabitants as having a conservative claim-manqué: they may gain a probationary period in which to develop intentional plenitude without state encroachment. This resolution may be particularly apt given that the inhabitants, by definition, do not already have a state, and so they may be unready to assume the bureaucratic and other obligations of statehood, even though they do have a strong interest in attaining statehood. A lack of intentional plenitude alone thus justifies a temporary injunction against encroachment. Finally, it is possible that the residents lack both forms of plenitude in at least some places. In this event, encroachment is justifiable in those places.

6.2.4 Type 4: revisionist (i) vs. radical

This sort of claim occurs when controllers want to settle a place that is also claimed by newcomers. Mutual validity assumes that each claimant has intentional plenitude; that the newcomers either lack a territorial base or have one that is already full; that the occupiers have not previously emptied the territory and their territorial base is also already full. Instances of this sort of dispute could occur when populations move across borders in search of safe harbor.

Assuming joint validity, there is no reason that the territory ought not to be shared, by partition, confederation, or some other arrangement. Neither side loses anything by not getting the entire territory to itself. Invalidity, however, complicates these sorts of claims. The radical claimants may, for instance, be refugees, in which case their lack of intentional plenitude may be due to a lack of the sorts of skills that statehood engenders in a population. If they are refugees claiming empty land, their claim resembles a type-ii revisionist one: they may be granted safe harbor without full territorial rights for some probationary period. In other permutations of this case, however, lack of plenitude undermines claims. It is important to remember, however, that invalidity of the controllers' revisionist claim does not entail that they may simply abandon the territory altogether, ceasing even to administer it. That desire would turn the current case into type 8 (section 6.2.8 below).

6.2.5 Type 5: revisionist (ii) vs. revisionist (ii)

This sort of case occurs when each of two resident groups seeks to attain territorial rights to a shared territory. Examples include diverse colonies under imperial rule. The assumption here is that a third, presumably colonial, state controls the territory but either does not lodge a competing claim (because it wants to decolonize, for instance) or would have an invalid claim if it did.

The criteria of validity for the two claimants are identical: intentional plenitude as well as empirical plenitude or imposed emptiness. In this circumstance the conflict should be resolved through mutual accommodation in partition, confederation, shared governance, or some other system that would be appropriate given the population distributions and other aspects of the particular case. With one wrinkle: in the case of imposed empirical emptiness, the fault might lie not (or not only) with the controllers but with the other revisionist claimant. How responsibility for imposing emptiness should function here depends on whether the perpetrators have a political body that acts on their behalf. If Quebec imposed emptiness on the James Bay Cree, its claim would be invalidated in much the same way that a type-i revisionist claim would be. But if the perpetrators lack a state or state-like apparatus, or act independently of that apparatus, then responsibility must ultimately be individualized. In that event, imposed emptiness serves as a valid excuse for the victims, but need not disqualify the group that harbors the perpetrators.

6.2.6 Type 6: revisionist (ii) vs. revisionist (iii)

Type-6 cases describe consensual decolonization and consensual secession. Provided both claims are valid (and all territories resilient), there should be no problem, since there is no dispute. We have seen how to deal with difficulties that arise when the residents lack intentional plenitude. If they lack skills because of colonial subjugation, then tutelage is appropriate; if they have plans to ethnically cleanse a competing group, then the case is type-5; if the residents suffer from imposed empirical emptiness, this should not be held against them. This leaves cases such as that where the residents lack empirical plenitude but this is not the fault of the departing empire. In this event – assuming there is no other group in the mix – assignment of empty regions may be for purely administrative purposes, for instance to avoid land rushes.

6.2.7 Type 7: revisionist (ii) vs. radical

In type-7 cases, residents without effective territorial rights confront newcomers – for example, Palestinians under Turkish rule facing the original waves of Zionist immigration. Of all the sorts of cases we have discussed, this one is the most likely to pit two oppressed groups against each other: each side may lack intentional plenitude because of the oppression it has suffered; the residents may suffer imposed empirical emptiness; the newcomers may lack a territorial base.

As we have seen, a valid type-ii revisionist claim looks like a conservative claim, and imposes the same rigors on newcomers. Radical claims thus gain their greatest force when the prior inhabitants' claim is invalid. If the residents lack intentional plenitude they still maintain a right to a probationary period in which to develop intentional plenitude. If the residents lack empirical plenitude, then their claim is demoted to a radical claim and the two claims are on par (section 6.2.9 below).

6.2.8 Type 8: revisionist (iii) vs. radical

These cases occur when newcomers seek to settle in a territory that the controller seeks to abandon. In this event there is no conflict. Difficulties arise when the newcomers lack intentional plenitude due to oppression. In such an event we may legitimately insist on a phased departure by the type-iii revisionists, to assist with the initial bureaucratic and other requirements of setting up a state. Invalid claims would exist when the newcomers lack intentional plenitude, but not because of oppression, or when they have a territorial base that is not full. In these events, their claim ought to be denied. This is perhaps counterintuitive; among the few settled intuitions regarding territorial rights is that if some territory is empty it should be permissible to settle there. But the difficulties with this intuition should by now be clear. Settlement that engenders mere dereliction is worthless. Settlement in empty territories must still meet the plenitude criterion.

6.2.9 Type 9: radical vs. radical

Finally, consider territories on which two sets of newcomers set their sights. If both claims are valid, then provided the two are compatible, a joint arrangement is the right solution. If one is invalid, then only one claim should be honored, although it need not justify territorial rights in the entirety of the claimed territory. If both are invalid then neither side should get the territory.

One wrinkle: each claim may be valid, but the two may be incompatible, such that granting one would require frustrating the other. The bias in favor of empirical plenitude prevents this from being a problem in other sorts of cases, but here, neither party has attained empirical plenitude and so all that remains are the two instances of intentional plenitude. It seems appropriate in this case of potential incompatibility to require negotiation to a mutually satisfactory conclusion, and to make reaching such a conclusion a necessary condition for the validity of either claim.

6.2.10 Remaining issues

Two other sorts of cases might arise. First is competition between upstream and downstream groups over access to, and the quality of, mobile resources such as water, air, wildlife, and other phenomena that provide vital ecosystem services. The migratory character of pollution and natural resources has led cosmopolitans, in particular, to insist that international regulation must overwhelm state control of environmental phenomena (Pogge 2002: 187). In contrast, nationalists typically do not address mobile resources at all.

It is often fruitful to see this as a special case of territorial conflict. Downstream effects constitute territorial conflicts because the two groups are attempting to impose incompatible in/out rules on the territory, with conflicting accounts of the appropriate permeability of the boundaries between places. In the case of waste, in particular, the upstream group uses the place as a dumping ground, while the downstream group seeks to prevent this. Treating such clashes as territorial conflicts is especially helpful in light of the principle of inclusiveness and subsidiarity. For the multi-scalar character of ecosystems otherwise (by cosmopolitan lights, in particular) poses a serious challenge to the prospect of maintaining control at smaller levels of governance.

If clashes between upstream and downstream groups are territorial conflicts, then downstream groups are type-ii revisionists, that is, inhabitants who seek to control, while upstream groups are type-i revisionists – controllers who seek to inhabit. Upstream groups have a certain control over the in/out rules of the downstream territory, and may use that control to undermine plenitude. Type-i revisionists are liable for emptying places, so in this case upstream groups are liable for downstream emptiness. Similarly, the theory does not blame type-ii revisionist or radical claimants for imposed empirical emptiness, and should therefore absolve downstream groups in the same way if long-term pollution, excessive water diversion, and other upstream harms have forced the downstream group to abandon fisheries, settlements, or whatever.

In the real world, however, this solution is too simplistic. Places that are upriver might be downwind, and vice versa, so there is not always a single overarching upstream-downstream relationship between any two places. Such places are linked parts of natural systems, so applying the basic upstream–downstream principle will require careful understanding of such systems to determine how the actions of one group affect other groups, and of how variables interact across scales. Demanding plenitude and resilience helps with this, since these criteria necessarily involve maximizing our understanding of natural systems. At the extreme – when the links between places within a system are especially dense and the two places are deeply interactive – it is unlikely that each place is independently resilient. They would then constitute at most one country, and be appropriate sites of statehood together or not at all.

A second remaining issue is that some states contain multiple ethnogeographic communities, and the state may lodge a conservative or type-i revisionist claim by appeal not to its main ethnogeography but to that of one of its minority communities. This sort of case has several distinct permutations. The state may be a confederation of multiple ethnogeographic communities in which one constituent group seeks independence against the state. This seems to describe a type-1 case. Alternatively, the state may have incorporated into its law a number of distinct ethnogeographies, each one ascendant in particular places, depending on how different lands are categorized (Bosselman 1994). This issue opens numerous cans of worms: who speaks for an ethnogeography? For whom does the state speak? If the state has carved out particular places, such as state wilderness areas, national parks, or rights-of-way for nomadic communities, and exempted these from the dominant ethnogeography, then it may be that the dominant ethnogeography is in fact part of a larger pluralist ontology recognizing multiple types of relationship between people and land. In this event the state's territorial claims should be evaluated in terms of this pluralist ontology. To be sure, the character of empirical and intentional plenitude in any given place will determine which ethnogeography is in play. It will hardly be convincing for the state to argue that a derelict section of a city is actually a national park. There may, of course, be difficulties along the edges – for instance, if ghost towns become historic sites or national parks allow for-profit resource exploitation.

Another possibility is that the state treats all non-dominant uses of land merely as insurance for its dominant use – for instance, using national forests as timber reserves to subsidize a wasteful timber industry. In this case the supposed minority ethnogeographies are subsumed under, not an overarching pluralist one, but the single dominant one. Territorial claims must then be evaluated in terms of that one, even if the state seeks to turn some claimed territory into a national forest. Finally, it may be that, even though the state has a single official ethnogeography, minority ethnogeographic communities have emerged unofficially within the state – for instance, agrarians within the US. If these smaller communities then seek territorial rights their type-ii revisionist claims would generate disputes of type 1, 3, 5, or 6.

6.3 The Israeli–Palestinian dispute

Over the course of the study we have touched on a number of real cases. This has helped us to understand the nature of ethnogeographic variability, the various ways that groups' claims may interact, and some concrete implications of the theory. It remains to apply the theory more rigorously in the hope of determining whether it is right and useful. This section addresses the Israeli–Palestinian dispute by breaking it into temporal stages and explaining what would be recommended at each stage. Obviously, no party has historically asserted claims in the way that our theory requires, so we must engage in a kind of productive anachronism. In the historical cases, the test of the theory is whether the solution proposed here would have been the right thing to do, even though it did not happen. In the contemporary case – which obviously must deal with the legacy of disastrously wrong answers at prior stages of this dispute – the test is whether our theory makes the best of a bad situation. I believe it does. I shall sketch the solution and defend it below. But first I shall argue that the two standard solutions – the cosmopolitan one-state solution and the nationalist two-state solution – are both unattractive.

6.3.1 Against standard solutions

As its name suggests, the one-state solution (sometimes ambiguously called bi-national) recommends a single, unified state with no official ethnic differentiation. It imagines that the state would be located in the territory of British Mandatory Palestine as it existed from 1923 to 1948: from the Mediterranean to the Jordan and from the Galilee to the Red Sea.[3] (See Figure 6.1.) The attraction of this proposal is that it would constitute the territorial foundation of a secular multi-ethnic democracy where all rights and privileges of citizenship were equal across the entire population. This is nothing to be scoffed at. But it has a number of problems. First, the solution refuses to recognize that the various claimants have distinct aspirations and, in our terms, ethnogeographies. The Israelis now have – although they previously did not – an Anglo-American ethnogeography, whereas many Palestinians have an agrarian one.[4] And each group has a claim to live in a territory reflecting its

---

[3] The British Mandate began in 1920 but in 1923 the British severed Transjordan (now Jordan) from Mandatory Palestine and recognized it as an independent state under the control of the former Sharif of Mecca, whom the Sa'ud family had chased out of Arabia. Prior to the British Mandate, there was no territory of Palestine.

[4] I believe that their ethnogeography is agrarian in the sense defined in section 5.1 above. That very many Palestinians are urban or crowded together in refugee camps does not change this.

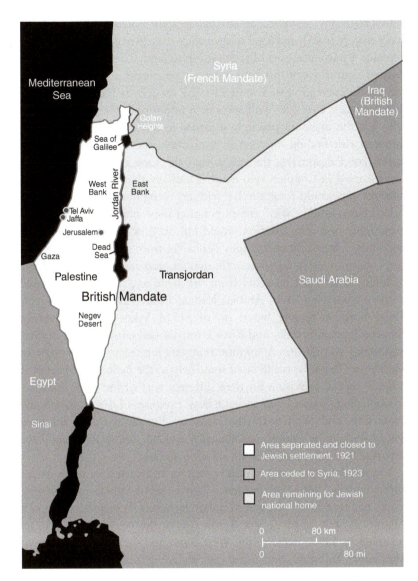

Fig. 6.1: The British Mandate, *Israel's Story in Maps*, Copyright Koret Communications. All rights reserved. www.israelinsider.com/maps. Used by permission.

ethnogeography. To reflect an ethnogeography would mean structuring economic, political, and legal relationships to land in a way that tends to promote a particular sort of relationship to land. The refusal to respect distinct aspirations of this kind is acutely problematic in different ways for the different groups. For Israelis, the concern is that demographic trends suggest that Jews will soon be a minority in the territory. Jews who left the diaspora precisely in order to avoid being a permanent minority risk finding themselves in precisely the same situation once again. For Palestinians, the risk is that the sorts of market pressures we discussed in Chapter Two make it unlikely that their agrarian ethnogeography could long survive without recognition as distinct. The Palestinians would "win" the population issue but "lose" the ethnogeographic one. The solution would fail most acutely for Palestinian Bedouins, whose ethnogeography is distinct from those of both sedentary communities. In addition to the market pressure just mentioned, the Bedouins would get no relief from the arbitrary, imperially imposed borders separating Saudi Arabia, Jordan, Israel–Palestine, and Egypt. These borders, largely based on the 1916 Sykes–Picot Agreement between France, Britain, and Russia, restrict Bedouins' pursuit of their traditional way of life. A solution that was limited to the territory of Mandatory Palestine could be of some help to the Bedouins, but only if it made special provision for their different way of life – for instance, guaranteeing rights-of-way through large expanses of desert, communal ownership, and other distinctive elements. But in that case, the state would in fact be ethnogeographically divided, and we would have departed from the cosmopolitan solution already.

The standard two-state solution proposes an Israeli state more or less within Israel's 1949–1967 borders – 77 per cent of Mandatory Palestine (or 20 per cent of the original Mandate including Transjordan) – and a Palestinian state more or less within two of the territories that Israel occupied in 1967, namely, the West Bank and Gaza (23 per cent of Mandatory Palestine, or 5.5 per cent including Transjordan). Because standard two-state proposals all default to the 1949 armistice lines (see Figure 6.2), I shall refer to all such proposals as "the 1949 solution" for clarity and simplicity. The attractions of the 1949 solution include respecting, in principle, two distinct sets of national aspirations (albeit ignoring Bedouins), and using separation to cool tempers over a generation or more while developing deep economic and political ties. But 1949 solutions have even more problems than cosmopolitan solutions.

Fig. 6.2: A 1949 solution reflecting Clinton ideas. Copyright 2004 by the Washington Institute for Near East Policy. From Ross (2004). Reprinted with permission.

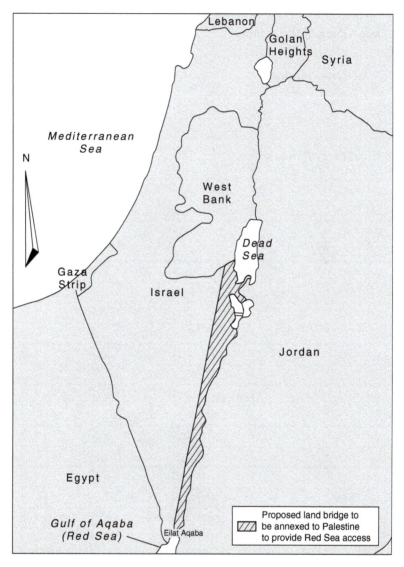

Fig. 6.3: Revised 1949 solution with land bridge to the Red Sea. Designed by D. J. Biddle, University of Louisville Center for Geographic Information Systems.

First, 1949 fails the Bedouins even more sharply, since it presupposes unchallenged Israeli sovereignty in the Negev, the region of primary Bedouin residency, essentially guaranteeing that necessary concessions to ethnogeographic differences will not be made. Second, the 1949 solution envisions a Palestinian state that is not a country, for several reasons. The West Bank is sandwiched between Jordan and Israel. If the population of that territory is to trade externally, it will either have to do so with its two neighbors, or it will have to rely on them for safe passage to seaports in the south or west. It would be possible to overcome this problem by carving a Palestinian land bridge between the West Bank and the Red Sea (Figure 6.3), extending Palestine southward and permitting the construction of a seagoing port between Eilat and Aqaba, or a conurbation for use by all three states. This land bridge, I would argue, should be an integral part of any 1949 proposal. But even if this were to happen, the territory of Palestine would be noncontiguous, with safe passage depending on Israeli good will. The RAND Palestinian State Study Team (2005: 8) argues that "none of the major conditions of success ... can be achieved unless Palestinian territory is substantially contiguous." RAND applies this conclusion only to the West Bank, but in effect suggests (*ibid.*) that contiguity is at least as important with respect to Gaza. Finally, in 1949 solutions the West Bank lacks control of its most vital resource: water. Palestine would depend for its survival on the forbearance of neighbors – Syria, Jordan, and Israel – which are also political and economic competitors and have a history of hostility to Palestinian interests.

The unfeasibility of the 1949 solution should be reemphasized, because it is the solution most widely touted by doves and moderates on both sides. Even those who dislike it in principle typically regard it as the only possible solution (Bose 2007: 286–9). Rejecting this solution thus makes one seem like an extremist or a dreamer. Obviously, there are reasons for the popularity of 1949: the distinct national aspirations, the idea that peace requires separation, the fact that it looks reachable with minimal departure from the status quo, and the certainty that Israel cannot, if it is to continue in anything like its current form, honor an effective right of return for all prior residents and their descendants.[5] But 1949 solutions make it very likely

---

[5] Khalidi (1992: 595) lists 347 total Israeli settlements on lands that formerly housed Palestinian villages within Israel's 1949 borders. These places are, unsurprisingly, concentrated in the most fertile and the most strategic land (*ibid.* 639). Palestinian return to these very places would cause Jews and Palestinians to be interspersed to such a degree that carving distinct national territories would be impossible.

that Palestine will be a failed state. Gaza is among the most densely populated and fastest-growing places on Earth, and would suffer absolute water scarcity even under better conditions (RAND 2005: 165). The RAND study, invoking Hong Kong and Singapore, suggests (2005: 93) that "the challenge of coping with increasing population density depends less on physical limits and more on how a society and its economy are organized and what financial and technical resources it has at its disposal." But to suppose that a basket of economic "best practices" (2005: 142) could even be implemented in the face of crushing physical and demographic pressures seems Panglossian. Israel's continuation in its current form must, then, be weighed against the real likelihood of state failure and all that it entails – including the prospect that even "land for peace" will not bring peace, because no one in Palestine would be in a position to guarantee it. We should for these reasons treat 1949 solutions, even with my land-bridge amendment, as a very much worse fall-back, behind not just the solutions I shall propose below, but also the cosmopolitan one-state alternative.

6.3.2 1880

Prior to the start of the Zionist movement the people of Palestine were religiously divided among Muslims, Christians, and Jews, but were ethnogeographically divided among sedentary and nomadic, inland and coastal. The sedentary populations may have shared an ethno-geography, but their land-use patterns were regionalized; each main city had its hinterland. Thus there was no single ethnogeographic community, because land-use patterns were not densely and perva-sively interacting. Moreover, much of the land was not full. Thus our theory would not have endorsed the creation of a state in the whole territory – or at least, no one group would have had a territorial right to the whole. Rather, there could have been numerous assertions of type-ii revisionist territorial rights, for instance by city-states (Haifa and its hinterlands, Jaffa and its hinterlands, etc.), against the Otto-man Empire. The Ottomans also could have made a type-iii revisionist or a conservative claim. Each of these claims could have been valid, and if so, our theory would have required some kind of settlement between the Ottomans and the inhabitants. Unilateral territorial change would have been rejected.

Against this backdrop, the first wave of Zionist immigration beginning in 1880 constituted a radical claim to agrarian settlements mostly on the coastal plain. If these claimants saw themselves as the vanguard of a movement unilaterally to take the whole country, their claim could not be accepted. But insofar as it was limited to specific places, it was plausible. Provided the new settlements were restricted to empty or fairly obtained land, intentional plenitude would justify this radical claim; the Zionist immigrants had no base territory, and were arriving in a place that was not full. The Zionists' motivations clearly included the historical attachment between Jews and the Land of Israel, as well as the permanence of European anti-Semitism, but as we have seen, these motivations had no direct role in the justification of the claim. By the same token, the facts that there had been no Jewish political control of the region for some two millennia, and that the European Zionists were newcomers, do not undermine or even weaken the territorial claim because, as I argued in Chapters Four and Five, these sorts of issues are irrelevant to the validity of a claim one way or the other.

6.3.3 Circa 1900

By the turn of the twentieth century the Zionist movement had attained intentional and empirical plenitude with respect to a number of places within the territory of what was to become Israel. These were primarily in the coastal region and west Jerusalem. Despite the Lockean turns of phrase appearing in some well-known Zionist writings, it is clear that the Anglo-American ethnogeography did not at the time define the Zionist movement. On the contrary, the emphasis on mutual transformation between people and land exemplified intentional plenitude in precisely the way that the Anglo-American ethnogeography rules out.[6] Nonetheless, essential to this notion of mutual transformation was the idea that the land was indeed empty or at least worthless in the absence of transformation. The Zionist ethnogeography was distinct from that of the prior inhabitants, but disputes,

---

[6] Kaplan (2005) points out that ascribing such views to the Zionist movement as a whole risks papering over political and philosophical rifts within that movement, particularly between Labor and Revisionist Zionism. The discussion here may be read, then, in terms of the Labor–Zionist wing of the movement.

such as they were, were clearly soluble due to the population and the demands that the various groups were making on the land. Both Jewish and Arab populations were increasing at a high rate, and in some urban areas, growing together (Isseroff 2007).

The radical Zionist claim remains valid in principle, for the reasons noted above. Due to the dense intermingling between Jews and Palestinians, however, it is doubtful that separate nation-states could be justified. Where intermingled, both groups were agrarian, differing in ethnicity and religion but not ethnogeography. By the turn of the century, then, assuming the independent resilience of each community, our theory could have justified several distinct states representing distinct ethnogeographic communities – a mixed Zionist–Palestinian state of the form just mentioned, agrarian Palestinian (including Muslims, Christians, and Jews), and Bedouin – in what became Mandatory Palestine. That these states would have been small is no argument against them, since, assuming resilience, they would have been countries. We should emphasize, though, that there is no reason to suppose that the boundaries of these states should have been limited to the territory that the Sykes–Picot agreement carved out as Palestine. The Bedouin population, in particular, covered the Sinai and Arabian peninsulas as well as (what became) Palestine and Jordan.

6.3.4 Partition

In 1938 the British Mandate's Peel Commission proposed a partition plan that would have divided the Mandate into three distinct territories: a Jewish state concentrated in a small coastal and northern section; a significantly larger Arab state in most of the rest of the territory; and a middle section, including Jerusalem and Bethlehem, to continue under the Mandate (Figure 6.4). This plan was shelved, but in 1947 the UN voted to partition Palestine into two states that looked more like the 1949 armistice lines (Figure 6.5). By 1947 the Zionist claim could be regarded as partly radical and partly type-ii revisionist, as Zionist settlement continued to expand geographically while the settled *yishuv* sought control from the British. Due to urbanization, industrialization, and population growth, as well as political separation from neighboring territories (Morris 2004, 17–22), the various non-Zionist Palestinian claims seem by now to have resolved into two – agrarian and Bedouin. The agrarian Palestinian claim was also

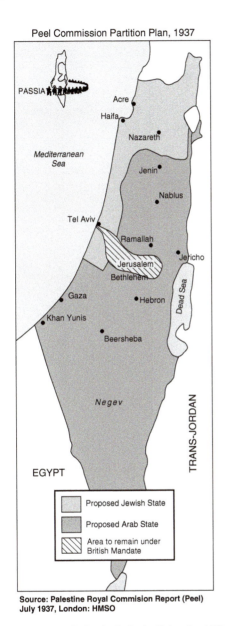

Peel Commission Partition Plan, 1937

Source: Palestine Royal Commision Report (Peel)
July 1937, London: HMSO

Palestinian Academic Society for the Study of International Affairs
(PASSIA)

Fig. 6.4: Peel Commission partition proposal, 1937. Copyright Palestinian Academic Society for the Study of International Affairs (PASSIA). Used with permission.

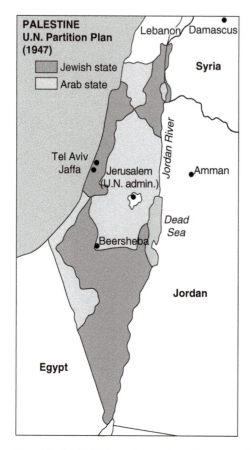

Fig. 6.5: 1947 UN partition plan. Courtesy of the University Libraries, The University of Texas at Austin.

partly type-ii revisionist and, insofar as it extended to all of Mandatory Palestine, partly radical as well. Bedouin communities were not yet (effectively) prevented from moving across borders, so their claim was type-ii revisionist, but it included parts of neighboring states outside the borders of the Mandate. And the British claim was type-iii revisionist.

The British claim was invalid, as an easily foreseeable mass flight partly due to intentional expulsions occurred upon their departure.[7] The

---

[7] Shahak (1975) lists 385 Arab villages (out of 475) within Israel's 1949 borders which were destroyed. He estimates expulsion of three-quarters of

initial justification for the Mandate was that the British were to prepare the inhabitants for self-rule. The British did the opposite, exacerbating the growing Jewish–Arab tensions (Bose 2007: 225) and encouraging Palestinian Arab society to become dependent on the Mandate (Morris 2004: 28). The British should not have been permitted to depart in the way they did – that is, knowing what would happen and simply trying to slink out without being pulled back in (see Ben-Porat 2006).

The type-ii revisionist Palestinian claims were valid, but insofar as these were organized into a demand for a unified state, rejecting partition while accepting the arbitrary Sykes–Picot and 1923 Mandate lines, they were less so. Such a state would have had to be imposed upon the Zionists and Bedouins, subjugating two distinct ethnogeographic communities. The ethno-national principle of organization, the rigid adherence to Sykes–Picot lines, and the hegemonic idea that at most two states could fit in the territory, were understandable errors, but such claims failed to meet our criteria of eligibility and plenitude. The Zionists' type-ii revisionist claim was also valid in parts of the territory, but similarly could not justify a unitary Jewish nation-state, certainly not in the entirety of the Jewish section of the Partition plan. Further, radical Zionist claims were invalid; much of the territory was empirically full for others upon whom the Israelis eventually imposed emptiness on a massive scale. Further, much of the claimed land lacked even intentional plenitude.

Against partition, our theory would recommend a confederation between agrarian communities, protecting and respecting each. This confederation would either include, or exclude by partition, a separate Bedouin community (or state) that should have extended outward into

---

the 73 Bedouin sub-tribes in the Beer Sheba district and mentions 16 other tribes most of which "cannot be traced now." See also Khalidi (1992). Morris (2004) gives an extensive account of the haphazard but in many places ruthless expulsion policy over the course of the war and during cease-fires, including a number of military operations with names like Operation Broom, Operation Cleaning, and Operation *Hametz* (Passover Cleaning). Haphazard or otherwise, however, the initial evacuations were cemented by a systematic refusal to permit return of those who fled. The moral assessment of the whole thus goes well beyond mere negligence, blunder, or even byproduct. That the expulsions were foreseeable is demonstrated in Morris (2004), chap. 2. Morris denies that the earlier texts advocating "transfer" caused the eventual development of the policy, but this is a separate question from whether the British should have seen the real possibility that such a policy would eventuate.

202 Land, Conflict, and Justice

desert regions of the Arabian and Sinai peninsulas as well as into Jordan. The problem with partition between Jews and Arabs was that Jewish settlement had not been concentrated in specific enclaves that would be exclusively or even large-majority Jewish, but had spread around the country such that it was impossible to carve out a country (i.e. a resilient juridical territory) that was majority Jewish, without including a significant minority of Palestinians rendered second-class citizens by the ethno-national organization of the state. The prospects for partition were undermined by the patterns of settlement. That said, the 1947 Partition did not even do the best possible under those circumstances, but arbitrarily added Bedouin territory to Israel and posited a non-contiguous Arab enclave in Jaffa, cutting off this major city not just from other Palestinian territory but from its own hinterlands. The UN seems to have recognized the unattractiveness of the 1947 plan by almost immediately going back to the table, but as it happened, events overtook this reconsideration (Diller 1991: 250; Bose 2007: 231).

6.3.5 Circa 1955

By the 1950s, the Israelis had imposed emptiness on much of the territory, some of which they then filled. But the imposition of emptiness undermined the validity of the Israeli claim to those parts of the territory. Thus the valid Israeli claim remained limited to those areas in which they already enjoyed empirical and intentional plenitude in 1947, or which were empty in 1947 but filled in the intervening years. In 1950, Jordan asserted a radical claim to the West Bank, but this claim lacked intentional plenitude as the Jordanians left a large part of the territory, particularly the refugee camps, in a state of dereliction.

As long as refugees maintain their ethnogeography the empirical emptiness of their former settlements remains imposed and does not count against them, but against those who dispossessed them. In the absence of ethnogeographic evolution, this claim never weakens. Clearly such evolution had not happened in the case of Palestinian refugees by the 1950s, so our theory would recommend a return of 1950s Palestinian refugee populations to their prior places and the creation of a single confederation or consociational state.

But what happens when their ethnogeography does evolve? As the ethnogeography evolves, the refugees' territorial claim dissipates because the empirical emptiness has been imposed, not on them, but on their ethnogeographic predecessors. We will consider the implications of ethnogeographic evolution below. (Even when territorial claims dissipate, however, nothing yet follows regarding personal property claims. These are independent of eligibility and attachment criteria, and may survive even when territorial claims do not, or may dissipate even when territorial claims survive. The theory is silent on this issue.) But by the 1950s at least, such evolution had not yet occurred. At that point, the refugees had a valid territorial right, based on a revisionist claim, to the parts of Israel from which they had been expelled.

But what of the populations that had settled in the place of the refugees? Many of these people were themselves refugees either from genocide in Europe or from suddenly inhospitable Arab countries in the region.[8] Assuming that return was undesirable or impossible, the overriding claim that these refugees had (aside, again, from personal property claims) was, I think, not a collective territorial one but a collection of individual claims to asylum and permanent resettlement in Israel. This claim could easily have been granted without derogating from any territorial claim.

6.3.6 After 1967

The 1967 War does not change anything from the theory's perspective. Insofar as Israel lodged a claim to conquered Egyptian, Jordanian, and Syrian territories, these were radical claims that were straightforwardly invalid due to the existence of empty places within Israel's borders. But the occupation of these territories eventually engendered a regime of settlement in Gaza, the West Bank, and the Golan (and even the Sinai, until the peace with Egypt).[9] The radical claims of these settlers were invalid, both because of the existence of empirically empty places in the territorial base and because of the emptiness imposed on the prior

---

[8] I do not mean to equate the cases of Jews from Europe, Jews from Arab countries, and Palestinians from Palestine/Israel. Each has distinctive features that may be relevant to moral assessments of their situation. For my purposes, though, what matters is that they were populations who left their homes in duress and asserted a claim to reside within Israel's 1949 borders. See Fischbach (2005) for discussion.

[9] To be sure, the regime of settlement was haphazard and subject to shifting strategic doctrines. Large-scale colonization did not become explicit Israeli policy until the accession of the Likud government in 1977. See Drysdale and Blake (1985: 296–98).

population. Insofar as the settlers remain responsible for imposed emptiness, their claim never becomes laundered, except possibly over time as the ethnogeography evolves. If the settler ethnogeography evolves then it will no longer be they who are responsible for the imposed emptiness, and their claim would become a type-ii revisionist one (insofar as they are under the control of the Israeli government or a Palestinian state, assuming that the settlers' evolved ethnogeography is distinct from each).[10] In 1988 the Jordanian government renounced its claim to the West Bank. This type-iii revisionist claim reversed the invalid radical claim from 1950. The situation for Palestinians has worsened dramatically since 1988, arguably in part because Jordanian abdication removed any established state's competing claim to the territory, making it possible for Israel to spend, as of this writing, nearly two decades undermining empirical and intentional plenitude in the West Bank through an acceleration of settlement and the creation of Bantustans (Figure 6.6).[11]

6.3.7 Today

Finally, as of this writing, several key questions remain open. The first is whether ethnogeographic evolution has indeed occurred among Palestinian refugees. If so, then their right of return would have dissipated as they developed new lives in new places. Among those who have escaped refugee camps for new lives elsewhere (and particularly

---

[10] I should emphasize that an ethnogeographic community's responsibility for emptiness is not the same as individual responsibility for crimes committed in the process of settlement, such as murder, theft, etc. So even if, *per* (almost) *impossibile*, the settlers' ethnogeography evolved extremely rapidly, this would still not absolve individual guilty parties of their crimes. Moreover, it is also almost impossible to imagine the settlers' lands being resilient, and so even if the settlers' descendants developed a type-ii revisionist claim, their lands would not constitute a country; independent statehood would be ruled out.

[11] One should not draw any direct line between the Jordanian departure and the intensification of occupation. It is impossible to know whether the intensification would have happened in the absence of a Jordanian renunciation of claims. If it would have all been the same, this just speaks to the worthlessness of the original Jordanian radical claim from 1950. If not, then the Jordanian type-iii revisionist claim was invalid for the reason stated in the text. Bose (2007: 244) suggests that the Jordanian type-iii revisionist claim had the salutary effect of preventing Israel from bypassing Palestinian negotiators in favor of Jordanian ones, once peace talks started. That may be, but as there were no regular negotiations in progress at the time, this can hardly have been anything more than a side effect.

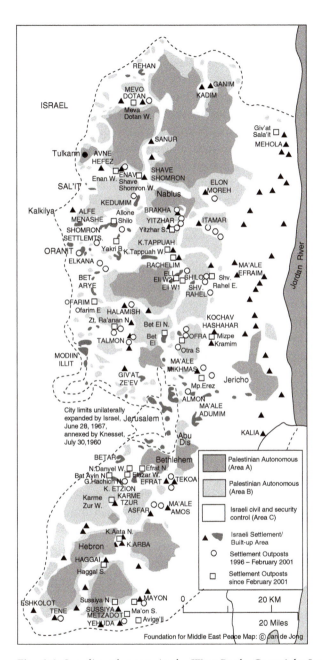

Fig. 6.6: Israeli settlements in the West Bank. Copyright Jan de Jong, used with permission.

for their children and grandchildren), this has surely occurred. As for the approximately four million who remain refugees, it is undeniable that the landscape of refugee camps has crucially influenced their social order (Peteet 2005). In some cases, as noted in Chapter Four, the refugees have reinscribed the lost landscape of Palestine onto the refugee camps themselves; "village areas [in refugee camps] have been the physical and symbolic memory, transmitting the space of Palestine to the present, giving the displaced a deep visceral and everyday connection to past time, place, and social relationships" (Peteet 2005: 112). Nonetheless, due to continual disruptions, expulsions, and reexpulsions, and the rise of a national movement, Palestinian identity has been nationalized in a way that it never was before (Peteet 2005: 115). And as the generation that actually remembers Palestine ages and dies, the link to the land has dissipated, partly undermining empirical plenitude as well (Fisk 2002: 22 provides an example).

The persistence of empirical plenitude in previously inhabited territory may depend on particular sub-group practices, such as practices in particular refugee camps or among people linked to particular towns or villages. Nonetheless, even for those who have lost empirical plenitude in the original territory, the refugee camps have not become the object of intentional plenitude – intentional plenitude applies to the lost land. Thus in addition to any individual rights of compensation or return of stolen property that may persist, Palestinian refugees have in some cases a type-ii revisionist claim (to places where they maintain empirical plenitude), and in some cases a radical claim, to return to areas from which they fled or were expelled. From this it does not follow that the refugees have a right to return to the specific houses, or even the specific town sites, from which they were evicted. That is a matter of personal property rights on which our theory is silent. Further, from the validity of the claim it does not yet follow that there is a right of return at all, for there is a competing claim the validity of which must be assessed, and which, if valid, constrains the implementation of any valid claim. Nonetheless, it is clear that in many cases the land on which Palestinian villages previously existed is empirically empty, and there is surely a prima facie reason to permit return to and rebuilding in those specific places.[12]

---

[12] Khalidi (1992) provides a comprehensive survey of former village sites. A number of these are desolate and overgrown. A right of return to such places

The second question is whether the Israeli ethnogeography has evolved such that that community cannot be held responsible for emptiness imposed by a predecessor. Clearly, evolution has occurred: the Anglo-American ethnogeography has taken hold, replete with a stark urban–rural population imbalance and the application of industrial logic to agriculture. So far from creating a "new Jew" through dense interaction with the land, the State of Israel has turned Jews of all origins into Anglo-Americans, turning the land into a neo-Europe. The only real exception to this characterization is the Negev desert in the south, most of which is empty from an Anglo-American perspective (Figure 6.7). This "Anglo-Americanization" of the Zionist ethnogeography has generated a great deal of empirical plenitude but, as we saw in Chapter Four, in the longer term it also creates empirical emptiness and is for this reason incompatible with intentional plenitude. As a result, the territory lacks resilience, a fact that is particularly evident in unsustainable depletion of the aquifer on which all residents depend (RAND 2005: 177). On the other hand, the fact of evolution severs the direct link (for purposes of territorial claims) between those guilty of ethnic cleansing in 1947–49, and those who currently inhabit the territory. The territory has been transformed, and the people with it. To return prior residents into the core areas of Israeli population density would have only symbolic value; it is not as though Israel is on the whole a country of stolen houses and traditional farms that can simply change hands from one community back to the other.

The theory would, then, propose to resolve the conflict as follows. Within Israel's 1949 borders, areas that are empirically full are subject to a conservative claim, even where Palestinians previously lived. The conservative claim is invalid due to the lack of intentional plenitude, but due to empirical plenitude, Israel would get a probationary period in which intentional plenitude should be developed. In the absence of ethnogeographic evolution, Palestinian refugees have a type-ii revisionist claim to places where they had attained empirical plenitude prior to their expulsion. Insofar as this claim features (in addition to

need not displace a single Israeli. Whether a more comprehensive solution should include or exclude this particular implementation of the right would, however, depend also on macro-level considerations such as the number of sovereign states involved, the location relative to other sites, etc.

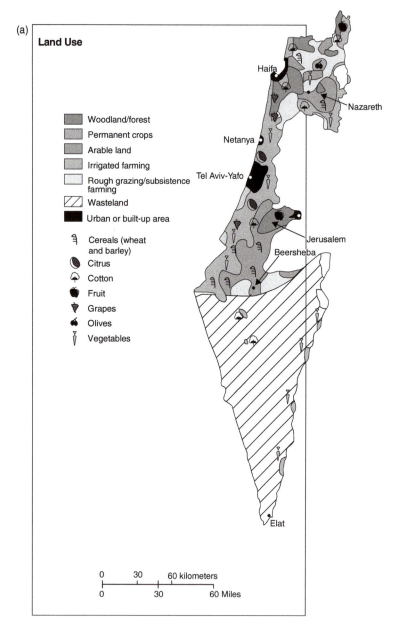

(a)

Land Use

Woodland/forest
Permanent crops
Arable land
Irrigated farming
Rough grazing/subsistence farming
Wasteland
Urban or built-up area

Cereals (wheat and barley)
Citrus
Cotton
Fruit
Grapes
Olives
Vegetables

Haifa
Nazareth
Netanya
Tel Aviv-Yafo
Jerusalem
Beersheba
Elat

0   30   60 kilometers
0   30   60 Miles

Fig. 6.7: Israel: land use (a) and population density (b). CIA *Atlas of the Middle East 1993.* Courtesy of the University Libraries, The University of Texas at Austin.

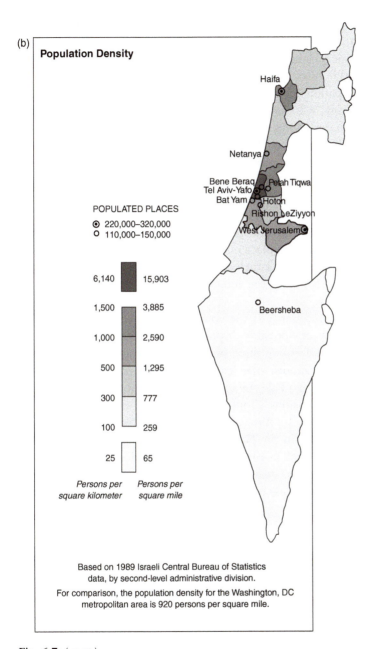

(b)

Population Density

Haifa

Netanya

Bene Beraq   Petah Tiqwa
Tel Aviv-Yafo
Bat Yam   Holon
Rishon LeZiyyon
West Jerusalem

POPULATED PLACES

⊙ 220,000–320,000
○ 110,000–150,000

6,140	15,903
1,500	3,885
1,000	2,590
500	1,295
300	777
100	259
25	65

*Persons per
square kilometer*   *Persons per
square mile*

Beersheba

Based on 1989 Israeli Central Bureau of Statistics
data, by second-level administrative division.

For comparison, the population density for the Washington, DC
metropolitan area is 920 persons per square mile.

Fig. 6.7: *(cont.)*

the imposed emptiness) intentional plenitude, it is valid. Further, inasmuch as Palestinian refugees lack a territorial base, they could lodge a radical claim to empty places either within Israel or anywhere in the world. Palestinians who are not refugees, but "merely" living under occupation, have a valid type-ii revisionist claim. Finally, Israeli settlers, if any, who have undergone ethnogeographic evolution such that they share land-use practices with neither the Israelis in general nor the Palestinians, could have a valid type-ii revisionist claim as well. Whether such settlers exist – that is, whether any of the settlers actually constitute an ethnogeographic community distinct from that of Israelis in general – seems highly unlikely (Drysdale and Blake 1985: 301–2). But just as a territorial right may exist independently of individual and collective responsibility for theft of land, so an individual right to stay in a place may exist independently of the territorial right. A finding against Israeli territorial rights in the West Bank says nothing about whether the individuals who live there ought to be allowed to stay.

The theory recommends the creation of one state that could recognize and respect – possibly through confederation, possibly through a pluralistic land law – three distinct ethnogeographies, namely, a suitably altered Zionist one (call it Ecological–Zionist), a Bedouin one, and an agrarian Palestinian one (see Figure 6.8 for a suggestion). Roughly, this envisions Zionist control of regions currently in the Jerusalem, Central, Tel Aviv, and Haifa districts (*mehozot*); Agrarian–Palestinian control in the North District, the West Bank, and Gaza; and Bedouin control in the South District. Bedouin control should extend through desert regions in Egypt, Jordan, and Arabia as well, though Jordanian access to the Red Sea through Aqaba would have to be guaranteed.

What does the envisioned ethnogeographic pluralism entail? In effect, Ecological–Zionist control involves (for instance) urbanization and industrialization, and the application of an industrial logic to land law and agriculture, as well as an effort to structure work weeks and other aspects of the economy around a particular religious tradition. Agrarian–Palestinian control involves land laws fostering viable agricultural lifestyles organized around market towns, and an ability to protect the integrity of a workshop economy against pressures from global capital and heavy industry. Bedouin control involves rights-of-way, collective ownership, and consideration of seasonal or

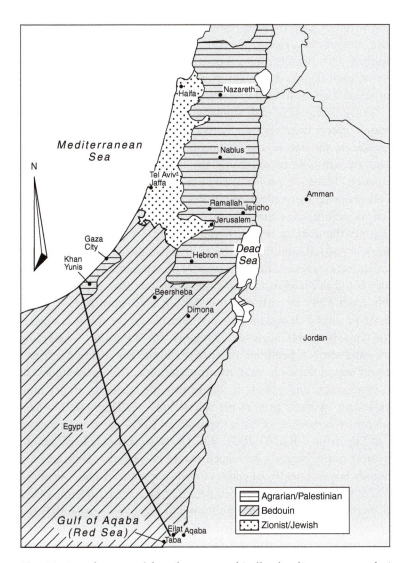

Fig. 6.8: Rough proposal for ethnogeographically pluralist one-state solution. Designed by D. J. Biddle, University of Louisville Center for Geographic Information Systems.

temporary settlement and agriculture when structuring economic, educational, and other institutions. By envisioning shared-but-pluralistic sovereignty rather than partition or unitary sovereignty, this proposal lowers the stakes of the dispute, opening up pathways to constructive or positive-sum resolution of issues such as water use, Jewish settlements, rights of return, trade, and the disposition of Jerusalem. For instance, the proposal does not require that the residents of each district be of any particular ethnicity or religion; it is compatible with the limited Palestinian right of return discussed above, but it is also compatible with allowing Jewish settlers in the West Bank to stay in place. Precisely because we have spent a great deal of time investigating the nature and significance of attachment to particular places, we are able to overcome the logic according to which the competing claims are zero-sum and existential.

This proposal for confederation or a pluralist state is distinct from the cosmopolitan one-state solution described above, precisely because it respects the distinct ethnogeographies and aspirations, and builds concern for sustainability into the political solution. If, however, the pluralist state is rejected due to insistence on separate sovereignties, the theory could fall back on a partition, albeit one that departs considerably from 1949 by virtue of transferring land from Israel's South District to joint Palestinian–Bedouin control (Figure 6.9 is a suggestion). This proposal achieves contiguity for Palestine – including Gaza – and respects Bedouins' distinctive claims. The shared Agrarian–Bedouin region would have to incorporate both ethnogeographies, in law, economics, and policy. It would provide currently empty land ("wasteland" with 65 persons per square km – see Figure 6.7) to help offset the overcrowding of Gaza in particular (3457 persons per square km and growing – RAND 2005: 93). On this proposal, Israel would cede most of the Negev – Beersheba would be shared – while keeping within its borders nearly its entire current population. The loss of the Red Sea port of Eilat could be compensated by a swap for some of the settlement blocs that the Clinton solution in Figure 6.2 envisions being annexed to Israel, and by sharply limiting or forswearing a Palestinian right of return to areas within Israel. With two major Mediterranean seaports and unhindered access to the Suez Canal, Israel has far less need than the Palestinians for a Red Sea port; as for the Dead Sea, the increase in sustainable economic activity and tourism attendant upon a just and lasting peace would far outstrip the lost industry of Dead Sea resorts – an industry that is in any case under serious ecological stress and would not likely survive a 1949 plan anyway. The multi-state solution ensures the contiguity of Palestine and, hence, increases the prospects of viability. The multi-state solution also respects the

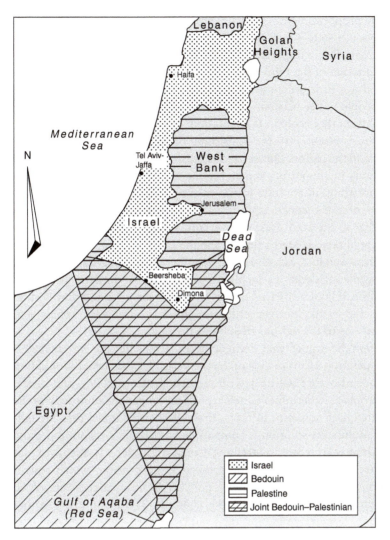

Fig. 6.9: Rough proposal for a multi-state solution. Designed by D. J. Biddle, University of Louisville Center for Geographic Information Systems.

Bedouin ethnogeography and is compatible – again, given continued Jordanian Red Sea access – with extending some level of Bedouin control through the Sinai, the Negev, Jordan, and Arabia. This would reverse an arbitrary closure that dates to the Sykes–Picot Agreement, and could spur an experiment in superseding orthodox sovereignty.

The proposals here – both the preferred confederation and the fall-back multi-state solution – are obviously distinct from most other proposals. But in important respects they are the same: they affirm that the situation of the refugees must be addressed, but that addressing it should not generate another round of dispossession; they affirm that the people under occupation must be accorded full territorial rights; they affirm that ecological adaptation, particularly with respect to the aquifer, is essential to the flourishing of eight million (and counting) people in the region. Our solutions, however, go further than the 1949 solutions in supporting repair for the expulsions of 1947–49, while also insisting, in contrast to the cosmopolitan solution, on the legitimacy of the distinct aspirations of the three communities bound together in the land. Despite overlaps, then, I have rejected both the cosmopolitan one-state solution and the 1949 two-state solution. They are ideas well lost. More viable than either of them, perhaps, would be a larger confederation, including all or part of Jordan, Syria, and Lebanon (Halper 2005). But this proposal for a Middle East Union lacks the virtue of respecting the distinct ethnogeographies and aspirations of the various peoples of the region.

It may be argued that confederation is no solution. In particular, confederation seems to give up on the basic idea that Israel should be a "democratic state with a Jewish majority" (Beilin 2006), and hence, my proposal undermines Israeli aspirations in just the same way as the cosmopolitan solution. In reply, it should first be noted that the fall-back multi-state solution is compatible with Beilin's vision. But more importantly, this way of framing Israeli aspirations is already a significant climb-down from the original Zionist vision, which sought to limit full citizenship to Jews, possibly by ridding the state of all or nearly all Arabs (Morris 2004, chap. 2). The Beilin vision rather amounts to gerrymandering on a national level – finding boundaries that ensure a Jewish majority in perpetuity. This has two important implications. First, it changes from an ethno-nationalist conception of the polity, where full citizenship depends on ethnicity, to a liberal-nationalist conception, where citizenship is universal. But it does this only by smuggling the ethno-nationalist commitments into the territorial demography, investing the Jewishness of the majority with fundamental significance, and making demographic shifts things to be feared and fought. In contrast, an unabashedly ethno-nationalist state at least has the distinct (theoretic) virtue of not pretending to be something it is not; that the majority in Kuwait or Saudi Arabia is composed of non-citizens creates no existential crisis for the citizens of those states.[13] (It is, obviously, fodder for a moral critique.) This shift away from open ethno-nationalism suggests that in the longer term, for Israel to remain a Jewish state it will, in addition to leaving the West Bank and Gaza and rejecting any Palestinian right of return, have to reverse or neutralize the so-called "demographic time-bomb" represented by the relative fertility rates of Jews and Arabs, or ultimately, renege on Beilin's formula and find yet another way of maintaining its Jewish character. It may do this latter either by reverting to an illiberal but at least forthright ethno-nationalism, replete with an ethnic or confessional criterion of (full) citizenship; by setting up a consociational state, on the model of Lebanon or (more hopefully) Belgium, which ensures national self-determination for both nations but sovereignty for neither (Gans 2003); by instituting a Fiji-style constitutional system that protects the Jewish minority and ensures that Israel remains, symbolically as well as in some basic commitments, their state (Carens 2000: chap. 9); or by revoking its claims in the Galilee, where Arab populations are highest. In other words, over the longer term, demographic trends are working against the delicate balance that makes Beilin's putative liberal nationalism credible.

The second implication of Beilin's putatively liberal–nationalist "democratic state with a Jewish majority" is that it is committed to ensuring that non-Jews will be a persistent minority on certain fundamental issues. We have seen, though, that the existence of a persistent minority constitutes at least a powerful challenge to state legitimacy. So in one sense, the new vision is worse than the old. Where the old vision was at least consistent with the problematic Wilsonian idea of national self-determination, Beilin's vision recognizes the inevitability that populations will be interspersed, and seeks to deal with that in a way that undermines the legitimacy of the state even in the absence of demographic shifts. It "rescues" the liberal–nationalist state by descending to nationalist illiberalism. The nationalist alternative to the solution proposed here is at most an illiberal stopgap, not an alternative at all. Its popularity cannot be explained by its quality.

---

[13] Compare Mills (1997: 73).

Perhaps its popularity is explained by the fact that all other options are worse. Sumantra Bose briefly discusses the idea of confederation but rejects it as impossible, insisting that "[t]here is simply no alternative to salvaging the most equitable two-state solution that is possible from the ruins of the peace process" (Bose 2007: 287). On his view, the quixotic Clinton proposal of late 2000 (see Figure 6.2) provides the best framework for moving forward. It should be noted that my multi-state solution has all the same virtues but fewer vices. Even if confederation is impossible, we can still do better than 1949 solutions such as the Clinton proposal. But notwithstanding his objections to confederation, Bose proposes "two interlinked sovereignties" that cooperate on a wide range of issues, given that they share "the same aquifers, the same highway network, the same electricity grid and the same international borders" (287; see also Benvenisti 1995: 232 and RAND 2005). Two things are clear. First, in the near term, sovereignty is of great symbolic importance to each people – and with reason, for each has a tragic history of suffering due to statelessness. Second, if the peoples can indeed salvage the most equitable two-state solution that is still possible, then the future holds for them a new kind of sovereignty, one that looks much more like confederation and regional cooperation than like traditional sovereignty. Where my proposal differs from Bose's is in the attention paid to the Bedouin in the south, and relatedly, in the concern for the land itself. My theory insists that Israel's Anglo-American ethnogeography must evolve in an ecological direction, and that the Palestinians' agrarian and Bedouin ethnogeographies must not be coercively dissolved in the name of political or economic development. In other respects, however, a Bosean two-state solution is much like a confederation, and with due attention to the land and the ecology, Bose's proposal differs from mine mostly in emphasis (see also Benvenisti 1995: 233).

6.4 Conclusion: indigenous land claims

Indigenous rights issues feature sharper versions of many of the same phenomena as the Israeli–Palestinian dispute, but are also importantly different.[14] In the Israeli case, assertions of sovereignty followed the

---

[14] Khalidi (1992: xxxi) provides a list of differences while arguing for an overall similarity.

initial waves of immigration – not least because European Jews were in no position to make or act on declarations of sovereignty to begin with. In contrast, European empires typically asserted sovereignty first and colonized thereafter. This is important because it shows the initial assertions of sovereignty to have been in most cases utterly, even ridiculously, invalid. As Rousseau quipped, flag-plantings no more generate territorial rights than would the "Catholic King['s]... tak[ing] possession of the universe all at once from his private room, excepting afterwards from his empire only what already belonged to other princes" (Rousseau 1987: 28). Such claims served merely as shots across the bows of other European sovereigns. Over the course of centuries, the project of mapping, colonizing, and defending may have generated plenitude in some of these regions, but the initial flag-plantings were, of course, normatively inert. Second, the settler states of the western and southern hemispheres are on the whole vastly larger than Mandatory Palestine. Even Ecuador, one of the smaller states of the Americas, is some ten times larger than Mandatory Palestine. Thus even though the population in 1492 was also much larger than that of Palestine in 1880 or 1947 (or even today), the sheer amount of space, not to mention the quality of the land for a variety of uses, was incomparably greater.

A third difference is that the exterminations perpetrated by European imperialists were of a kind and degree incomparably worse and more total than even the most egregious Israeli expulsions of Palestinians. The Europeans perpetrated this unfathomable crime in three principal ways. First, they engaged in an inexorable, albeit centuries-long, military and political steamrolling of all in their path (Jennings 1976; Brown 2001); second, they used, with varying degrees of intention, exotic diseases to exterminate the prior population (Crosby 1993: chap. 9); and third, they engaged in ethnobiological cleansing, sowing exotic plants and importing grazing animals and pests, thereby transforming the entire biome of the temperate parts of the New World into neo-Europes.

The disease issue is particularly horrific but also particularly vexing. Lack of prior exposure to Old World diseases practically ensured that the very fact of contact would visit epochal pestilence upon the indigenous peoples – especially in regions of higher population density. For this reason there is a risk of some naïveté in supposing that the Europeans could have settled peacefully in even a small part of the

New World. If anything, the recognition that in early cases such as that of the Canary Islands, the indigenous population was wiped out by pestilence (Crosby 1993: 92–4) supported an obligation on Europeans to quarantine themselves. David Lyons (1977) and others have suggested that considerations of economic need justified some European settlement, but the serious risk of a pandemic would arguably override or at least constrain the pursuit of economic fairness in this case. Nothing like this risk applies to the European Jews arriving in Palestine.

Fourth, while the common experience of dispossession and societal breakdown is shared among most if not all indigenous groups, these groups have for a number of reasons not cohered into a single nationality seeking a single state – even, in many cases, when they find themselves in the same general regions. On the contrary, indigenous populations are separated into hundreds of distinct bands, tribes, and nations on hundreds of reservations and territories, some with tiny populations and no prospect of developing the kinds of political institutions that statehood entails (Cairns 2005: 16–18). Thus, whereas Palestinian identity was nationalized by the common experience of trauma, indigenous identity was on the whole not; and where Palestinian and Jewish histories have both imbued sovereign statehood with great symbolic significance for many on each side, the indigenous struggle has in most cases not.

Finally, the Europeans' destruction of entire civilizations in the western and southern hemispheres happened much longer ago, and was much more total. As a result, hundreds of millions of people now live on the stolen land, and the indigenous populations of the temperate neo-Europes, which once numbered in the tens of millions, are by comparison tiny.[15] Among other things, this means that insofar as indigenous peoples are incorporated into the electorates of the settler states, they are virtually guaranteed to be persistent minorities.

The differences between the cases make it more obvious that the indigenous struggle defies straightforward application of either

---

[15] There are just over two million indigenous Canadians (Statistics Canada 2008), 350,000 indigenous Australians (Memmott and Moran 2004), and under five million American Indian and Alaska Natives in the US (US Census 2001). These three states alone amount to about 27 million square kilometers of territory. By contrast, there are now approximately eight million Palestinians worldwide. Mandatory Palestine covered about 27,000 square kilometers.

nationalist or cosmopolitan logic – respectively, sovereign statehood, and full integration into the liberal political–economic system. Indeed, the indigenous rights agenda, as developed in every settler state as well as in international forums, looks much more like my proposal for the Israeli–Palestinian dispute than like either standard solution to that dispute. That is a significant fact. The cosmopolitan should prima facie support total integration of indigenous peoples – perhaps appended to a choice theory of secession – even though this would in most cases doom them, as a small minority, to being engulfed and dissolved over a few generations. The inappropriateness of this result in indigenous rights cases tends to disconfirm cosmopolitanism. On the other hand, the fact that indigenous sovereignty is typically an assertion of political rights within or alongside the state, with little or no prospect of (and overall, little desire for) independent statehood, suggests that nationalism also seems to miss the right result. Though I cannot make the case here, I believe that my theory is more promising as an approach to indigenous rights than these other approaches.

I have offered an attachment theory of territorial rights based in plenitude. I have argued that this theory meets all the desiderata of theories of territory and territorial rights, and that it is systematically and attractively applicable to at least one ongoing and contentious territorial dispute, proposing new and on reflection preferable solutions, as well as affirming aspects of familiar solutions. I believe the theory has emerged in good shape, and that its proposals compare favorably to other available solutions. Like much else in the current theory, these applications would benefit from further empirical and conceptual work that is impossible here. The theory is offered, then, as an approach toward a theory of territorial rights and the just resolution of territorial disputes.

Works cited

All on-line sources are on file with the author.

Alfred, T. 1999. *Peace, Power, Righteousness: An Indigenous Manifesto.* Toronto: Oxford University Press.

Anderson, B. 2006. *Imagined Communities: Reflections on the Origin and Spread of Nationalism*, revised edn. London: Verso.

Aristotle 1995. *Politics* (trans. Ernest Barker, rev. R. F. Stalley). Oxford University Press.

Australian Government. 2007. "Land Use – Australia." Australian Natural Resources Atlas, updated 7 December 2007. www.anra.gov.au/topics/land/landuse/index.html.

Barry, B. 1973. *The Liberal Theory of Justice.* Oxford University Press.
    1982. "Humanity and Justice in Global Perspective," in Pennock, J. R. and Chapman, J. W. (eds.) *NOMOS XXIV: Ethics, Economics, and the Law.* New York University Press: 219–52.

Beilin, Y. 2006. "Black or White Folly," *Yediot Ahronot* (9/28).

Beinin, J., and Hajjar, L. 2000. "Palestine, Israel and the Arab–Israeli Conflict: A Primer," Middle East Research and Information Project (MERIP). www.merip.org/palestine-israel_primer/intro-pal-isr-primer.html.

Beitz, C. 1999. *Political Theory and International Relations*, revised edn. Princeton University Press.

Ben-Porat, G. 2006. *Global Liberalism, Local Populism.* Syracuse, NY: Syracuse University Press.

Bennell v. State of Western Australia. 2006. Case FCA 1243 (19 September).

Benvenisti, M. 1995. *Intimate Enemies.* Berkeley and Los Angeles: University of California Press.

Bern, J., and Dodds, S. 2000. "On the Plurality of Interests: Aboriginal Self-government and Land Rights," in Ivison, Patton, and Sanders (eds.): 163–79.

Berry, W. 1977. *The Unsettling of America: Culture and Agriculture.* San Francisco: Sierra Club Books.
    2002. *The Art of the Commonplace.* ed. N. Wirzba. San Francisco: Counterpoint.

Bishai, L. 2004. *Forgetting Ourselves: Secession and the (Im)possibility of Territorial Identity*. Lanham, MD: Lexington Books.

Blaut, J. M. 1979. "Some Principles of Ethnogeography," in Gale, S. and Olsson, G. (eds.) *Philosophy in Geography*. Dordrecht, Boston, and London: Reidel: 1–8.

Blomley, N. 2003. *Unsettling the City*. London: Routledge.

Bose, S. 2007. *Contested Lands*. Cambridge, MA: Harvard University Press.

Bosselman, F. 1994. "Four Land Ethics: Order, Reform, Responsibility, Opportunity," *Environmental Law* 24: 1439–511.

Boyarin, J., and Boyarin, D. 2002. *Powers of Diaspora*. Minneapolis: University of Minnesota Press.

Brock, G. 2005. "Egalitarianism, Ideals, and Cosmopolitan Justice," *Philosophical Forum* 36: 1–30.

Brown, D. 2001. *Bury My Heart at Wounded Knee* (Thirtieth Anniversary Edition). New York: Henry Holt.

Brown, P. 2000. *Ethics, Economics, and International Relations*. University of Edinburgh Press.

Bryan, B. 2000. "Property as Ontology: On Aboriginal and English Understandings of Ownership," *Canadian Journal of Law and Jurisprudence* 13: 3–31.

Buchanan, A. 1993. "The Morality of Inclusion," *Social Philosophy and Policy* 10: 233–57.

1997. "Theories of Secession," *Philosophy & Public Affairs* 27: 3–31.

2000. "Rawls's Law of Peoples: Rules for a Vanished Westphalian World," *Ethics* 110: 697–721.

2004. *Justice, Legitimacy, and Self-determination*. Oxford University Press.

Cairns, A. C. 2005. *First Nations and the Canadian State: In Search of Coexistence*. Kingston, Ont.: Institute of Intergovernmental Relations.

Callicott, J. B. 1997. *Earth's Insights*. Berkeley and Los Angeles: University of California Press.

Canadian Broadcasting Company (CBC). 2006a. "Harper won't call Quebec a nation," (23 June). www.cbc.ca/canada/montreal/story/2006/06/23/qc-harper20060623.html.

Canadian Broadcasting Company. 2006b. "Quebec as 'nation' divides Liberal candidates," (21 October). www.cbc.ca/canada/story/2006/10/21/liberal-leadership.html.

Canadian Broadcasting Company. 2006c. "How Each MP Voted on Quebecois Nationhood," (28 November). www.cbc.ca/news/background/parliament39/quebecnation-mpvotes.html.

Caney, S. 2001. "Cosmopolitan Justice and Equalizing Opportunities," *Metaphilosophy* 32: 113–34.

Carens, J. 2000. *Culture, Citizenship, and Community.* Oxford University Press.

Carpenter, S., Walker, B., Anderies, J. M., and Abel, N. 2001. "From Metaphor to Measurement: Resilience of What to What?" *Ecosystems* 4: 765–81.

Casler, S. D. 1992. *Introduction to Economics.* New York: HarperCollins.

Cassese, A. 1986. *International Law in a Divided World.* Oxford: Clarendon Press.

Christiano, T. 1996. *The Rule of the Many: Fundamental Issues in Democratic Theory.* Boulder, CO: Westview Press.

2006. "A Democratic Theory of Territory and Some Puzzles about Global Democracy," *Journal of Social Philosophy* 37: 81–107.

Cohen, G. A. 1996. *Self-ownership, Freedom, and Equality.* Cambridge University Press.

Copp, D. 1995. *Morality, Normativity, and Society.* Oxford University Press.

1999. "The Idea of a Legitimate State," *Philosophy and Public Affairs* 28: 3–45.

Costanza, R., DeGroot, R., Farber, S., Grasso, M., Hannon, B., Limburg, K., Naeem, S., O'Neill, R. V., Paruelo, J., Raskin, R. G., Sutton, P., and van den Belt, M. 1997. "The Value of the World's Ecosystem Services and Natural Capital," *Nature* 387 (15 May): 253–9.

Cresswell, T. 2004. *Place: A Short Introduction.* Oxford: Blackwell.

Crosby, A. W. 1993. *Ecological Imperialism.* Cambridge University Press/ Canto.

Cumbler, J. T. 1989. *A Social History of Economic Decline.* New Brunswick, NJ: Rutgers University Press.

Daniels, R. 2000. "The Crisis of Police Brutality and Misconduct in America," in Nelson, J. (ed.) *Police Brutality: an Anthology.* New York: W.W. Norton: 240–60.

Davidson, D. 1983. "On the Very Idea of a Conceptual Scheme," in *Inquiries into Truth and Interpretation.* Oxford University Press: 183–98.

Diller, D. C. (ed.) 1991. *The Middle East,* 7th edn. Washington, DC: Congressional Quarterly.

Drysdale, A., and Blake, G. H. 1985. *The Middle East and North Africa: A Political Geography.* Oxford University Press.

Dryzek, J. 2000. *Deliberative Democracy and Beyond: Liberals, Critics, and Contestations.* Oxford University Press.

Dworkin, R. M. 1977. *Taking Rights Seriously.* Cambridge, MA: Harvard University Press.

2000. *Sovereign Virtue.* Oxford University Press.

Federation for American Immigration Reform (FAIR). 2002. "The Population–Environment Connection." www.fairus.org/site/PageServer?pagename=iic_immigrationissuecentersfd36.

Fischbach, M. R. 2005. "Palestinian and Mizrahi Jewish Property Claims in Discourse and Diplomacy," in Lesch and Lustick (eds.): 207–24.

Fisk, R. 2002. *Pity the Nation: The Abduction of Lebanon*, 4th edn. New York: Nation Books.

Föllesdall, A. 2006. "Subsidiarity, Democracy, and Human Rights in the Constitutional Treaty of Europe," *Journal of Social Philosophy* 37: 61–80.

Forth, G. 2000. "Following the Yellow Brick Road and the Future of Australia's Declining Country Towns," First National Conference on the Future of Australia's Country Towns (June 2000). www.regional.org.au/au/countrytowns/ideas/forth.htm.

Freeman, S. 2006. "The Law of Peoples, Social Cooperation, Human Rights, and Distributive Justice," *Social Philosophy and Policy* 23: 29–68.

Gans, C. 2003. *The Limits of Nationalism*. Cambridge University Press.

Gardiner, S. M. 2004. "Ethics and Global Climate Change," *Ethics* 114: 555–600.

The Guardian. 2006. "Aboriginal Groups Deny Australia Land Grab," 9/22. www.guardian.co.uk/australia/story/0,,1879070,00.html.

Goodin, R. E. 1988. "What is So Special About Our Fellow Countrymen?" *Ethics* 98: 663–86.

1992. *Green Political Theory*. Cambridge University Press.

Haack, S. 1996. "Reflections on Relativism: From Momentous Tautology to Seductive Contradiction," in Tomberlin, J. (ed.) *Philosophical Perspectives 10: Metaphysics*. Cambridge, MA: Blackwell: 298–314.

Halper, J. 2005. "Israel in a Middle East Union: A 'Two-stage' Approach to the Conflict," *Tikkun* 20:1 (January/February): 15.

Hampton, J. 1996. *Political Philosophy*. Boulder, Colorado: Westview Press.

Hargrove, E. 1980. "Anglo-American Land Use Attitudes," *Environmental Ethics* 2: 121–48.

Held, D. 1995. *Democracy and the Global Order*. Palo Alto, CA: Stanford University Press.

2004. *Global Covenant*. Cambridge, UK, and Malden, MA: Polity Press.

Heyd, T. 2005. "Sustainability, Culture, and Ethics: Models from Latin America," *Ethics, Place, and Environment* 8: 223–34.

Hobbes, T. 1998. *On the Citizen*. Tuck, R., and Silverthorn, M. (eds.) Cambridge University Press.

Hobsbawm, E. 1992. "Mass Producing Traditions: Europe 1870–1914," in Hobsbawm, E. and Ranger, T. (eds.) *The Invention of Tradition*. Cambridge, UK: Canto, pp. 263–307.

Imbroscio, D. 2006. "Shaming the Inside Game," *Urban Affairs Review* 42: 224–48.

Isseroff, A. 2007. "Population of Ottoman and Mandate Palestine: Statistical and Demographic Considerations," *Mideast Web*: www.mideastweb. org/palpop.htm.

Ivison, D. 2002. *Postcolonial Liberalism*. Cambridge University Press.

Ivison, D., Patton, P., and Sanders, W. (eds.) 2000. *Political Theory and the Rights of Indigenous Peoples*. Cambridge University Press.

Jennings, F. 1976. *The Invasion of America*. New York: Norton.

Joffe, P. 1995. *Sovereign Injustice: Forcible Inclusion of the James Bay Crees and Cree Territory into a Sovereign Quebec*. Nemaska, Eeyou Astchee (Quebec): Grand Council of the Crees (of Quebec).

Jones, P. 1999. "Human Rights, Group Rights, and Peoples' Rights," *Human Rights Quarterly* 21: 80–107.

Kaplan, E. 2005. *The Jewish Radical Right*. Madison, WI: University of Wisconsin Press.

Keneley, M. 2004. "The Dying Town Syndrome: A Survey of Urban Development in the Western District of Victoria, 1830–1930," *Electronic Journal of Australia and New Zealand History* (22 March). www.jcu.edu.au/aff/history/articles/keneley3.htm.

Khalidi, W. (ed.) 1992. *All That Remains*. Washington, DC: Institute for Palestine Studies.

Knox, P. L., and Marston, S. A. 1998. *Places and Regions in a Global Context*. Upper Saddle River, NJ: Prentice-Hall.

Kofman, D. 2000. "Territorial States: What are they Good For? Who Needs Them?" in Calder, G., Garrett, E., and Shannon, J. (eds.) *Liberalism and Social Justice*. Aldershot, UK: Ashgate: 209–230.

Kolers, A. 2000. "The Lockean Efficiency Argument and Aboriginal Land Rights," *Australasian Journal of Philosophy* 78: 391–404.

  2002. "Territorial Rights in Cosmopolitan Justice," *Social Theory and Practice* 28: 29–50.

  2006. "Subsidiarity, Secession, and Cosmopolitan Democracy," *Social Theory and Practice* 32: 559–69.

Krugman, P. 1997. *Development, Geography and Economic Theory*. Cambridge, MA: MIT Press.

Kukathas, C. 2006. "The Mirage of Global Justice," *Social Philosophy and Policy* 23: 1–28.

Kuper, A. 1999. *Culture: The Anthropologists' Account*. Cambridge, MA: Harvard University Press.

Kymlicka, W. 1993. *Liberalism, Community, and Culture*. Oxford: Clarendon Press.

2001. "Territorial Boundaries: A Liberal Egalitarian Perspective," in Miller and Hashmi (eds.): 249–75.

Lee, R., and Wills, J. (eds.) 1997. *Geographies of Economies*. New York: John Wiley & Sons.

Lesch, A. M., and Lustick, I. (eds) 2005. *Exile and Return*. University of Pennsylvania Press.

Levin, N. 1977. *While Messiah Tarried*. New York: Schocken.

Levy, J. T. 2000. *The Multiculturalism of Fear*. Oxford University Press.

Locke, J. 1988. *Two Treatises of Government*, ed. P. Laslett Cambridge University Press.

Lomasky, L. 2001. "Toward a Liberal Theory of National Boundaries," in Miller and Hashmi (eds.): 55–78.

Lyons, D. 1977. "The New Indian Claims and Original Rights to Land," *Social Theory and Practice* 4: 249–72.

Maaka, R., and Fleras, A. 2000. "Engaging with Indigeneity: Tino Rangatiratanga in Aotearoa," in Ivison, Patton, and Sanders (eds.), 89–109.

Mabo and Others v. Queensland. 1992. 175 CLR 1 F.C. 92/014.

Malpas, J. E. 1999. *Place and Experience*. Cambridge University Press.

Margalit, A., and Raz, J. 1990. "National Self-Determination," *Journal of Philosophy* 87: 439–61.

McDonald, M. 1976. "Aboriginal Rights," in Shea, W. R., and King-Farlow, J. (eds.) *Contemporary Issues in Political Philosophy*. New York: Science History Publishers: 27–48.

McGirr, L. 2001. *Suburban Warriors: The Origins of the New American Right*. Princeton University Press.

Meisels, T. 2003. "Liberal Nationalism and Territorial Rights," *Journal of Applied Philosophy* 20: 31–43.

2005. *Territorial Rights*. Dordrecht: Springer Law and Philosophy Library.

Memmott, P., and Moran, M. 2004. "Indigenous Settlements of Australia," Department of the Environment and Heritage. www.environment.gov. au/soe/2001/publications/technical/indigenous/index.html.

Miller, D., 1995. *On Nationality*. Oxford University Press.

2000. *Citizenship and National Identity*. Malden, MA: Polity Press.

Miller, D. and Hashmi, S. (eds.) 2001. *Boundaries and Justice*. Princeton University Press.

Mills, C. W. 1997. *The Racial Contract*. Ithaca, NY: Cornell University Press.

Moellendorf, D. 2002. *Cosmopolitan Justice*. Boulder, CO: Westview Press.

Montmarquet, J. A. 1985. "Philosophical Foundations for Agrarianism," *Agriculture and Human Values* 2: 5–14.

Moore, M. 2001. *The Ethics of Nationalism*. Oxford University Press.

Morris, B. 2004. *Birth of the Palestinian Refugee Problem Revisited.* Cambridge University Press.

Morris, C. 1996. *An Essay on the Modern State.* Oxford University Press.

Moskowitz, K., and Romaniello, C. 2002. *Assessing the Full Cost of the Federal Grazing Program.* Tucson: Center for Biological Diversity. www.biologicaldiversity.org/swcbd/Programs/grazing/Assessing_the_full_cost.pdf.

National Alliance to End Homelessness. 2007. "First Nationwide Estimate of Homeless Population in a Decade Announced," www.end-homelessness.org/content/article/detail/1443.

Nielsen, K. 1997. "Cultural Nationalism, Neither Ethnic nor Civic," *Philosophical Forum* 28: 42–52.

Novak, M. 1972. *The Rise of the Unmeltable Ethnics.* New York: Macmillan.

Nozick, R. 1974. *Anarchy, State, and Utopia.* New York: Basic Books.

Nussbaum, M. C. 2000. *Women and Human Development: The Capabilities Approach.* Cambridge University Press.

Olwig, K. R. 2002. *Landscape, Nature, and the Body Politic.* Madison, WI: University of Wisconsin Press.

O'Leary, B. 2001. "The Elements of Right-sizing and Right-peopling the State," in O'Leary, Lustick, and Callaghy (eds.): 15–73.

O'Leary, B., Lustick, I., and Callaghy, T. (eds) 2001. *Right-sizing the State: the Politics of Moving Borders.* Oxford University Press.

O'Neill, O. 2000. *Bounds of Justice.* Cambridge University Press.

Parfit, D. 1984. *Reasons and Persons.* Oxford University Press.

Patz, J. A., Campbell-Lendrum, D., Holloway, T., and Foley, J. A. 2005. "Impact of Regional Climate Change on Human Health," *Nature* 438: 310–17.

Peteet, J. 2005. *Landscape of Hope and Despair: Palestinian Refugee Camps.* University of Pennsylvania Press.

Pinder, L. H. 1999. "The Carriers of No," *Index on Censorship* 28: 65–75.

Pogge, T. W. 1989. *Realizing Rawls.* Ithaca, NY: Cornell University Press.
  1994. "An Egalitarian Law of Peoples," *Philosophy and Public Affairs* 23: 195–224.
  2002. *World Poverty and Human Rights.* Cambridge, UK, and Malden, MA: Polity Press.

Pollan, M. 2006. *The Omnivore's Dilemma.* New York: Penguin.

Pratt, S. L. 2001. "The Given Land: Black Hawk's Conception of Place," *Philosophy and Geography* 4, 109–25.

Prugh, T., Costanza, R., and Daly, H. 2000. *The Local Politics of Global Sustainability.* Washington, DC: Island Press.

Quine, W. V. O. 1969. *Ontological Relativity and Other Essays*. Cambridge, MA: Harvard University Press.

RAND Palestinian State Study Team. 2005. *Building a Successful Palestinian State*. Santa Monica, CA: RAND Corporation.

Ranjeva, R. 1991. "Peoples and National Liberation Movements," in M. Bedjaoui (ed.) *International Law: Achievements and Prospects*. Dordrecht: Martinus Nijhoff: 101–12.

Rawls, J. 1993. *Political Liberalism*. New York: Columbia University Press.

1999a. *A Theory of Justice*, revised edn. Cambridge, MA: Harvard University Press.

1999b. *The Law of Peoples*. Cambridge, MA: Harvard University Press.

Rieber, S. 2004. "Democracy and Territorial Rights," *Journal of Social Philosophy* 35: 529–43.

Roemer, J. 1996. *Egalitarian Perspectives*. Cambridge University Press.

Ross, D. 2004. *The Missing Peace*. New York: Farrar, Straus, and Giroux.

Rousseau, J-J. 1987. *On the Social Contract* (trans. Donald Cress). Indianapolis: Hackett.

Russell, D. C. 2004. "Locke on Land and Labor," *Philosophical Studies* 117: 303–25.

Sack, R. D. 1986. *Human Territoriality*. Cambridge University Press.

2003. *A Geographical Guide to the Real and the Good*. New York: Routledge.

Sagoff, M. C. 1988. *The Economy of the Earth*. Cambridge University Press.

Sassen, S. 1998. *Globalization and its Discontents*. New York: The New Press.

Scalet, S. 2000. "Liberalism, Skepticism, and Neutrality: Making Do without Doubt," *Journal of Value Inquiry* 34: 207–25.

Scheffler, S. 2000. *Boundaries and Allegiances*. Oxford University Press.

Shahak, I. 1975. "Arab Villages Destroyed in Israel," in Davis, U. and Mezvinsky, N. (eds.) *Documents from Israel 1967–1973: Readings for a Critique of Zionism*. London: Ithaca Press: 43–54.

Shapiro, I., and Brilmayer, L. (eds.) 1999. *NOMOS XLI: Global Justice*. New York University Press.

Simmons, A. J. 2001. "On The Territorial Rights of States," *Philosophical Issues* 11: 300–26.

Simon, J. 1998. "Scarcity or Abundance?" in Westra, L. and Werhane, P. (eds.) *The Business of Consumption*. Lanham, MD: Rowman & Littlefield: 237–45.

Slaughter, A-M. 2004. *A New World Order*. Princeton University Press.

Smith, A. D. 1999. *Myths and Memories of the Nation*. Oxford University Press.

Statistics Canada 2002a. *Census 2001: Population and Dwelling Counts, for Canada, Provinces and Territories, 2001 and 1996 Censuses – 100% Data.* www12.statcan.ca/english/census01/products/standard/popdwell/Table-PR.cfm.

Statistics Canada 2002b. *Census 2001: Canadians on the Move.* www12.statcan.ca/english/census01/release/release4.cfm.

Statistics Canada 2002c. *Census 2001: Mode of Transportation.* www12.statcan.ca/english/census01/release/release6.cfm.

Statistics Canada 2002d. *Census 2001: Families and Living Arrangements.* www12.statcan.ca/english/census01/release/release3.cfm.

Statistics Canada 2003. *Census 2001: Mode of Transportation.* www12.statcan.ca/english/census01/release/release6.cfm.

Statistics Canada 2008. *Census 2006: Aboriginal Peoples Highlight Tables.* www12.statcan.ca/english/census06/data/highlights/aboriginal/index.cfm?Lang=E.

Steiner, H. 1999. "Just Taxation and International Redistribution," in Shapiro and Brilmayer (eds.): 171–91.

Stone, C. D. 1972. "Should Trees Have Standing? Toward Legal Rights for Natural Objects," *Southern California Law Review* 45: 450–501.

Tan, K-C. 2000. *Toleration, Diversity, and Global Justice.* University Park, PA: The Pennsylvania State University Press.

Tesón, F. 1998. *A Philosophy of International Law.* Boulder, CO: Westview.

Thompson, J. 2002. *Coming to Terms with the Past in Australia.* Cambridge, UK: Polity Press.

Tully, J. 1994. *An Approach to Political Philosophy: Locke in Contexts.* Cambridge University Press.

   1995. *Strange Multiplicity: Constitutionalism in an Age of Diversity.* Cambridge University Press.

Umberger, M. 2006. "Third Wave: For Some, First and Second Homes Just Aren't Enough," *Chicago Tribune* (February 17).

United States Census. 1995. "Urban and Rural Population – 1900–1990," www.census.gov/population/censusdata/urpop0090.txt.

United States Census. 2001. "The American Indian Population: 2000," www.census.gov/prod/2001pubs/mso01aian.pdf.

United States Census. 2006. "Housing Vacancies and Home Ownership: Annual Statistics 2006," www.census.gov/hhes/www/housing/hvs/annual06/ann06ind.html.

United States Interagency Council on Homelessness (USICH). 2007. "12% Reduction in Chronic Homelessness Announced by Administration," 7 November. www.ich.gov.

Vasquez, J. 1995. "Why Do Neighbors Fight? Proximity, Interaction, or Territoriality," *Journal of Peace Research* 32: 277–93.

Vincent, A. 1998. "Liberalism and the Environment," *Environmental Values* 7: 443–59.

Waldron, J. 1992. "Superseding Historic Injustice," *Ethics* 103: 4–28.

2003. "Indigeneity? First Peoples and Last Occupancy," *New Zealand Journal of Public International Law* 1: 55–82.

Walker, B. and Salt, D. 2006. *Resilience Thinking: Sustaining Ecosystems and People in a Changing World*. Washington, DC: Island Press.

Walzer, M. 1983. *Spheres of Justice*. New York: Basic Books.

1990. "The Communitarian Critique of Liberalism," *Political Theory* 18: 6–23.

1992. *Just and Unjust Wars*, 2nd edn. New York: Basic Books.

Wellman, C. H. 2005. *A Theory of Secession: The Case for Self-Determination*. Cambridge University Press.

Wilcox J. 2006. "Statement of Justice Wilcox" regarding *Bennell* v. *State of Western Australia and Others* and *Bodney* v. *State of Western Australia and Others*. Federal Court of Australia. www.austlii.edu.au/au/cases/cth/federal_ct/2006/1243.html.

Wiredu, K. 1996. *Cultural Universals and Particulars*. Bloomington, IN: Indiana University Press.

Wright, A., and Wolford, W. 2003. *To Inherit the Earth: The Landless Movement and the Struggle for a New Brazil*. Oakland, CA.: Food First Books.

Wunderlich, G. 2000. "Hues of American Agrarianism," *Agriculture and Human Values* 17: 191–7.

Young, I. M. 1990. *Justice and the Politics of Difference*. Princeton University Press.

Index

West Bank, 21, 24, 76, 153, 156,
192, 195, 202, 203, 204, 205,
210, 212, 215
White Australia Policy, 144
world state, 47, 48
worldview axis, 24–26, 163–64, 166
Levy on, 25

Yellowstone-to-Yukon Ecoregion, 109,
110, 113

Yugoslavia, 91

Zionism, 104, 112, 168, 169, 186,
196, 197
Zionists, 125
ethnogeography of, 190, 197,
206–07, 210, 216
territorial claims of, 197,
198, 201
Zurich, 50

For EU product safety concerns, contact us at Calle de José Abascal, 56–1°,
28003 Madrid, Spain or eugpsr@cambridge.org.

www.ingramcontent.com/pod-product-compliance
Ingram Content Group UK Ltd.
Pitfield, Milton Keynes, MK11 3LW, UK
UKHW020331140625
459647UK00018B/2103